About Pfeiffer

Pfeiffer serves the professional development and hands-on resource needs of training and human resource practitioners and gives them products to do their jobs better. We deliver proven ideas and solutions from experts in HR development and HR management, and we offer effective and customizable tools to improve workplace performance. From novice to seasoned professional, Pfeiffer is the source you can trust to make yourself and your organization more successful.

Essential Knowledge Pfeiffer produces insightful, practical, and comprehensive materials on topics that matter the most to training and HR professionals. Our Essential Knowledge resources translate the expertise of seasoned professionals into practical, how-to guidance on critical workplace issues and problems. These resources are supported by case studies, worksheets, and job aids and are frequently supplemented with CD-ROMs, websites, and other means of making the content easier to read, understand, and use.

Essential Tools Pfeiffer's Essential Tools resources save time and expense by offering proven, ready-to-use materials—including exercises, activities, games, instruments, and assessments—for use during a training or team-learning event. These resources are frequently offered in loose-leaf or CD-ROM format to facilitate copying and customization of the material.

Pfeiffer also recognizes the remarkable power of new technologies in expanding the reach and effectiveness of training. While e-hype has often created whizbang solutions in search of a problem, we are dedicated to bringing convenience and enhancements to proven training solutions. All our e-tools comply with rigorous functionality standards. The most appropriate technology wrapped around essential content yields the perfect solution for today's on-the-go trainers and human resource professionals.

www.pfeiffer.com

Essential resources for training and HR professionals

"Elaine's practical zest of 'yes, you can do it now—here, let me show you how' takes you by the hand to build the marketing plan of your business and gets you into action immediately. An easy read and helpful resource that makes marketing the game to play."

—Aviv Shahar, president, Amber Network

"What a treasure of proven marketing insights! Elaine Biech has the market cornered on advice for successful consulting, and her latest effort is rich with tips and tricks of the trade. She asks the right questions to guide the consultant to a new understanding of a true marketing approach. I recommend this book to every consulting professional as a must-have reference."

—Rex Gatto, Ph.D., Gatto Training Associates

"The subtitle of this book could be 'The Great Idea Dream Factory.' Imaginative tips fill each page. Elaine's marketing lessons are useful and easy to apply to every consulting practice. If you are starting a career as a consultant Monday morning, be sure to read this book by Sunday night."

—Jean Lamkin, director of career development, Landmark Publishing Group

"For anyone who has had a great service or product, you learn painfully fast that it's the marketing that makes it viable. This book is a great 'how to' in making marketing easier and more engaging than you thought possible. I have been a client of ebb associates for years and have personally experienced these 'tips.' The actionable tips in this book make ebb stand out from the crowd."

—Shirley Krsinich, executive and management talent consultant, American Family Insurance

"I continue to utilize techniques learned from Elaine and ebb associates when they first worked with Lands' End: organization, analysis, research, creativity, and simplicity are a few of the principles. These concepts once again come through in this publication. She continues to make complex ideas simple and enjoyable. This book is a great resource to focus priorities to market your consulting business."

—Mindy Meads, executive vice president, Lands' End

"Marketing is the key ingredient to any successful business. Elaine makes the marketing process for consultants easy. I recommend that if you must market, keep this book on your desk. It is that good—and that indispensable."

—Maribeth Kuzmeski, author, *Red Zone Marketing*

"Elaine Biech has done it again! Like her other books, *Marketing Your Consulting Services* is bursting with ideas that any professional can implement immediately. This is an indispensable guide for anyone who is building a consulting business. I'm convinced that even people who thought that they dreaded marketing will get inspiration from the perspectives and practical suggestions in this book."

—Diane Hessan, president and CEO, Communispace Corporation

"If you entertain the assumption that there is nothing new in 'marketing,' then this book both confirms and denies that mind-set! Elaine Biech does it again—she adds an additional 'P' to the marketing lexicon: practical. I especially enjoy her 'Fast Fourteen' and the 'Quick tips' as common sense reminders of what we often forget when we struggle with the marketing dilemma."

—Ronald E. Galbraith, CEO, Management 21, Inc.

"I could have used this book when I was a marketing manager at Apple, marketing 'programs.' As Biech points out early on in this fascinating book, consulting is a profession unlike any other. Therefore, you need a marketing plan that is different from someone who sells a tangible product like, say, computers. Let *Marketing Your Consulting Services* teach you how to get your service, expertise, knowledge, and experience in front of the prospects that are the right fit for you."

—Sue Fox, author, *Business Etiquette For Dummies,* and former program marketing manager, Apple

"In her new book, Elaine continues her contribution to consultants' success, giving very practical, usable, and time-tested information and ideas. There is definitely something for everybody in *Marketing Your Consulting Services*, whether you're just starting out in consulting or have been in the field for years. A truly valuable handbook!"

—Linda Growney, vice president of strategic development, CUNA Mutual Group

"This book replaces the twenty-five books on marketing currently on my shelf. Within the first five minutes of reading this book you are guaranteed to get practical, actionable ideas to grow your business. Elaine knows what to do, when to do it, and takes 'I am not a marketer' off of every consultant's lips. Want to grow your business? Buy this book + read it + use just 10 percent of what you learn = marketing success. Why wait?"

—Ann Herrmann-Nehdi, president, Herrmann International

"Successful consultants must market themselves twenty-four hours a day, 365 days a year. Sure, it sounds daunting. Yet somehow, Elaine Biech makes the process seem as natural as breathing. Her creative tips and techniques—many of which can be done on a shoestring budget—will have you rolling up your sleeves and digging into the dreaded task of marketing your services with more enthusiasm than you've felt in a long, long time!"

—Celia Rocks, author, *Brilliance Marketing Management*

"Another surefire winner from Elaine Biech that takes the mystery out of successful marketing. Elaine can make anything doable and this book is just another example of her all-inclusive but down-to-earth guidance that demystifies a key element of business for the ordinary and the extraordinary entrepreneur. Insightful! Practical! Comprehensive!"

—Edie West, executive director, National Skills Standards Board

"This book is a must-read for any independent or small consulting company that is far more interested and skilled in doing the work than in getting the work. This easy-to-read book provides practical suggestions and methods that will go a long way in keeping less marketing-oriented colleagues aware of what marketing really is and how to go about it."

—Hank Karp, co-author, *Bridging the Boomer-Xer Gap*

"In competitive sports the game plan is rarely divulged. So, too, in the consulting arena, trade secrets are usually well-guarded, because maintaining the competitive edge is seen as key to success. Not so with Elaine Biech (ebb), a star of the business. In her latest book, *Marketing Your Consulting Services,* she dares to reveal her proven, practical, and fun marketing techniques to anyone who will heed and apply them. As a client, a competitor, and ultimately a co-operative of ebb over the past fifteen years, I can testify that these techniques really work—and you can take that to the bank."

—Captain Garland F. Skinner, United States Navy (Ret), and former CEO, The Skinner Group, Inc.

"A readable, and useful book with stand-alone chapters and specific advice to guarantee success."

—Lieutenant General Carol Mutter, United States Marine Corps (Ret), and consultant

"Elaine has done it again. This is not only an extremely practical hands-on approach to marketing your consulting business and generating clients, it's also a great overview of the entire process. Whether you're new or a veteran, struggling or successful, you'll find this book packed with lots of tools, techniques, advice, and directions that you can use right away. Elaine doesn't withhold any secrets; she shares all the successes as well as the failures, and provides a range of approaches that you can choose from. This book needs to be on your desk right next to *The Business of Consulting*."

—Joe Willmore, president, Willmore Consulting Group, and author, *Managing Virtual Teams*

"*Marketing Your Consulting Services* takes the mystery and complexity out of marketing. If you're as tired of the marketing mystery and rhetoric as I am, this book will restore your faith."

—Pamela J. Schmidt, executive director, Instructional Systems Association

"Elaine Biech gives new meaning to marketing as she shares her experiences as well as her insights into the world of marketing. It's a book that every consultant should read and offers a wealth of information including great tips and what pitfalls to look for. A very readable book that provides simple details on how to make marketing fun."

—Kathleen Talton, program manager, Precise Systems, Inc.

"Once again, Elaine has written a book that provides valuable, practical tips for consultants. I have a marketing background, and I am still challenged marketing my consulting services to clients. I learned many useful ideas that I employ today to increase my client base. As consultants, we are nothing without the clients we serve. Elaine shares her many years of successful marketing tips for getting clients. Don't put together this year's marketing plan without reading this book. Put it on your book shelf if you are a consultant!"

—Maureen Moriarty, consultant and executive coach, Pathways to Change

"Elaine has written another must-have book for consultants! Full of useful and concrete steps to identify how to conduct a successful marketing campaign, she presents a creative and compelling plan to develop a marketing strategy. She removes the fear and intimidation factors surrounding the concept of marketing by providing a clear practical how-to guide. Elaine shares her many years of professional experience with her competition. We are all the beneficiaries of her generosity."

—Maggie Hutchison, consultant

"Elaine promises practicality, and she delivers! From the 'Fast Fourteen' to the concept of marketing all the time, she presents surefire ideas to fit any consultant's marketing comfort level."

—Judith Free, senior consultant, Free Associates, Inc.

"Elaine's dynamic personal style comes through in this book. It's high energy, refreshingly straightforward, creative, and just packed full of useful information."

—Kathy Armstrong, illustrator and designer

"As with all her previous books, Elaine has again written a very practical, straightforward, and easy-to-read guide for consulting professionals that will bring immense and immediate value to them and their practices."

—Bob Sautter, consultant

"Elaine Biech is the consummate pro at consulting. Her earlier books establish her credentials; watching her in practice proves her mastery. Now she closes the loop with practical advice on how to select and win the clients who will benefit from skilled, capable consultancy."

—Joseph Wojtecki, Center for Risk Communication

"Elaine has done it again! *Marketing Your Consulting Services* is the best practical guide available for new and experienced consultants alike. How often have I said that I hate to market and sell, that I just want to consult? Elaine takes that attitude and shows how the marketing challenge is really an easy and practical exercise even for those of us who shun the very idea. Instantly useful, applicable, and practical, this book avoids the theory and jargon of marketing that make it a foreign and frightening concept. *Marketing Your Consulting Services* complements Elaine's previous volumes that guide the consultant to a successful business practice."

—Barbara Pate Glacel, Ph.D., principal, The Glacel Group, and author, *Light Bulbs for Leaders*

"Elaine has done it again—a book chock-full of ideas, tips, and techniques specifically targeted to help your consulting business grow. Elaine distilled boring, humdrum marketing theory, combined it with her experience, and shares her knowledge in a practical, engaging way. A must-have for any consultant who wants clients!"

—Kristin Arnold, president, Quality Process Consultants, Inc., and author, *Team Basics* and *Email Basics*

"As always, Elaine promises to be practical, and, as always, Elaine delivers what she promises! This book is practical from the start. A busy individual can open this book to any page and gather new, practical ideas. The 'Fast Fourteen' have helped me stay current and in touch with existing clients and have helped me build a dynamic potential client list. This book is an easy read and it gets two thumbs up from me!"

—Steve Kuper, managing partner, Kuper/Kemen & Associates, LLC

"This book is more than Marketing 101 for consultants. It's a recipe for success in a very competitive field! Thanks for sharing your secrets in a way anyone can grasp. Bravo Elaine! No wonder you are one of the busiest and most successful consultants out there!"

—Linda Byars Swindling, J.D., Passports to Success, and author, *Get What You Want* and *Set the Standard & Meet the Challenge*

"With all the noise and hubris surrounding the topic of marketing, it was refreshing to discover Biech's shining jewel, *Marketing Your Consulting Services.* Whether you are a sole practitioner just starting out or the starch-shirt managing director of a solidly entrenched firm, this is a must-read if you are interested in thoughtfully growing your enterprise."

—James Olan Hutcheson, CEO, ReGENERATION Partners, and author, *Portraits of Success: 9 Keys to Creating Sustainable Success in Any Business*

"I have purchased and used two of Elaine's books already, *The Business of Consulting* and *The Consultant's Quick Start Guide.* Both books have proven to be invaluable as I moved my consulting practice from Washington, D.C. (where I grew up and had worked for 20 years), to Seattle. Her experience and practical advice made starting up in a new town with no networking in place so much easier! I am obviously looking forward to her newest release, *Marketing Your Consulting Services.*"

—Lynne A. Lazaroff, Action Management Training & Consulting

"Are you a consultant? Then you need this book. Whether you're a one-man shop devoted to helping start-ups get off the ground or a thriving firm who serves Fortune 500 corporations, Elaine Biech's been-there-done-that advice will help you find (and keep) the clients you need to keep your practice growing. And in these lean economic times, that's no small feat."

—Greg Smith, lead navigator and president, Chart Your Course International

"Ever practical and pragmatic, Elaine Biech offers easy-to-implement, innovative approaches to marketing that will help consultants be more successful."

—Lynn McManus, project acquisitions manager, Milmanco Corporation

"The hardest part of my business is marketing. I never took a course in college about how to market and sell. Elaine's book makes soooo much sense and gives me great ideas that I can put to use immediately. I recommend it to anyone who needs to—but doesn't want to—market."

—JR Holt, JRH Associates, Inc.

"Elaine consistently offers practical information that works. She packs her books with down-to-earth solutions that start with A (for action) and end with A (for more action!). Elaine provides bottom-line advice to consultants who aren't afraid to be creative and want to have fun growing their businesses."

—Lola Hilton, marketing and events planner, First Flight Centennial Celebration

Marketing Your Consulting Services

elaine biech

Foreword by Geoff Bellman

Pfeiffer

A Wiley Imprint
www.pfeiffer.com

Published by Pfeiffer
An Imprint of John Wiley & Sons, Inc.
989 Market Street, San Francisco, CA 94103-1741   www.pfeiffer.com

Pfeiffer books and products are available through most bookstores. To contact Pfeiffer directly call our Customer Care Department within the U.S. at (800) 274-4434, outside the U.S. at (317) 572-3985 or fax (317) 572-4002.

Pfeiffer also publishes its books in a variety of electronic formats. Some content that appears in print may not be available in electronic books.

Printed in the United States of America

ISBN: 0-7879-6543-X

Library of Congress Cataloging-in-Publication Data

Biech, Elaine.
  Marketing your consulting services / Elaine Biech ; foreword by Geoff
Bellman.
      p. cm.
  Includes index.
   ISBN 0-7879-6543-X (alk. paper)
   1. Consultants—Marketing. I. Title.
  HD69.C6B44 2003
  001'.068'8—dc21
                                        2002156553

Acquiring Editor: Matthew Davis
Director of Development: Kathleen Dolan Davies
Editor: Rebecca Taff
Production Editor: Nina Kreiden
Manufacturing Supervisor: Bill Matherly

Associate Art Director: Bruce Lundquist
Interior Design: Claudia Smelser and Gene Crofts
Cover Design: Laurie Anderson and Hatty Lee
Illustrations: Lotus Art

Printing   10   9   8   7   6   5   4   3   2   1

For Shane and Thad,

who marketed all

their ideas

to me first

CONTENTS

LIST OF FIGURES AND EXHIBITS

ELEVEN

TWELVE

FOREWORD

If consultants did not have to market and sell themselves, I am sure that the number of consultants would at least quadruple. Just the thought of submitting our work and ourselves to the judgment of others scares many people away from making a living as an independent consultant. Marketing and sales helps define the boundary between those who choose to consult and those who do not. I've been on my own for years, and I am still uneasy about new encounters with potential clients. The phrase "standing naked before strangers" captures my worst fears.

Elaine Biech wrote this book to provide me and you with some of the consultant clothing we need. And not just our outer attire (yes, she does tell us how to present ourselves in person and in print), but also the "inner attire": the habits of mind and heart that give us the confidence we need to present ourselves in the marketplace. I dearly needed this guidance twenty-five years ago when I was starting my business in the basement coal-bin-converted-to-office that was the "world headquarters" for my new consulting firm. I found it very difficult to get out of that coal bin and go find the clients. Elaine deals directly with these new consultant dilemmas by telling you what you could do, helping you decide, and then getting you up off your laurels to do something about it.

You will not read long before Elaine puts you to work. She is particularly good at offering many actions for you to choose from, or add to. In her immediate, almost hands-on guidance, she intends to move you to action. Don't just study marketing and sales; do something about it! And soon! I agree with Elaine. You can take a year to put together the best consulting marketing plan in the world, and then not have the time and money left to implement it. Early on, find ways of investing more of your energy getting out there with your potential clients, instead of hanging back, buried in your books and research. (If this is the fourth marketing book you've read in the last two weeks and you have not reached out to one potential client, chances are, you are not on the path to consulting success!)

This book is useful in its suggested actions, and in its many questions. The author repeatedly asks you what *you* think. I didn't always like this, and I suspect you won't either. But to be honest, when I didn't like the questions, I usually didn't have very good answers. Elaine's questions are pointed, relevant, and maddeningly useful. She puts dozens before you, and more than once you will look at a question—pen poised ready to answer—and you will have NO idea what to write! When her searching questions meet your blank mind, there lies opportunity.

What I especially value about each of Elaine's consulting books is captured in this sentence: "I've done the research for you and boiled it down to its key elements; now read it and do something, dammit!" She does this with a twinkle in her eye. She draws on her own marketing experience; she offers charts, lists, and frameworks to fit over the apparent chaos of the marketplace; and she helps us learn and face what we need to know to be successful consultants.

Each month, I am contacted by four or five people who are either new consultants, or are considering making the leap to consulting. We spend an hour or so together talking about their aspirations and their attractions to consulting, and marketing concerns are almost always part of these conversations. While helping them, I get a privileged look into their lives. There is something quite wonderful about having people tell me about what they want from their lives, their hopes and dreams, and their concerns and fears. I am the invited guest at their life table. Visiting with them causes me to think again about my own life, how I got where I am, and how my choice to be a consultant figures in all of that. And, what do I find myself saying, time after time, to these people who come to me with their questions? Here are a few samples that might be useful to you:

- Consult for love of the work, not for the money. Money will likely come, but see it as the frosting on the cake of doing work you love to do.

- Create work that asks you to be your better self. Do not build a role for yourself that is so artificial that you have to put it on each day like a lead suit.
- Respect and care for your clients. It is possible to make a living while disliking, punishing, or ridiculing your clients, but you cannot make a good life.
- Take good care of yourself. You cannot serve your clients well by living and working in ways that conflict with what you would advise them to do.
- This choice is about life first, not work. Create a life for yourself; use this work to help you do that.

Well, at least I *hope* that's what I say to people. When I follow my own guidance (I often do not), I live a better life, do better work, and more clients invite me back. Some of the best marketing I've done is based on the advice I give to others: Build a practice that is a part of the life you want to create.

Succeeding in this work means finding and keeping clients, no small feat—especially in today's world where the marketplace is filled with consultants parading, displaying, and revealing their wares. There are more consultants than ever before, all acting like they know what they are doing. Your challenge is to know what *you* are doing, to find clients who value what you do, and to consult in a way that fits with your larger life. Use this work of consulting to become your better self.

March 2003

Geoff Bellman
Author, *The Consultant's Calling*

PREFACE

It is rare that I am writing this preface prior to starting this book. I have always written this part last to provide you with a roadmap of what to expect or to discuss insights I've had while writing the book. However, I find myself writing this preface now facing the very reason that I decided to write this book. It is the fact that there are probably more business books written about marketing and selling than about any other topic. Yet few portray marketing as practical and enjoyable. This is frustrating.

Before I write a book I usually read as much as I can about the topic. As I write this book, I am surrounded by stacks of marketing books—eighty-seven volumes to be exact. In addition I have a stack of marketing periodicals and the past year's issues of four different newsletters. Many of them lack the practicality that I search for.

Few of these resources will make it into the marketing reading list that you will find at the end of this book. Why? Because most are theoretically based and contain few practical ideas. In some cases the practical ideas are there, but you spend much time digging for them and may even miss them if they are buried in a chapter of text.

In my reading I examined graphs that display the demand curve and fluctuations; wouldn't you prefer to know how to get your clients to refer you to other clients?

I examined a three-dimensional grid that displays product life cycles and marketing strategies; wouldn't you prefer a few inexpensive marketing tools?

I examined rules for qualifying sales questions; wouldn't you prefer a list of practical questions to ask clients?

I examined charts explaining major segmentation of consumer markets; wouldn't you prefer knowing how to find new clients?

I examined lists of 162 closing techniques; wouldn't you prefer several practical excuses for getting in touch with dormant clients?

I examined a diagram of a "need-driven sales process"; wouldn't you prefer to learn how to develop creative marketing ideas?

I read admonishments to those of us who do not know the difference between advertising and marketing. I have been chided for not knowing the real definition of promotion, and insulted for not taking the time to qualify a client. I think you want to know how to make marketing fun and practical. Well, that's what I promise: fun and practical.

I PROMISE PRACTICAL

I am certain that you bought this book to learn something about marketing. But my guess is the real reason you plunked down the money is because you want to know the fastest, cheapest, most effective way to drum up business for your consulting company. Here's what I promise you.

- I promise to discuss only enough about market research to give you a basis for building a solid plan.

- I promise to provide an easy, but thorough, process for developing your marketing plan.

- I promise to identify tools you can use and what you may wish to consider for each.

- I promise to discuss the advantages and disadvantages of marketing for a small consulting firm.

- I promise to help you cut through to the most critical selling concepts.

- I promise to show you how to retain the customers you have today and why this is your best marketing strategy.

- I promise to teach you creativity tools that will help you to invent your own clever marketing ideas.
- But most of all: I promise practical.

I will live up to my promise to make this book practical and easy-to-use. And I will fill it with the kind of useful guidance, practical ideas, special consulting considerations, and creative tips I think you want.

"Practical and fun is just what I need," you say, "but I can't wait! I need to do something today!"

BUT I NEED TO DO SOMETHING TODAY

You will find hundreds of ideas throughout this book that you can implement immediately. If that is your main reason for picking up this book, here are a fast fourteen marketing ideas. Select one and do it today.

What about a plan? What about research? What about determining the best way to invest my marketing dollars? Yes, planning will save you money and a focus on your niche will save you time. But neither will guarantee your success. You should have a "market all the time" mindset. But if you are not doing any marketing and you need to do something today, any one of these ideas will get you started as you read the rest of the book. Most of these fourteen ideas will require fewer than eight hours of your time. Most of these fourteen ideas cost little or no money.

Fast Fourteen to Do Today

1. Print mailing labels for fourteen of your best clients; then purchase fourteen appropriate (funny, thank you, thinking of you) cards from your local card shop. Write a sentence or two in each and mail them off.

2. Find a great article in a recent business magazine issue. Purchase fourteen copies of the magazine and mark the article with a Post-it® and a note from you. Send it to fourteen potential clients.

3. Attend your next professional or service organization meeting. Select fourteen people and give each person two business cards—one to keep and one to pass on.

4. Call people you know and ask them to suggest others you might help. Do not stop until you have fourteen names and phone numbers.

5. Call the fourteen names provided to you in the previous idea. Ask for time on their calendars to chat with you about how you might be able to help them.

6. Add fourteen names to your mailing list. Send each a brochure with a note from you.

7. Identify fourteen dormant clients (people you have not spoken to in two years) and call them to see what they have been doing.

8. Read a good book? Seen a great website? E-mail the title and author or the website address with fourteen words about why you liked it to fourteen people who could refer you to new clients.

9. Write a fourteen-paragraph article for your website. Then contact fourteen clients and ask them to read it and provide you with feedback.

10. Take fourteen minutes to decide how you could improve your answering machine messages. Then implement the ideas.

11. Go to your local bookstore. Scan at least fourteen of the newest books that focus on your area of expertise. Identify phrases, concepts, and thoughts you could use in your next prospecting letter.

12. Identify fourteen events, such as conferences, meetings, or social gatherings, that will occur in the next year, where you could touch base with potential clients. Add all fourteen to your annual calendar.

13. Identify fourteen strangers to whom you would like to sell your services. Skip ahead and read Chapter Seven to determine how to prospect.

14. Identify fourteen journals, magazines, and newspapers to which you could submit an article or a press release.

Select one of these items and do it today. Follow up with a call or another next step fourteen days from today. And in between begin to read this book so that you can learn the rest of the marketing story.

Tips

Several tips are highlighted in each chapter. Most are not dependent on the chapter, so you may use them as stand-alone ideas. Many will initiate thoughts you may not have had in the past. Try some of them. Use others as thought-starters for your own ideas.

One Last Thing

I have lots of last-minute thoughts, so you will find many of the chapters end with one last idea—kind of a p.s. to the chapter. In addition, each chapter ends with a list of Marketing Actions. You should consider adding the actions to your daily to-do list. Take action toward your marketing plan.

March 2003

elaine biech
ebb associates inc
virginia beach, va

ACKNOWLEDGMENTS

Every author needs a supporting cast of many who coach, critique, and encourage. I am fortunate to have found that in the Pfeiffer publishing team:

- Kathleen Dolan Davies, director of development, who carries a big stick but has a soft touch. She trusts me to meet deadlines, yet pushes me when she must. She has become a friend and confidante.
- Nina Kreiden and Dawn Kilgore, production editors, who skillfully keep all the pieces of the puzzle together to ensure a tight production schedule. An author could not ask for better communication and support.
- Susan Rachmeler, development editor and word maestro, for going above and beyond to provide her expertise and insight.
- Rebecca Taff, who manages my stray sentence structure, prods my prepositions into place, reduces redundancies, corrects capitalization, and still manages to ferret out all the "gets."
- Jeanenne Ray, whose marketing magic will create another success story with this book.
- Matt Davis, acquisitions editor, who agreed to take a chance at yet another book about consulting.
- Cedric Crocker, publisher, for creating a synergistic climate in which the publishing team excels.

Thank you all.

Celia Rocks, publicist, thanks for your brilliance-to-be on yet another project.

Thanks also to the people who kept the rest of my life in order as I wrote: Maggie Hutchison, Emma Meredith, and my family who stayed in touch while I ignored them.

Thank you clients who have always allowed me to explore creative marketing ideas with you.

And especially, Dan, love of my life, who took care of me for a month so that I could write—no one has ever done that for me.

Marketing

What's It All About?

Many consultants never think about marketing . . . until something goes wrong. The company that was your bread and butter has just been bought out by its competitor. The person who hired you to conduct an organizational assessment was offered a better job and the new guy wants to bring in his own consultant. The market has taken a downward turn and your regular clients are not calling you. Guess it's time to think about marketing!

MARKETING 101

My college marketing class dictated that the market must first be identified using *research* and surveys by experts. The next step was to *reach* the market using huge outlays of time and money in the form of advertising. Consultants may interpret this as follows: They will rent a mailing list from the industry to which they consult (research) and then mail a pricey four-color brochure (reach) to everyone on the list. They may accompany this with a full-page ad in the industry's journal. They pat themselves on the back and sit back and wait for the calls to roll in. When no one calls they are at a loss about what happened.

Market Research and Market Plans

What is marketing? Must it really be research-based? Should consultants have marketing plans? Marketing is everything you do to find or keep a client. Most successful consultants know more about marketing than they believe they do. That's because if you keep all the jargon out of marketing it can be an intuitive process.

To be the most successful, marketing is generally based on some research, even if that research is unsophisticated and subjective. For example, you as a consultant decide to contact one client over another, or to write one proposal over another, and you make those decisions based on the "research" you have done. Do you have some inside scoop about one client? Perhaps you spoke to the director of human resources and you know they are looking for some sales training, your specialty. Is the other client notoriously late with payments to other consultants? The answers to these questions will lead you to the next step.

You will most likely plan some marketing strategies to use with the first company. Perhaps you will write a personal letter to the vice president of sales that shows you are familiar with the company and outline your credentials and what you do. You may follow up with a telephone call that leads to a sales call. You plan carefully what you will say during the sales call: What questions you will ask, what information you will share, and how you will position yourself to ensure that you are hired for the job. Congratulations! You have just completed your market research and market planning for one client.

Now how did you choose to respond to one proposal over another? Again, you conducted some minimal amount of research. Perhaps you called a colleague to learn more about one of the organizations. Perhaps you looked the organization up on the Internet. Once you read the Request for Proposals, you learned which one would utilize your skills more. Again, this is the research. Your marketing plan will be to write the best proposal they've ever seen, showing how you will solve the organization's problem, add value to their mission, and do it all for a reasonable price and within their time frame.

Guarantee Your Business Success

Want to guarantee the success of your business? You can essentially predict success if you do two things: (1) Research and answer the following questions correctly and (2) plan and implement the effort to accomplish the actions suggested by the questions.

- What does your business do? What do you do well? What do you not do well?
- What do your customers want? How do you ensure excelling at meeting their needs? How do you predict their future needs?
- Who is your competition? What do you do better than they do? How do you stay ahead of your competition?
- How do you keep yourself in front of your customers?
- Where is your business heading? What is your vision? What do you need to do to get there?
- What will you do differently once you get there?

The answers to these questions should be found in your business plan. It is a working document that you keep in front of you and your staff. When done thoughtfully, it becomes your roadmap to success. It is also the precursor for your marketing plan. If you have not completed a business plan, you will want to back up and complete one before moving forward. If you need a format to follow, use one of my earlier books, either *The Business of Consulting* or *The Consultant's Quick Start Guide.* Both provide guidance for writing a business plan.

Alan Kay, author and consultant, has said that the best way to predict the future is to invent it. Do you want to predict your success? This is the way to invent it.

The 4 Ps

Probably one of the things you remember from your marketing classes is the 4 Ps. *Product, price, placement,* and *promotion* are the four elements of the marketing mix. Manipulating them in the best way brings the greatest number of sales. "Whoa!" you may say, "I don't have a product to sell. How can marketing help me?"

The 4 Ps were first presented in an article titled "The Concept of the Marketing Mix" in the *Harvard Business Review.* The author, Harvard professor Neil Borden, coined the term "marketing mix" to describe the variety of different marketing elements that must come together to produce an effective marketing plan. The 4 Ps seem to work well for planning a marketing campaign for products such as toothpaste, computers, and Halloween masks. In the consulting business you will need to expand the definition a bit.

On the other hand, the fact that consulting is a service rather than a product is not a reason to think marketing will not work. Just because your client doesn't receive something to put in a box, it doesn't mean there is no value. However, your clients can't see, hear, taste, smell, or feel your services before they purchase them. So what are they buying? They are buying a promise that your consulting will solve their problems. They must have faith that you will deliver as you state in your proposal.

People buy solutions, not products. The tried-and-true example is the hardware store that sells drills. People really don't buy drills; they buy holes. They want a hole in a particular place and of a particular size. So the hardware store owner is selling solutions: holes. As consultants we are in the solution-selling business.

How do the 4 Ps relate to consulting? Let's look at each one.

Product As mentioned earlier, a consultant's product is the service you offer your clients. Whether you are a consultant in real estate, publishing, electrical engineering, computer-aided design, finance, weddings, or dog grooming, your product is *you* and the expertise, knowledge, and experience you bring to your clients.

Price Price is always a hot topic for consultants. In my seminars I always have more questions about pricing consulting services than anything else. For an in-depth discussion about how and what to charge, see one of my earlier books, *The Business of Consulting,* published by Jossey-Bass.

What is most interesting to contemplate here is that if clients cannot see your expertise, cannot touch your knowledge, cannot hear your experience, it may be difficult for them to make a decision. How can they know the value you have placed on the service you will offer?

Clients have a difficult time understanding why we charge as much as we do; it's even more difficult when they must have faith in the outcome. Clients usually like and trust you before they agree to your price.

Quick tip . . .

> When your clients purchase your consulting, they are buying a promise of satisfaction. Why not give them a 100 percent money-back guarantee. Nervous about doing that? Think about how your client may feel. If you don't believe in yourself, who will?

Placement Placement is another concept that is difficult to explain in the service arena. In product sales, placement is actually distribution. But what is placement in consulting? Whether you work alone or with other consultants, the service resides within the people who are delivering it. Your services are inseparable from you.

Another way to look at placement is where you complete the services. Do you do all, some, or none of your work at the client's place of business? This may affect price in the market mix. For example, if you are an executive coach you may charge one price for the time you spend in your office compiling data, designing questionnaires, and putting materials together. You may charge a much higher price when you work one-to-one with the executives.

Promotion Typically when marketing products, the term promotion refers to things like coupons that push sales or persuade buyers to ask for a brand. We can broaden the definition of promotion of services. For example, in consulting it includes all the marketing methods available for you to use in marketing your consulting services. What mix of personal sales, publicity, advertising, direct mail, and telemarketing should you use?

CONSULTANTS AND MARKETING

Consultants in my workshop, So You Want to Be a Consultant, made the following statements. How would you respond to these consultants?

- "Marketing takes too long and it doesn't work for consultants anyway!"
- "I am not a salesman and I would never have become a consultant if I knew I had to market and sell!"
- "Marketing? It's a mystery to me. Isn't that what big companies like Coca-Cola do; they have entire departments and they conduct research, do taste tests, and study the buyers' habits to know what kind of ads to buy and how to sell more Coke."
- "I've been in business for nine months and have already spent thousands of dollars on my brochure. I don't see a payoff."
- "I don't do any marketing. It's too expensive and takes too much time. Besides, my clients wouldn't like it if I became a pushy salesperson."

If any of these consultants are successful, they have done some kind of market analysis, goal setting, market planning, and customer sales. They just may not call it that. Whether you like it or not, you are marketing all the time. Your present clients are making judgments about your work and at least subconsciously are deciding whether they would hire you again or whether they would refer you to another colleague. Anyone you come in contact with at work, while shopping, in an airplane, at church, or at Rotary is a potential client or could lead you to a potential client.

So the argument goes, if you are researching, marketing, and selling anyway, why not organize it in a way that you can draw on lessons learned, make decisions based on data, and plan the most efficient path to success. Let's get back to our consultant comments.

- "Marketing takes too long and it doesn't work for consultants anyway!"

Marketing does take time. It takes time in two ways. You must invest time in marketing activities and it takes some time before you will see results, perhaps six months to a year or more. We maintained a relationship with one client for three years before something came to fruition. This is common for consultants, for a couple of reasons. First, we sell a high-ticket item and it generally takes longer to make a decision about a large purchase than a small one. Second, what we sell is intangible. In many cases we sell ideas and concepts. It is sometimes difficult for people to buy what they can't see, so they ask us to write proposals. This gives them something tangible to hold. It does take time, but like every other business, you'd better market some way or you won't be in business for very long.

- "I am not a salesman and I would never have become a consultant if I knew I had to market and sell!"

You are a salesman. We are all salesmen and women in all that we do. Your first day as a salesman was the day you first tried to convince your parents to purchase a box of cereal because it had a treasure buried deep inside the box of flakes. You were directly affected by the cereal company's marketing, and you did exactly what they hoped you would. You became a miniature salesperson for them by begging your parents to purchase the cereal. Now you regularly sell your ideas about local politics to your friends; sell your rationale for why they cannot stay out past midnight to your children; and sell your need for a new car to your spouse. Face it, you are a salesperson.

Post a positive affirmation about marketing where you can see it every day: on your computer, in your Day-Timer®, in your wallet's clear window.

- "Marketing? It's a mystery to me. Isn't that what big companies like Coca-Cola do? They have entire departments and they conduct research, do taste tests, and study the buyers' habits to know what kind of ads to buy and how to sell more Coke."

Marketing is all of these things and more. For the consultant, you will do some research about your clients and your competition. You also need to assess yourself. Once you put your data on paper, you will be able to develop a solid marketing strategy for your consulting business. But it's not a mystery. You can follow the ABCs of marketing and select some effective as well as enjoyable marketing tools and activities. You will learn a lot about how to market in this book. You will not learn a great deal about marketing theory. My intent is to make creating your marketing plan as easy as drinking a Coke!

- "I've been in business for nine months and have already spent thousands of dollars on my brochure. I don't see a payoff."

Brochures alone will not sell your services. I learned that the hard way. We designed and printed a great brochure to market a product. But it failed. The entire campaign barely paid for the brochures! What went wrong? Lots. Timing was bad. The price point was too high. The concept was too difficult to sell in a brochure. But there is good news too. We learned a huge amount with that failed effort. As Tom Peters is fond of saying, "Fail faster!" Fail faster and get on with the successes.

- "I don't do any marketing. It's too expensive and takes too much time. Besides, my clients wouldn't like it if I became a pushy salesperson."

This is the comment of an uninformed person. Must you become a pushy salesperson to sell your consulting services? Of course not. In actuality, if the person who was quoted above has any business at all, some marketing is happening. It may be subtle personal marketing, but marketing is occurring. Do you believe you add value for your clients? Do you have vendors that add value for you? Do you welcome those vendors' calls? If you answered "yes" three times, the message should be clear. If you view yourself as a pest, it will undermine your persistence. This book will show you how to help your clients see that you add value.

Do all consultants have the same attitude? Absolutely not! Although I do remember when I fell into this same uninformed category. In business for five years, I made a sales call (though I refused to call it that) to Coopers and Lybrand. I scheduled the "visit" with Ian Littman by phone and corrected him when he called it a "sales call" by saying, "I don't do sales and marketing, but I will come and talk to you." After we reached an agreement on what we would do for them, Ian said, "Well, that was the best non-sales call sale I've ever been a part of." His tongue-in-cheek comment felt like someone had dumped a pail of cold water over me! I got it. I had a great sales and marketing routine going and I needed to recognize what I was doing. As consultants, our main job is to help our clients. However, we can't help them if they don't know what we can do, or even that we exist! And that's what marketing is all about.

My real estate consultant, Marianne Scott, has a very healthy attitude about marketing and selling her services. When she learned that I was writing this book, she said, "Marketing is all about selling yourself and you need to use what you do best to market. Some real estate consultants are good at baking chocolate chip cookies, some are good at cold calling, and some know how to hang a banner from an airplane to drum up business; I know people who have done all of those things. I don't do any of them because I'm not good at them. I am knowledgeable about the real estate market and the area, and providing service. My marketing strategy is to go after referrals and repeat business by providing excellent service." And it must be working, because 90 percent of Marianne's business is from referrals and repeat clients.

Marketing for Consultants Quiz

1. Marketing is a peripheral part of consulting; the only thing that's important is doing the best work for your clients.

2. A marketing plan is critical for large consulting firms, but I can get along without one since I practice alone.

3. Marketing is expensive and takes a great deal of time if you are going to do it right.

4. I am just getting started and already have more work than I can handle, so marketing now would be a waste of my time.

5. Marketing is a mystery to most people, and the techniques must be studied carefully before developing or implementing a plan.

6. Selling will ruin the professional image my partners and I have created.

7. My clients already know what we do, so there is no reason to market.

8. Marketing on the web is only for big consulting companies.

9. It's best to hire an outside firm to develop your marketing plans.

10. Word-of-mouth marketing is the only thing a consultant must do.

Many consultants have some or all of these thoughts. It should be clear that each of these statements is false or mostly false, but why are they false? Let's explore some of the reasons.

1. Yes, it is critical that you do a superb job for your client, but marketing is more than a peripheral part of what a consultant does. No marketing; no work. Do remember that one of the best things you can do is to get your satisfied clients to provide referrals for new business for you. So if you do good work, ask for more business. That's marketing.

2. Consultants are busy. You need to put your plan on paper or you will not do what needs to be done.

3. This book is filled with fast, easy, and free marketing techniques and ideas.

4. Eventually that work will be completed and then what will you do? The most important time to market is when you are too busy to do so.

5. Like most topics, marketing is filled with theory. You do not need to know all the theory to start. In fact, you will learn throughout this book how much you know already. Marketing can be practical. It is common sense with a dash of creativity thrown in for fun.

6. If your attitude about selling is that you are helping your client, it can only enhance your image. Isn't that what you are trying to do? You have a product or service that can help your clients if they take advantage of it.

7. Yes, your current clients probably do. But you won't be working for your current clients forever. You need to inform potential clients what you do so they can make an informed choice.

8. Marketing on the web is perfect for small companies. Asking for your web address is almost as common as asking for your telephone number.

9. You will want to hire an expert for certain things, such as designing your logo and your business stationery, but you can develop your own marketing plan.

10. Word-of-mouth marketing is the best kind of marketing a consultant can have. However, word-of-mouth marketing does not appear out of thin air. The consultant did something first—completed a difficult task that resulted in a satisfied client or perhaps gained a reputation as an internal expert. Eventually, the consultant sold services. In either case, that word of mouth must be maintained in order to continue to grow the business. It's going to need a little help from a marketing plan.

Marketing Pitfalls for Consultants

There are four common pitfalls for consultants. I see these occurring over and over. We will examine each of these throughout the book. Decide whether or not you have fallen into any of these. If so, why has this occurred? Next, think about why I might be calling these pitfalls.

- Obtaining a big contract that doesn't allow you the time for marketing.
- Conducting sporadic marketing activities rather than regularly scheduled events.
- Having a plan but not on paper.
- Avoiding cold calls at all cost.

Watch for the reasons throughout the book.

THE ABCs OF MARKETING

So what's a consultant to do? Well, unlike the consultants that you heard about at the beginning of the chapter, you do not wait until your business is in trouble to market—after you've lost your key client, after your sponsor has left the company, or after the market goes south. You must plan ahead. You must have a marketing plan in place.

Must it be a time-consuming, difficult process? The answer is "no." It can be as easy as ABC. To be successful you must have *assessed* your situation, *built* a client base, and *contacted* potential clients. I call these the ABCs of Marketing. With these in place you will safeguard yourself against the potential perils of owning your own business.

Let me introduce each of the ABCs here, as shown in Figure 1.1. Following this chapter, the book is organized in four parts. The first three sections correspond to the ABCs of marketing and will expand beyond the description I provide here. They will also present practical implementation plans for each phase. The fourth part of the book introduces additional support.

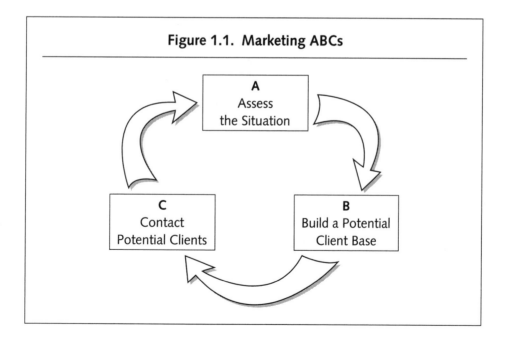

Figure 1.1. Marketing ABCs

A
Assess
the Situation

B
Build a Potential
Client Base

C
Contact
Potential Clients

A: Assess the Situation

Assessing the situation means examining from an internal and an external perspective. Internally you will examine your consulting company. Externally you will examine your competition and your customers.

Why an internal assessment of you and your consulting company? A solid marketing plan will be based on where you are today and where you want to be in the future. Before developing a marketing plan, review your business plan and strategy. They will provide a foundation for your marketing plan. If you have recently completed or updated your business plan, you may not need to do much here. Starting with who you are, what services and products your company offers, what unique position your company holds to set it aside from your competition, as well as what financial situation exists, creates a basis from which many assumptions are made.

For example, if you are the only computer consultant in your small city, you have a unique advantage that probably allows you to charge a premium price for your services. On the other hand, if your specialty is time management and your local community college offers a time management class for $75, you will need to keep its competitive price in mind when you set fees and when you determine who you will target as your audience. What strengths and weaknesses define your present company? What opportunities and threats could define your future company?

Why assess your competition? You may be surprised about who your competitors are. In addition to consulting firms that are the same size, in the same location, and who deliver the same services, you will want to consider those that are larger who can offer more services and those in other states whose employees don't mind traveling. You may want to consider other organizations such as colleges, associations, and retail stores that provide consulting with the products they sell. You will want to examine your competitors' positions in the marketplace and how you might position yourself against their weaknesses or in spite of their strengths. For example, a waste-management consulting firm may have a national reputation and employees who have written a book that is respected by the industry. You may be able to underbid them if you have a smaller organization with lower overhead. Consultants frequently overlook college professors as possible competitors, when in fact they can be a strong competitive force for several reasons. First, they have a university name behind them and second, they can easily underbid you, since they already have a full-time job and no overhead. Frequently, universities encourage their professors to consult to obtain practical experience and to gain community exposure.

Why assess your customers? You will want to assess your present as well as your potential clients. Examine your present clients. Where are they now? Where do they want to be? And how can you help them get there? What services do they use now and what services do you offer that they have not utilized? Is there some opportunity for cross-selling? For taking your services to another department? Look for new clients. Who is in your geographic area that you have not contacted? Perhaps you have been reluctant to call on the larger companies in your area. What can you offer them? If you focus on a specific industry, have you marketed to all the companies in the industry? How about related industries? An assessment will remind you of the many marketing opportunities available to you.

After completing an internal and external assessment of your firm, your competition, and your clients, you will want to assess the messages you are already sending to clients and potential clients. The message is your image or what the client sees and hears from you already. It is important that the image be clear and consistent. Your assessment provides the input you will need to build a strong client base.

B: Build a Potential Client Base

Building a potential client base will require that you complete three key actions. First, you will analyze the data you gathered in the Assessment Phase. Second, you will develop a marketing plan. Third, you will target and identify specific clients or groups of clients. This phase can be a lot of work. It can also be confusing. But it is also exciting.

It is a lot of work because you will analyze what you learned in the Assessment Phase to determine which clients you should target. You cannot pursue every potential client in the universe, so you will need to make difficult decisions to narrow the field. Put everything you learned in Phase A about you and your company, about your competitors, and about your potential clients in the mix. Then begin to look for the opportunities. The analysis will lead you to the answer.

This phase can also be confusing. Unless you are a marketing major, you may have many questions about all the marketing tools available to you. What's the difference between advertising and publicity? What are promotional activities? What's the relationship between PR, publicity, and a press release? What's a media blitz and do you need one? Is there a marketing mix that's best for consultants? Should you buy a mailing list? What about a brochure? Business cards? Pricing? Direct mail? Telemarketing? Trade shows? Or does any of it matter? There are many marketing tools available to you. Try to see this as many opportunities rather than confusing. Consulting is a unique profession that requires a unique marketing plan. Although all of the options can be confusing at first, a little common sense and a lot of creativity will help you make practical decisions.

In the end, however, this phase is exciting. It is now that you will prepare a marketing plan—putting your ideas on paper. Don't be dismayed if you have a small (or even non-existent) marketing budget. You will be surprised about how much you can do with very little money. You will also begin a plan for prospecting for new clients and new opportunities. Starting something new is always exciting.

C: Contact Potential Clients

This is actually the sales part of the marketing process. In this phase you contact potential clients and convince them to use your services. You will come across concepts such as opening and closing sales, cold calls, client-centered selling, and rainmaking. This is the place in the process when you will also want to figure out how you can get your clients to market and sell for you and how to find more repeat business.

As I stated, this is the "sales" step in the process. In a sense, selling is the culmination of the marketing process when you are increasing work with present clients and convincing new clients to use your services. The words "sales" and "marketing" are often linked. They are separate and distinct activities, and yet they are so related that it is difficult to tell when one ends and the other begins.

This book presents marketing as prior to sales. Typically a consultant would put together a marketing plan; then a potential client would hear about the consultant due to the marketing and contact the consultant. After meeting with the consultant, the client might decide to purchase the consultant's services.

Now when does the "marketing" end and the "sale" begin? Is it when the potential client hears about the consultant? When the client contacts the consultant? When the consultant meets with the client? When the consultant opens a sales pitch? When the client decides the services are necessary? When the client agrees to purchase the consultant's services? When the consultant closes the sale? When the consultant sends the proposal? When a contract is signed? When the consultant delivers the services? When the client writes the check? It could be any of these. For a consultant, these actions may occur over several weeks. For larger sales, the actions may even occur over several months.

It is difficult to clearly determine the exact point where marketing and sales split. And this is good. If you can accept how intertwined the two processes are and how dependent on each other they are, you will appreciate how important marketing your business is. If you absolutely need to define the difference, I think of marketing as focusing on many people and organizations at once; I think of sales as focusing on only one person or organization. Marketing is a broader effort; sales is a specifically defined, concentrated effort. Even with my definition, it is still difficult to determine whether a particular activity is sales or marketing. Even though many large organizations have separate sales and marketing departments, I firmly believe that both are occurring all the time no matter what the size of your business.

To expand on this, remember that what happens both during the delivery of services and after the sale is completely over and the consultant has cashed the check are all marketing moments. As a consultant you are always "on" with respect to marketing. You are marketing during delivery of services when you are on time and under budget. You are marketing during delivery if you are honest, ethical, and easy to work with. You are marketing after the work is completed when you have given more than you promised or when you follow up to ensure that progress continues. On the other hand, you are also undermining any marketing efforts when you are rude or short with employees, when you bad-mouth the competition, when you miss deadlines, or when you deliver shoddy work. The point is that marketing and selling consulting services never stops. You are selling you. And that means there is only one time to market: all the time.

MARKETING FROM DAY ONE

The most successful consultants recognized the importance of marketing and started marketing activities long before they had their business cards printed, in fact long before they became consultants. Actions you have probably taken since starting your consulting practice will be helpful now as you develop a solid marketing plan. From the start, from day one you should:

- *Start a mailing list.* Every person you come in contact with who has the potential of being a client or knowing someone who could be a client should be on this list. As the list grows, you will organize it so that you can easily print labels for specialty mailings, for example, CEOs, personal contacts, female executives, petroleum industry, or retail contacts.

- *Start a file of marketing ideas.* If you see an AT&T ad, a Dilbert® cartoon, an item in a catalog, or hundreds of other things that suggest marketing ideas, file them in one place. You will be busy with other things, and you will forget them if you don't clip them right away. We use an accordion file. The extra space gives us room to add small items that could be sent, such as pins, clips, or small toys.

- *Print business cards early.* The least costly, high-impact marketing tool you have is your business card. It will take a few months to work with a designer to create a logo and design for your stationery. Therefore, print a few hundred cards to get you started. However, do not let these cards be a substitute for high quality very long. They send a message and project your image. Ensure that they are as professional looking as possible and start working with a designer as soon as you can.

- *Begin a testimonial file.* Your clients will begin to rave about your work. Collect those statements. You may receive unsolicited thank-you letters or notes. Place them in a file. If clients compliment your work verbally, you may ask them to put it in writing. You will use these testimonials for brochure copy, in prospecting letters, or in proposals.

Initiating these activities from the first day you are in business ensures that you will be better prepared to implement many of the marketing tools presented in Chapter Five.

So what's marketing all about? It's about getting your name in front of clients and keeping it there. It's about keeping work flowing and your consulting practice growing. It's all about staying in business. Part One of this book will ensure that you assess your situation adequately.

―――――

MARKETING: TAKE ACTION

1. The 4 Ps of marketing are Product, Price, Placement, and Promotion. What could you do differently in each that might expand your client base?

2. What was your score on the Marketing for Consultants Quiz? How satisfied were you with your score? What do you think you need to do about it?

3. The ABCs of marketing are Assess the Situation, Build a Potential Client Base, and Contact Potential Clients. How would you rate what you do in each of these three areas? What will you need to do to improve in each area?

4. As a consultant you are always "on" with regard to marketing your business. In what areas, when, and where might you improve your attention to marketing?

5. Examine the four common pitfalls. Have you fallen into any of them? What do you predict will be discussed about each?

Assess the Situation

Internal Assessment

What's Your Company's Marketing Success?

How do you get started with a marketing plan? What do you do? How do you do it? Like the consultants in Chapter One, you cannot just send brochures to a purchased mailing list, then sit back and wait for clients to call. To be a successful consultant, you must market your services—getting the word out to the right people. Granted, you may market to whomever and to whatever extent you would like. But you cannot successfully market to the world. You must get the word out, but you need to narrow your scope.

You might be the best consultant in the world, know the most innovative solutions, be the most knowledgeable in your field, and provide the most return on investment of any in your area. But if no one knows you exist, how will clients find you? You need to let people know that you and your business are available to serve them. You need to promote yourself. And as stated at the end of the last chapter, you need to do it *all the time*. However, before you promote yourself you need to determine exactly what you are promoting and to whom. You have established a strategy in your business plan. It is time to reassess that strategy now from a marketing perspective.

As mentioned earlier, a marketing class will most likely cover market research and market reach. This chapter begins to explore the research phase—the A: Assessing the Situation Phase as I defined it in the last chapter. You will conduct research by assessing your consulting company, competition, and clients. This chapter focuses on your consulting company.

WHY MARKET RESEARCH?

You probably do very little in life without conducting some form of research and then devising a plan. For example, if you are planning a party, you will conduct research in your mind that might include some of the following data points:

- Whose parties have you recently attended?
- Who gets along with whom?
- Which of your friends know or do not know each other?
- What statement do you want to make with refreshments?
- What happened at the last parties you attended?
- What is on your personal or the community calendar in the near future?

Next you will devise a plan for the party that may include some or all of these items:

- Date and time you will hold the party.
- List of people you will invite.
- Food you will serve.
- Location of the party.

Here's another example. Think about the last time you took the car to have its oil changed. You determined the date and mileage of the last oil change (research). You decided whether you would take the car in after work or wait until Saturday morning (plan).

This exercise demonstrates how you research and plan almost everything you do. Therefore, shouldn't you do the same when it comes to marketing your business? Yet many people do not and then wonder why they have not been successful. Research and planning provide the foundation for a successful marketing execution.

ASSESSING YOUR CONSULTING COMPANY

The first step in the Assessing the Situation Phase is to assess your company. This in essence is researching yourself. Consulting is a personal service business. Therefore, if you are a single practitioner, this may mean assessing your personal desires, qualifications, successes, and failures as well as those of your company.

The next few pages will help you assess your business.

Define Your Business

Begin by defining your business with a narrative. As mentioned earlier, if you have recently completed your business plan, you may review and/or revise it. The following narrative will help you think through the basic information about your consulting business and prepare you to use the diagnostic tools that follow.

Demographics What's the name of your business? The address? Telephone and fax numbers? What's the e-mail address? What's the website? Who is the owner(s)? What's the business structure and, if incorporated, where?

General Information What business are you in? What are the mission, vision, and purpose of your consulting business? That is, why are you in business? What work do you conduct? Where is your business located?

Changes What information is important about the start of this business? For example, is it a new business or an expansion of an existing business? What was the start-up date?

The Work What specific activities does the business conduct to raise revenue? What services and/or products does it provide?

Success Expectations How successful is your business? How do you measure success? Why do you believe your business will continue to succeed? Do you believe the business will grow? How will it grow? What relevant experience do you bring to the business of consulting?

Reputation How are you perceived in the marketplace? How satisfied are your clients?

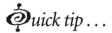*Quick tip . . .*

> Subscribe to the *Wall Street Journal* and *Fortune* magazine to continue
> to be knowledgeable about what is happening in the industries you are
> serving. Knowing what is happening will help you predict what your
> clients will need and what you might need to change in your strategy.

Future Plans What plans do you have for your business? What are your goals for
the business? Are your goals specific, measurable, and time bound?

Pull this section together by completing this statement.

I am a consultant who helps my client to _____

_____.

This benefits them _____

_____.

Define Your Management Plan

Defining your management plan will help you think through the resources you
have to construct and implement a marketing plan for your consulting business.

Management Who are the key players in your business? What are their duties,
compensations, and benefits? If you are the sole employee, how do you manage all
that needs to be completed? What is your salary?

Support Staff When do you expect to hire additional personnel—if ever? How
often do you use specialty contract assistance to complete the work? What percent
of your income is spent on support personnel? What percent of the time do you
believe you are using your time wisely?

Expertise What experience do you have in marketing, sales, managing a business,
and other supporting roles? What is your education level? What professional support do you use, such as an attorney, accountant, or banker? What banking services do you use and where? What process are you using to establish credit?

My management plan suggests:

- Amount of time I have available for marketing is _____.
- Amount of expertise I have for marketing is _____.
- Other expertise I have available to me is _____.
- Kind and amount of expertise I will call upon is _____.
- Ideas for managing the time required to implement marketing: _____
  _____.

Define Your Company's Customer Base

Defining your company's customer base will clarify the kind of customers you now serve. You should begin thinking about whether you have limited yourself through size, industry, or scope of work. You will want to think outside these parameters when you create a new marketing plan for your consulting business.

Companies Who are your current customers? How many clients do you serve now? Who are you serving in those companies? Which departments and/or divisions are you serving? Who are your potential customers? How satisfied are your customers?

Corporate Demographics What is the size of each of the companies you serve? Where are your customers located?

Customer Demographics At what level of the organization are you working? Are you working with individuals, teams, departments, or the entire company?

Industry What industry or industries are you targeting? Are you in a stable, growing, or declining industry? What is the primary geographic location of the industry? How are the companies you serve perceived in their industry?

Future What is occurring now or is expected to occur in the future that will affect your business? How will it affect your business? Is this a negative or a positive change? What is the size of the entire potential market? What percent do you expect to penetrate?

My customer base suggests that:

- The kind of companies I presently serve are _____
  _____ .

- The industries I focused on are _____
  _____ .

- My expectations for customers are _____
  _____ .

Define Your Financial Situation

Examining your financial situation will help you think through the resources you have available to implement a marketing plan for your consulting business. A large investment does not determine success. Your creativity and a wise plan will be more important.

Income Are your gross sales increasing, decreasing, or remaining the same? What percent of your income is profit? Are profits increasing, decreasing, or remaining the same? Why? Are expenses increasing, decreasing, or remaining the same? Why?

Market What is the estimated total market in dollar value of the industry you are serving? Is this market and/or industry in a growth or declining mode?

Projections What assumptions are you making at this time, such as market health, gross profit margin, required overhead, payroll, and other expenses? What are your cash-flow projections for each month of this year? What are your three-year cash-flow projections?

Emergency Funds Do you have a line of credit? How much? What is your personal net worth as displayed in a financial statement? What personal funds can you tap if necessary? What other resources are available if you need assistance?

My financial situation suggests:

- The income trend is _____
  _____ .

- The opportunities for the market are _____
_____.

- The challenges for the market are _____
_____.

- Investing in a marketing plan is _____
_____.

Summarizing Your Narrative Assessment

Now that you have defined your business, your management situation, your customer base, and your financial situation, you are in a better position to establish successful marketing strategies and tactics.

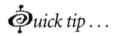 *uick tip . . .*

> Ask another consultant to read your strategy and your analysis to
> determine whether you have missed an opportunity or if you have
> forgotten something in your assessment.

SWOT YOUR COMPANY

As a consultant you have perhaps conducted a SWOT analysis on other organizations. Now it's time to conduct one on yourself. SWOT stands for strengths, weaknesses, opportunities, and threats. The strengths and weaknesses typically focus on internal factors such as service quality, financial situation, available technology, and expertise. Your strengths might be that you provide the highest quality possible and that your small size allows competitive pricing. Your weakness might be that you lack capital for expansion.

The opportunities and threats typically focus on external factors such as market demand, competitors, suppliers, the economy, social changes, or government regulations. Opportunities available to you might include a change in regulations that will require internal training by your clients or a growing dissatisfaction with the services provided by your competition. A threat might be that a new consulting firm is entering the market. Use your narrative responses from the last section to complete your SWOT analysis on Exhibit 2.1.

Exhibit 2.1. SWOT Analysis

Strengths	Weaknesses

Opportunities	Threats

Marketing Your Consulting Services

The most difficult part will be to remain objective during this analysis. You may ask a colleague to spend an afternoon challenging you to complete each section of the SWOT analysis. The two of you may want to use a creativity technique to gain another perspective. Try this: Imagine that your business is actually your own competitor. How would you view your business from a competitor's vantage point?

Whatever process you select, answer the following questions about your business:

1. What are your company's major strengths?
2. What are your company's major weaknesses?
3. What are your company's major opportunities?
4. What are your company's major threats?

Summarize these responses and prioritize the top two to four factors in each area. Hold these to use as a part of the analysis you will conduct in Chapter Five.

OTHER DATA REQUIRED

You will want to gather other data as a resource as you design your marketing plans.

- Gather historical data that might include why you formed your business and the philosophical perspective on which it was based. This will help to position your business against your competition.

- List the income and expense data that defines the profitability of each of your services and products for the last year or two. This will help you determine the most profitable focus for your business.

- Break down your sales by geographic area and company.

- Outline your present marketing plans and the results. This will help you decide what has worked best in the past.

- Gather cost of marketing projects you completed during the past year or two.

- Gather customer comment cards, training evaluations, letters of endorsement, or other customer feedback. This will explain what your customers like most about your services.

> One of the easiest and fastest measures of the effectiveness of your marketing strategy is to ask all new contacts how they heard about your company. Track the responses, and soon you will see trends about the strongest marketing paths to your door.

- Ask your employees or colleagues about their views of trends and how well you are meeting the needs of the marketplace.

CLARIFY YOUR PRESENT PREFERENCES

One of the reasons you are an entrepreneur is that your preferences can guide your business strategy. This section will assist you to clarify the type of clients and business you would like to acquire. The three activities will provide clarity about your business preferences, your skill preferences, and your personal preferences.

Business Preferences

You may change your marketing strategy in the next phase, but for now you will probably want to clarify the business preferences that have defined your strategy to date. These questions should provide you with your strategy definition. Answer the questions to the best of your knowledge. If you do not have definitive answers at this time, simply jot down what you believe has been behind your choices to date. Your responses will help you clarify how you have been thinking about your preferred client base—even if it hasn't been declared in a specific marketing plan.

- Describe your market niche in detail.

- Where is your business heading?

- What size companies do you want to serve?

- What specific geographical area do you want to serve?

- Do you want to work for government, non-profit, or for-profit organizations?

- In what industry are you specializing? What is desirable about this industry? Should you change or expand industries?

- Do you wish to serve groups or individuals?

- Do you wish to serve special markets such as start-ups or mergers?

- What is your pricing strategy and structure? How do your pricing strategy and structure differ from your competitors'?

- What kinds of projects do you want to conduct?

Your answers to questions like these will reflect the kind of business you wish to develop. For example, your strategy may be to focus on medium to large financial institutions, located along the East Coast, that are facing mergers and need assistance working toward efficient, shared visions of the future.

Skill Preferences

The knowledge, skills, and talents you use on each job help you to enjoy the work you do. The Skill Preferences Chart in Exhibit 2.2 will help you analyze some of the tasks you do for various clients. The degree to which you prefer one kind of work over another will guide you to the kind of work you will want to repeat for other clients.

Complete the Skill Preferences Chart to help you identify the kind of work you would prefer to do with clients in the future. What does your completed chart tell you about the kind of work you prefer?

Exhibit 2.2. Skill Preferences Chart

Identify projects you've completed for various organizations. Then identify the skill, knowledge, or talent required. Prioritize the list according to which you liked the most.

Project	Company	Skills, Knowledge, or Talent Used	Priority

Personal Preferences

Although your personal preferences will not seem as critical to your marketing plan as some of the other data, if you are not happy with your schedule, income level, and partnering opportunities, you may ask yourself why you are in business at all. It will eventually affect your work; your clients will notice; and business will begin to deteriorate. Or as the saying goes, "If Mama ain't happy, ain't nobody happy!" Your personal preferences are very important to your overall personal and professional success.

Complete the Personal Preferences Chart in Exhibit 2.3 to help you identify those aspects of consulting you wish to guide your future plans. In most instances these items will relate to your personal goals. What does your completed chart tell you about the kind of work you prefer?

In the next chapter you will assess your competition and your clients. In the chapter after that you will examine the image you presently project. After you have completed each of these (assessed your business, your competition, and your clients and assessed the image you project), you will begin to analyze what you learned and determine whether the strategy you defined in this chapter still makes sense. This will help you generate a list of potential customers with whom you want to do business—ensuring your company's marketing success.

MARKETING: TAKE ACTION

1. Review the assessment of your company.

   - If you have not written a marketing plan, what are you presently doing to attract business? How much time is devoted to attracting business? What percent is paying off? What opportunities are you missing?

- If you are currently using a marketing plan, what are you doing that is attracting the business you desire? What are you doing that is attracting business you do not desire? What are you not doing that could attract the business you desire?

2. What did the examination of your management and financial plan uncover about your company?

3. What did you learn about your company from the SWOT analysis?

4. After a preliminary examination of your present marketing strategy, what opportunities do you think you might be missing?

5. Analyze with care your responses to the Skill Preferences and Personal Preferences charts. What is most important for you to consider as you develop your marketing plan?

Exhibit 2.3. Personal Preferences Chart

Rate the following items using the following scale:

4 – A high priority for me
3 – A medium priority for me
2 – A low priority for me
1 – Neutral
0 – Prefer never to do this

_____ International travel
_____ Travel out of the state
_____ Travel out of the area
_____ Overnight travel
_____ Work in single industry
_____ Deliver same topic
_____ Obtain additional education
_____ Team with others
_____ Work for various firms
_____ Observe religious practices
_____ Maintain current income
_____ Increase current income
_____ Reduce living expense
_____ More leisure time
_____ Combine work and leisure
_____ High-risk jobs
_____ Many short/small projects
_____ Few large projects
_____ Build personal relationships with clients
_____ Weekends free
_____ Forty-hour work week
_____ Regularly scheduled vacations
_____ Awards and recognition
_____ Volunteer work
_____ Professional growth opportunities
_____ Tap my creativity
_____ Pursue my hobbies
_____ Time for family

External Assessment

How Do Your Competitors and Clients Stack Up?

The last chapter impressed on you the importance of research to any marketing effort. We are still in the Assessing the Situation Phase. And while the last chapter started you down the research path by having you conduct an internal assessment of your own consulting company, this chapter will move you along your research trip by having you conduct external assessment of your competition and your clients.

How do you check out your competition? How do you check up on your clients? And more importantly, why assess both of them? Living in the competitive society that we do, it is easy to understand that the last thing you want is for your consulting competitors to offer a better value to your clients and potential clients than you do. Your goal is to provide a unique service that is higher quality, completed faster, and more economical than what your competition offers. You must also be certain that you know what services your customers need—preferably before they know—as well as the quality they expect, the turnaround time they desire, and the cost that they believe is acceptable. We will begin by assessing your competition.

ASSESSING YOUR COMPETITION

One of the most important, but also one of the most difficult, aspects of your marketing research is to learn as much as you can about your competition—those organizations that are competing for the same consulting dollars that you are. Identifying the strengths and weaknesses of your competition will help to illuminate the unique attributes of your company. It will also help you define your niche later in this chapter.

Competitive Analysis

You should spend some time examining the competition you have now as well as the competition you expect to face in the near future. Your competition consists of more than just other consulting companies. Remember to include colleges and universities, industry associations, non-profits, governmental agencies, and those located outside your immediate geographical area.

You can compile your data in three different formats. You may wish to use the questions here to tell a story and put it in a narrative format. A second option would be to use the Competitor Comparison Form shown in Exhibit 3.1. I suggest that you expand the form to at least two or three times the size in this book in order for you to have enough space to list everything you will need. I like to do this on a flip-chart page, using a small marker. A third option is to use the SWOT format from the previous chapter and complete one on each of your competitors.

1. Who is your competition?

2. How do you describe your competition in the geographical area you service?

3. How do you describe your competitors' ability to deliver in the specialty areas you have targeted?

4. How do your consulting products and/or services differ from your competitors'?

5. How do your competitors' pricing structures compare to yours?

6. How much experience do your competitors have?

7. How strong is each of your competitors' name recognition?

8. What share of the market do these competitors have?

9. Is your competitors' business increasing, decreasing, or remaining steady?

10. Why would someone buy from them instead of you?

11. How do your competitors market themselves?

12. What are your comparative strengths and weaknesses in sales or marketing?

13. What differentiates you from your competitors?

Temper any industry statistics, sales information, and other information that you may have with your experience and a dose of common sense as you fill out the form.

	Exhibit 3.1. Competitor Comparison Form			
	Your Practice	**Competitor 1**	**Competitor 2**	**Competitor 3**
Name				
Location				
Fees Charged				
Time in Business				
Specialty Area				
Client Type				
Client Location				
Why Clients Use				
Client Loyalty				
Name Recognition				
Marketing Plan				
Image				
Quality of Service				
Financial Strength				
Personnel				
Other				

Where to Get the Scoop

Where can you find information about your competitors? First check out their own advertising. The junk mail that appears in your mailbox is valuable. It's a marketing research gift. Also check out the journals from industries they serve. You may find ads or articles written by them. Check the Internet, of course, and also make friends of your local librarians. They can direct you to resources you may not have known existed.

When you attend conferences, listen to your competitors' speeches. If they participate in a trade show, visit their booth and talk to their sales reps. Check the newspapers for press releases and news stories. Can you obtain additional information from former employees, customers, suppliers, other competitors, or your employees? Each of these has very different levels of reliability and you need to consider that fact. Remember that every bit of information will help.

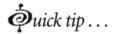

Quick tip ...

> Know your competition. Read the direct mail pieces from your competition. Visit their booths at trade shows. Attend their presentations at conferences. Read their ads and articles in your trade journal.

Assessing Beyond Your Immediate Competitors

Okay, so you've dug up all the dirt on your competitors that you can, but you know there must be some data about consulting in general that is available to include in your assessment. Where can you find it?

Your market analysis will be more beneficial if you can quote general statistics about consulting, your consulting specialty, or the industry you have chosen. This will help you determine how distinctive or similar you are compared with other consulting firms. You may find some of this data in industry journals or on the Internet. *Training* magazine and the American Society for Training and Development conduct research each year that might provide data for some of you. Kennedy Publishing is another good source for data about consulting firms.

ASSESSING YOUR CLIENTS

The second aspect of external research is assessing your clients' needs and their level of satisfaction. It goes beyond just knowing what they *need* to knowing what they *desire,* what *motivates* them, and how *satisfied* they are. Client research will give you insight into what your clients will purchase and why.

If you have been in business for any period of time, you should have some customer data from evaluation forms, testimonial letters, client satisfaction reports, or just informal comments from your clients. You may want to take time now to conduct a more formal client needs assessment or customer satisfaction survey.

Are you thinking about conducting a needs assessment? You do not have to have sophisticated software to track the results. You can use a simple Excel® spreadsheet to track responses. Our first collection process utilized colored index cards. What is more important is to ensure consistency. Ask the same questions in the same way to a large enough sample of clients. Answers to open-ended questions are always delightful to read and provide ideas and insight. The problem is quantifying the responses so that you have some baseline established for comparison the next time. You can use "yes" or "no" questions or provide a 1-to-5 rating scale to quantify level of agreement or satisfaction. The solution is to use a complementary mix of both kinds of questions—open-ended and quantitative.

What might you ask about?

- The kinds of services they need now

- What they anticipate needing in the future

- The criteria used to select one product/service over another

- What process is used to make purchasing decisions

- What they expect to happen within their own organizations

- Their preferred marketing methods for finding consultants or learning about your services

- Who your competition is

- Their past experience and satisfaction with you and/or others

- Their ideas and suggestions for improving the quality of service

If you decide that the survey will focus mostly on customer satisfaction, you may want to consider asking a two-part question. First, how well does your company meet customer expectations and, second, how important is it to the customer? For example, you may ask about how well you do on speed and meeting deadlines. Clients may rate you as excellent, but they may say that speed is only slightly important. That may be hard to imagine in this day of speed, but it may be a message that suggests that your clients want you to spend more time with them, rather than being totally focused on the job.

You might also hire an external resource to conduct focus groups for you. If you decide to do this, think about a time when many of your clients might be in the same area at the same time—at an industry convention, for example.

One last idea is one that I prefer because it is personal and we are a small company: I write a letter to our clients letting them know that we are gathering information that will help us improve our services. I enclose a second sheet with four questions and ask them to take a couple of minutes to complete it and place it in the self-addressed stamped envelope that is also enclosed. The questions are:

- What do you like about working with ebb associates?
- What would you like us to do differently?
- What would you like us to continue to provide for our clients?
- What would you like us to add to what we do now?

We thank them and let them know that they do not need to sign the page, but that we would like to talk to them if they are interested.

Never stop asking your clients questions. They are the best source of information for ensuring that you offer and deliver the things that they want.

$\mathcal{Q}$uick tip . . .

> Need to conduct customer service research, but don't have the time or resources? Contact your local college or university to utilize business students to design and conduct the research. Be sure to plan far enough in advance, since it may take longer than if you hired a marketing firm or if your company completed the research.

WHAT'S THAT POSITION THING?

In Chapter One we discussed the 4 Ps: Product, Price, Placement, and Promotion. Positioning is a fifth P that is critical to your marketing plan. Your position is how you are presently perceived by your clients and competitors. The concept identifies various dimensions that set you and your competition apart. Where you appear on these dimensions is your *position*. To determine position you need two pieces of information. First, what is unique about the products and services you deliver? Second, what is unique about what your competition offers?

Positioning and Your Niche

Your niche is related to your position; however, it is where you *wish* to be perceived. People often refer to finding a hole and filling it. If you can determine whether there is a niche, "the hole" that is not filled for your clients, you will have a ready-made market. You need to identify what your clients need that is not readily available to them.

Your niche is the place you wish to occupy that will set you apart from most of your competition. It might be the specific services you provide, how you provide those services, the people to whom you provide the services, or even the expertise and/or experience you have when providing these services. *Your niche is the unique position you hold when compared to the rest of your competition.* Your niche is your unique combination of components that gives you an unfair advantage over your competition. A combination of your position and your niche defines how you portray yourself and the services you offer to your targeted marketplace. So your consulting company's position will be determined by the niche you have selected.

One of the reasons new consulting companies fail is because they are unable to identify a specific niche. They print business cards, begin to network with potential clients, land a few contracts, and then when they need to move out to the next circle of clients, they have difficulty finding work. Part of the reason is that they have not established something unique that they offer. If a consultant is just like the rest of the pack and the other consultants arrived at the client's door first, the new consultant has little chance of landing new work. Start-up companies do best if they narrow their focus to a specifically defined market. Sometimes that seems scary to new companies that worry that a narrow niche will not generate enough business to sustain them.

If you are a small company, it is usually easier to create your own position than to compete against larger companies for theirs. In *The 22 Immutable Laws of Mar-*

keting, authors Ries and Trout claim, "If you can't be the first in a category, set up a new category that you can be first in."

When ebb associates first started in the late 1970s, we decided to offer customized training programs. We had no idea whether the niche we had chosen was unique. This was a time when the giants were selling training programs accompanied by videotapes and training manuals. Videotapes were created with a huge budget and training materials were designed generically to use in many organizations. Trainers were scripted and activities were timed. It was a time before PCs and easy tailoring. In fact, I remember using a Kroy headline machine that was like a giant typewriter on which we typed titles on clear tape and pasted them on paper to create large title pages and headers for overhead transparencies. Desktop publishing was a dream of the future.

Indeed, it was a time when the concept of customization was too difficult and too costly—at least for the large training consulting firms. A small company like ebb associates could focus on one client at a time and offer a special service, customizing exactly what the client needed. We offered the service and clients hired us. One of the most finely customized training programs we designed was a time management module for janitors on a specific ward in a hospital.

How did we know there was a need? As a trainer, I had heard complaints from participants for years that they could not transfer what they learned in training sessions. How, they would demand, could they be expected to transfer examples from a candy bar manufacturer back to their job as an environmentalist? The training gurus of the time were adamant that the required skills were the same, so the transfer of skills should be natural. We decided that no matter who was right, learning would not transfer to the workplace if the learner did not believe it would. Richard Bach's quote in *Illusions* sums up the situation, "Argue for your limitations, and sure enough they're yours."

So the niche we had chosen met the criteria for potential success. There was a hole to fill. The industry leaders were not filling it. Clients were asking for the hole to be filled. And it appeared that a small company like ours could accomplish fast delivery of the service. This was a recipe for success and it launched ebb associates quickly.

You, too, can position yourself and create your own niche. Use this process to discover where your competition is, what potential clients want, and how you determine your own niche.

Determine Your Position and Identify Your Niche

Positioning may sound complicated, especially if you read about how 7-Up® positioned itself against the cola market as the UnCola. Or how Close-Up® positioned itself as the toothpaste for young adults who care more about relationships than cavities. The position grid in Exhibit 3.2 shows how Close-Up created a unique niche away from its competitors.

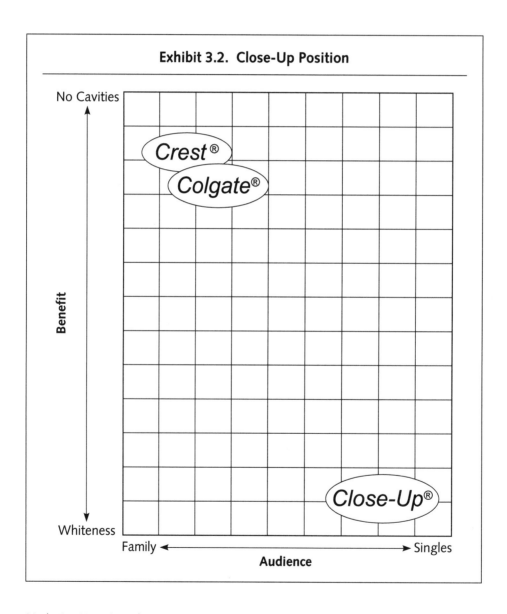

Exhibit 3.2. Close-Up Position

It doesn't have to be that difficult. Think about positioning as a way for you to clearly identify what you do better than your competition. Are you the low-cost alternative? Are you the premium quality leader? Are you the full-service provider? When you talk to your clients, they compare you to other consulting groups. How? What comparisons do they use?

The following process will assist with your thinking. Use the instructions below and complete the form provided in Exhibit 3.3.

Exhibit 3.3. Positioning Process

1. Identify your competitors.

2. Identify attributes for each competitor.

3. Identify the attributes that are used for selecting consultants.

4. 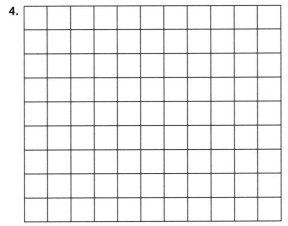 Position your competition on this grid.

5. Identify your unique advantages and place yourself on the grid.

6. Identify anything your clients might desire that competitors do not provide.

7. Describe your proposed niche in one phrase.

To complete the form, first identify everyone who is competing for your clients. Yes, you will list all the consultants who live in your geographic area, but remember also those who come from out of town, out of state, perhaps even out of the country. Also remember universities, colleges, and other schools that may conduct classes or offer services that may take potential clients away from you. Remember, too, the professors who have sideline businesses that compete with you. Sometimes your professional association may offer similar services.

Next, briefly describe the position of each competitor by identifying a couple of attributes for each. You may use some of the information that you gathered on your Competitor Comparison Form in Exhibit 3.1. That might include how the service is delivered: fast, inexpensively, high quality, and so on. Identify who receives the services: a specific industry, level in the organization, and so forth. Describe the basis of the service: research based, experience based, creative, customized, repeatable. Consider also how the competitors are perceived, such as their image, size, or reputation.

Examine the attributes you defined in the second step and determine which ones clients seem to use most often to select consultants. You will use these in the next step to create a grid for consultants in your area. For example, one axis might be high quality or price. A second axis might be to whom services are provided with executives at one end and line workers at the other.

Now select the attributes as names for the two axes. Estimate where the consultants you listed in step one would be positioned.

Identify your unique strengths and place yourself on the grid. You may need to try this a couple of times before you discover what's unique to you. Some of the things you might consider include your time in the market, number of prestigious clients you serve, your business philosophy, your industry experience, your community involvement, and your professional affiliations. If you have difficulty pinpointing your position, you have probably not been specific enough about your niche. If this is the case, you may want to revisit your vision and mission. If you think you just need to do some tweaking, move to the next step.

Next examine the consultant's positions and what they offer to clients. Is anything missing? Do you hear clients requesting attributes that are not being met? If so, is this a "hole that needs to be filled"? Is it a potential niche for you?

Last, describe your proposed niche. What benefits do you offer your clients? This can be a takeoff of your elevator speech (describing what you do in sixty seconds or less), but may be shorter and has a marketing twist to it. It identifies what you are known for and of what you are most proud. It may also include the industry you work in. These might include:

- The most successful change management process for Fortune 500 companies
- The fastest audit in the state
- The most accurate audit in the region
- The premier provider of human resource services
- The most creative computer graphics for the music industry
- The fastest time-management design
- The most practical team-building skills program

Discovering your niche and positioning your company is the first step. Next you must back it up with action by delivering what you say you will. To drive your position home to clients, you will sell your niche. Every aspect of your marketing plan should embody the unique niche you fill for clients. Your niche becomes your company's personality.

EXPLORE OTHER MARKETS

Now that you have established a niche and position for yourself, let's consider what clients you might focus on. Identify individual clients that you do not serve that you believe could use the attributes you offer. Identify industries that you do not serve that you believe could use the services and attributes you offer.

Did you describe the size of client you would like to serve? If not, don't limit yourself to small clients if you are a small company. I tell all consultants to "Go after the big fish because it takes the same amount of time to bait the hook." That means that it will take the same amount of time to market to large clients and the payoff may be greater in potential repeat business. If you think you might be questioned by potential clients about why you could do the job better, there are many answers. Over the years I have found these reasons to be important to my clients.

First, we are faster. We are small, so there is no bureaucracy or delays. The customer will know everyone's name in our company. They will get fast turnaround time and quick responses. Since we are small, almost anyone who answers the phone can provide information with the first call.

Second, the client will have our undivided attention. Because we are small, we handle fewer clients at one time and the client will not be competing with numerous other clients.

Third, we are less expensive. Since we bid a fixed price per project, there is no meter running, no additional fee for a phone call, no billable hours to contend with, no quotas to reach. In addition there is no huge overhead, partner perks, or extensive administrative support to pay for.

Fourth, the client will have the best expertise. The client will work with a principle and not deal with a handoff to a junior employee. We provide experts on an as-needed basis. So the client does not pay the overhead for expertise that is not used.

I am sure you can identify many similar advantages of working with your firm. The point is, don't rule out large clients because you are small. It does take the same amount of time to bait the hook for the big ones, but you will also need to know where the big fish swim before you catch them. So you should start thinking now about large companies that you may have avoided in the past due to their size. Know where the large ones are so that you can cast your marketing net to catch them.

The next chapter addresses your image—another critical aspect of your total assessment before you begin to design your marketing plan.

MARKETING: TAKE ACTION

1. The assessment of your competitors revealed a great deal about them. Completing those tasks also revealed a great deal about you and your consulting practice. What did you learn about yourself and the services you offer while assessing your competitors?

2. Most consultants offer similar services. What advantages do you offer over your competitors? Have you identified all the reasons your clients would pick you over your competitors?

3. List characteristics of your current customers and your desired customers. How do they differ? What does this tell you about your marketing plans now? What might you do differently to attract the desired customers?

4. Think about the attributes of your company's niche. What is unique about what you offer? How many of your competitors offer a similar service or product? Do you know whether clients would pay more for this special attribute? How could you find out?

5. Identify at least five potential clients who are large—much larger than the ones you now serve.

Marketing Image

What Message Do You Send?

When consultants think about marketing, often the first thing that comes to mind is a brochure. Quite honestly many consultants are successful without ever designing a brochure. You should be aware that many other items send messages to your clients as well. "Send" in this case means in the mail and/or in person. You will want to ensure that all of your messages, on paper or in person, are consistently professional.

Developing a powerful, consistent marketing message that establishes the image you desire is critical. Doing so provides repetition for potential clients, and repetition is what helps people remember you. You send marketing messages by means of who you are, what you do, and what your marketing materials look like. Your consulting company's image will influence those who hire you.

CONSISTENCY IS CRITICAL

One of the biggest marketing mistakes new consultants make is sending inconsistent messages to potential clients. This is done inadvertently. They don't mean to do it, but as their businesses evolve, their marketing strategies do too. A consultant may start out with a white business card with black ink—practical and inexpensive. She later finds folders in a nice shade of blue. A couple of months into the business she has enough money to have stationery professionally designed. The designer convinces the consultant that gray stationery with burgundy ink looks very professional. Each of these evolutions is good, but when you put all of these together, the result is an undefined look and a confused client. No, of course clients won't know they are confused, but you certainly have not left them with an image that's easy to remember.

Repetition and consistency are the keys to ensuring that potential clients remember you. If clients see the same colors and logo often enough they will remember you. Sometimes they may not remember your name, or your business name, or what you do, but they will remember you. That is why "who you are" must also be consistent with the image you are sending your clients. Consistency means that all your paper products look like they belong together. Consistency means that you project an image that is congruent with the work you do. Every time a note from you crosses a desk, every time someone looks at your business card, every time someone sees your logo on your holiday gift he or she will think of you.

MESSAGES YOU SEND IN PERSON

You may be wondering what your appearance has to do with marketing. Everything. You are your company. Your company is you. The image you project is the image your company will be known for. What do you need to consider?

Appearance

Consider your appearance, not just what you wear, but everything that adds to or detracts from your professional image. Arrive at your first meeting with a new client early enough to stop at the restroom to take a look in the mirror. Dandruff on your new blue suit? Wind-swept hair? Need a lipstick touch-up? Take care of it. And what should you wear? The best rule is to try to match your appearance to that of your potential client. When in doubt wear the better of your two choices.

In addition, keep your briefcase organized and nearly empty. Use two briefcases if you must—one to use when you visit clients and another that is stuffed with your laptop, your current file folders, Post-its, your PDF, and your airline tickets.

Carrying an overstuffed briefcase, as I sometimes do, may make you look more like a pack horse than a consultant. Also consider using a leather portfolio for taking notes. No one will notice if it's leather; they may notice if it's not. And certainly think twice before using one with any advertising on its cover.

A friend of mine consults with pharmaceutical companies. He had lined up a meeting with the vice president of sales in a company that he had not worked with. His greeting was professional, his handshake was firm, and during small talk he learned that they had something in common. Both liked to fly fish in the same stream in a neighboring state. He sat down, placed his portfolio on the table, and began to ask about the company's needs. The vice president was staring at his portfolio. He looked at it as well and was mortified to see the logo of the company's arch rival. It was the portfolio that the other pharmaceutical company had given away at its last trade show. Don't let this happen to you.

Style

Next consider your style and any mannerisms that project who you are. Always shake hands firmly. Introduce yourself to others and look people in the eye. Address people by name. These will all send a message to your clients at your first introduction and each time you meet afterward.

Attend every meeting well-prepared. Know what questions you wish to ask and listen well. Remember, if you are doing most of the talking you have most likely lost the sale.

Activities Outside of Work

Next consider your life outside of work. How much of your time do you spend meeting and greeting others outside of your work life? Are you known as a family man who attends piano recitals and soccer games? Are you a mother who balances her career and home life and still has time to give to Rotary? Are you a member of a service organization? This says something about you. Do you volunteer at the community center, give blood when it's needed, or lead fund-raising drives? Does your professional organization depend on you to assist them at conferences or local chapter meetings? Giving back to the community or your professional organization is not just a noble thing to do; it enhances your image as well.

You may also serve on advisory boards or boards of directors for the local hospital, non-profit organizations, or corporate businesses. This kind of involvement is a valuable marketing tool—showing that you are in a respected advisory role. It's important to note that all of these are opportunities to be around people who are potential clients. Even more important, however, is the image you project to others about who you are—someone who cares about your community and your professional organization, as well as someone whose advice is sought and respected by others.

MARKETING MESSAGES ON PAPER

Continue your professional look on paper. Your business cards, stationery, brochures, and other paper products all tell your present clients and potential clients something about you and your business. They project an image—be sure it is the one you want. I do not recommend that you purchase the identity packages that are available at office stores or from catalogs. They are bland and uninspiring and usually printed on mediocre paper, although a professional image need not be expensive.

Business Cards and Stationery

Your business card is often the first contact someone has with your business. It is also the least expensive, yet the most important marketing tool you have. Don't take shortcuts. Don't cut quality to save money. It will cost you in the end. Have it printed on heavy card stock—at least 80 pound. Use a professional to help you design your business card and your stationery. You can expect to pay $500 to $5,000 or more for a corporate identity design. Printing will be additional.

There are many philosophies about business cards. Again, you will need to determine the image you are trying to project. I prefer something that sends a quiet, professional message. Thus we use gray ink on light gray paper and all lowercase letters. Some of you will want to add an accent color. You could try some of the new tactile papers or stick with the classics: laid or linen. If you can, consider at least two ink colors to add impact. Be sure to include all the pertinent information and then proof it several times and give it to someone else to proof.

Use the name you want to be called on your business card, for example, Bill instead of William.

Imagine you have handed your card out at the last conference you attended, along with 13,000 other participants. You gave business cards to one hundred participants and now they are sifting through the cards they collected. What is going to make someone stop and look at your card a little longer? Heavier card stock? A unique paper or color? A great logo? If you want something that stands out among other cards, try some of these ideas:

- Try a vertical layout
- Print your picture on the card
- Add embossing or foil stamping for an elegant look
- Treat the edges creatively, deckled for example
- Use card stock that has a different color on each side
- Design a folded card that might look like a miniature brochure
- Use unusual paper, perhaps with flecks of color (remember if you use this for stationery it will not copy well)
- Have your cards cut larger or smaller
- Print a quote on the front or back
- Print tips that relate to your business on the back
- Give yourself an unusual title
- Add a picture of a book you've written
- Add a tag line, a four-word description of what you do

The choice is yours. You've got to love your business cards. They are the best marketing tool you have. You should challenge yourself to give away as many as possible. The easy way to do that is to ask others for a business card and then hand them yours. You might even hand the person two—one for a friend.

⊘uick tip ...

> If you might use your letterhead as the front page of a bound proposal, ensure that the left margin will be wide enough to accommodate the binding system you use.

Once you have figured out your business cards, the rest is easy. Select paper stock like the card stock you used for your business cards. Have your designer create letterhead, envelopes, note cards (to jot off a quick note), and mailing labels. Note that you will probably be able to save money by having your business cards and stationery printed at the same time. Pay as much attention to your envelopes as to the other items. Clients will see these first, so ensure that they recognize that something came from you.

⊘uick tip ...

> When you print stationery, print cards approximately 3¾ by 5½ inches. You can use this as a note card inside an envelope or as a postcard and use the back for the address.

Presentation Materials

If you use presentation materials at seminars, speaking engagements, or even sales calls, print them on the best paper you can get your hands on and, of course, remember to put your company name and complete contact information on the cover. Make it easy for potential clients to reach you. If you have a logo, it should also be on the cover.

The Name

You have probably selected a name for your company. There are no rules about naming your company. You should consider two things. Your name should be easy to remember and it should project the image you desire.

The name of your company should also tell a prospective client something about what you do. One of my favorites in this category is Toys "R" Us. If your name does not explicitly state what you do, like mine, you may want to add a "tag line." A tag line is three or four words that explain what you do. My tag line is "consulting, training, design" to better define the work we do.

The name can also project size. "Connie Sultant, Inc." is clearly a one-person shop. This limits your clients' perception to one person. Even if you have a dozen employees, the name does not project that fact.

What plans do you have for changes in your company's future? Will they include more people than you? "Connie Sultant and Associates" suggests that there are more consultants than Connie. However, it also suggests that Connie is the owner. This may be a problem for those who work for her now or if someone joins her firm in the future. Since all clients want the best, they will assume that Connie is the one they want without even knowing the skills of other people in the firm. On the other hand, if you have strong name recognition, such as "The Tom Peters Group," you may want to take advantage of it.

"Sultant Associates" or "CSS Consulting" conjures up a group of people working together with less emphasis on Connie. Another consideration is that the second one tells you what the company does. "Sultant Website Designers" or "Sultant Marine Engineers" clearly defines each company's area of expertise. Be sure that the names do not limit you for future growth. For example if "Sultant Website Designers" wants to branch out to software design, computer security, or general computer graphics, the name will no longer be inclusive of the work they perform.

Some company names are related to the location. Again, just be sure you do not limit yourself. "Midwest Marketing" may have a certain ring to it, but when you gain a reputation, will the name project an image that will encourage a store on Madison Avenue to hire you?

Also remember that your name will be a marketing tool, and even though you want something that is easy to remember, you do not want to be too cute. Select a name and add a graphic that adds to your marketing image, rather than detracts from it. For example, "Get Better" for a wellness training company or "Bank On Us" for a financial management consulting firm might project a less professional image than either of the companies desires—especially if they intend to provide services to Fortune 500 companies.

Your logo may be more important than the name. McDonald's golden arches are a great example. You don't need to be as big as McDonald's to have name recognition through your logo. I have had people say, "the consultant with the three little letters," referring to my lowercase name, which is an important part of my image. And although they did not remember the company, they remembered the logo and knew with whom they wanted to work.

If you are not satisfied with your name, it is never too late to change it. After being in business for four years, I was less than satisfied with the name of my company. At the time, I thought I could not change it since I had a client list and a good reputation. Now after being in business for almost a quarter of a century, I look back in amazement about how small the reach of that reputation actually was and how much easier it would have been to change it then, rather than now. In fact, although I am not contemplating a name change, I now see it as a potential marketing opportunity!

One last thing: If you have not yet done so, ask your attorney to determine whether the name you choose must be registered with the Secretary of State's office or whether it is already registered to someone else.

Logos

A logo identifies your business to the public. Like the name of your company, your logo should say something about your consulting business. It should be easy to find a designer who can create your logo for you as well as design your business cards and stationery. Your logo should be displayed proudly on your business cards, letterhead, envelopes, mailing labels, fax sheets, invoices, presentation materials, folders, table tents, t-shirts, newsletters, and advertising specialty items. Have your designer provide you with your logo in a format for your desktop. You will be surprised at how many opportunities arise for you to use it.

Let me expand on advertising specialty items. You've all seen them. They are the pens or calendars that you receive during the holidays. If you decide to send one of these items to your clients, have fun with it. Don't send them another pen. How about a stress reducer ball, or a yo-yo that lights up, or a mug filled with anything (jaw breakers, gold paper clips, coffee beans). Then create a card to go with it. For example, the yo-yo could be accompanied by a card that says, "It's been a year of ups and downs. Hope this lights up your New Year." The idea is to be creative, stand out from the crowd, and keep your name in front of your clients. Choose carefully and these will build your image quickly.

One last idea: Have your logo printed on stickers. Ours are 1½" by 1¾". We use them on the outside of folders for seminars and on some marketing materials. Like your company name, you should discuss your logo with your attorney, who will advise you about filing it with the U.S. Patent and Trademark Office in order to protect it.

Brochures

A brochure is a big step for most consultants. Our first brochure was a long iterative process that lasted over six months. It was worth it. Many consultants never have a brochure. We realized we needed one as a "leave behind" when we called on prospective clients. Potential clients often asked if I had something about the company that they could read. Again, this is one more time people will be reminded of you, so it must send the same message as the rest of your materials.

A brochure is a critical piece of your entire marketing package, and it will most likely be the most expensive. Therefore you should hire a professional designer—preferably the same one who designed your business cards. In fact, if you can afford it, design all your stationery and your brochure at the same time.

Select a designer who takes the time to ask questions about what you do and how you do it. Be certain the designer is knowledgeable of marketing and sales strategy. In addition the designer must be a good writer, or work with a good writer. It is a good sign if the designer is interested in helping you and your consulting practice overall, as opposed to simply wanting to design a brochure. Your professional will help you, but here are a few things to think about:

- Before you begin, gather some of your competitors' brochures to examine.
- Create a brochure that is flexible and timeless yet communicates enough to make a purchase decision.
- Project professional confidence, not just an expensive image.
- Use action-oriented words such as "results you can document," "seize new opportunities," "profits you can measure."
- Consider using questions instead of prose; questions increase the odds that the reader will read on to get the answers.
- Colored printing escalates the cost; avoid printing in four color when black and white could be more effective.

- Produce just enough brochures; don't let a printer convince you to print five thousand (for just a small difference) if one thousand will do. Most likely they will need to be updated by the time you get through one thousand.

- Pitch brochures that are dated; it's better than outdating you or your business.

A brochure is a serious decision for a consultant. It sends one of the strongest and longest-lasting marketing messages. It should represent you and your business in the best way possible. If you can't do it well, don't do it at all. Your brochure should project professional confidence—both in how it looks and in what it says.

Less Expensive than a Brochure

What if you are just starting out and you cannot afford to hire a designer to assist you? You could go to your local college and hire a design or marketing student. Professors are often looking for projects for their classes. In this case the brochure's schedule will conform to the class, not to your needs. One thing to remember, if you do have a student or the entire class working on your brochure, logo, business card, or whatever, you will need to be the expert in the content. Unlike a professional designer, you cannot count on students to pull out of you the powerful message you want to send. One last thing, realize that in the end you may not like the final product at all. Professional designers will ensure that they are heading in the right direction by discussing options and gathering input from you along the way. Students or a class may not have the kind of experience and expertise needed to deliver an acceptable product that delights you.

A second option if money is short is to print a one-sheet promotional flier. You may choose a tri-fold design or a single page. Keep a single page short. Nevertheless, remember to put all essential information on the front, that is, who you are, what you do, and how to reach you. Busy prospects may skim the front and make an instant decision. The following hints will help you produce a useful tool. Use bold headers to help them key in on what's important to them. Identify what you do, the benefits you provide, and some of the clients you have served. Add credibility by including your credentials, certifications, and awards. You may want to add your company's vision and mission statements. Add testimonials from satisfied clients who rave about your work. If you include a photo, you might consider an action shot instead of simply a head shot.

Promotional Package

A promotional package is a portfolio (or a two-pocket folder) containing a résumé or bio sketch, an introductory press release, a list of references or a client list, and a company history and description. You might also include a list of publications you've written and a list of your services and/or products. Testimonials can be used effectively here. Include either a page of your clients' rave reviews or several letters written by your clients on their letterhead. If you are just getting started as a consultant, ask your former employer to write a testimonial letter. You may also be able to obtain testimonials from people for whom you are doing small start-up projects or even pro bono work. Add photos and a brochure to complete your package if you have them available.

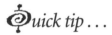*uick tip . . .*

> Collect testimonials from satisfied clients to use in your marketing pieces. You cannot start too soon.

You could print the pocket folders or purchase one off the shelf and buy stickers imprinted with your logo to add to the front. Stickers can be a part of your entire stationery design plan. We use Stephen Fossler Company (800/762–0017) in Crystal Lake, Illinois. They are probably the best in the business. Give them a call for a catalog and samples.

Your promotional package will be used by publicity folks. In fact, they expect you to have a promotional package. If you are speaking or presenting a seminar covered by the media, you will want to take it along. You could probably get by without one. However, I do mention it here because with a slight variation it could serve you well until your brochure is printed.

As your business grows, your image will evolve. If you cannot afford a complete marketing package at once, plan ahead and try to maintain one look as much as you can. You may pay for the design of a logo, business cards, and a brochure but print only the business cards at first, adding the other pieces as you have money. This will ensure a singular image. Besides projecting the image you desire, you also want your business to be easily identifiable from others. You will need to find the right balance between looking professional and standing out from the crowd.

Your Bio Sketch

If you've been a consultant for even a short time, you probably have a bio sketch. A bio may be used in proposals, as an introduction to corporate personnel, or to simply answer the question, "Who are you?" A well-written bio gives you credibility and is a practical marketing tool, usually printed on high-quality paper (or you can use the second page of your stationery). It describes you and your business to all who might hire you. Yet all too often a consultant will dash one off with little thought and no plan for updating it.

Your bio should tell the potential client that you have the experience and expertise for the job. You are writing this for the client. So what do clients want to know? Clients will want to know what companies you have worked with and whether those companies are in the same industry. Clients want to know whether you are a recognized expert and in what areas. Clients will want to know what experience you have had. Clients will also use your bio to determine whether there is a fit between their task and your skills. This is one of those times you need to brag about yourself, but not exaggerate. Be sure to include publications, awards, memberships, patents, speaking engagements, and citations. Plan to update your bio at least annually. Perhaps you should pull your bio out now and see if it conveys what it should. Consider these tips for writing or updating your bio:

- Keep it to one page.
- Use a professional, crisp tone.
- Write in complete sentences.
- Use the third person and active voice.
- Define acronyms.
- Use Mr., Ms., or Dr. rather than your first name.
- Specify the names of organizations and publications.
- Do not include employment or graduation dates.

If you are a new consultant, you may rely on your internal work and other experience to start a bio. The bio in Exhibit 4.1 is for someone who has internal experience and has just started her consulting firm.

Exhibit 4.1. Sample Bio Sketch for a New Consultant

Ms. Trey Hutchison is the president of the Unison Group, Inc., a firm specializing in human performance and teamwork.

Ms. Hutchison is a former assistant VP for loans at Towne Bank in Virginia Beach, Virginia, where she worked for fifteen years. She has managed both line and staff functions and had gained the reputation as the organization's team builder. Ms. Hutchison led the Towne Bank buyout of Southeast Virginia Bank and coordinated the redesign of the human resources function to serve all employees. Her expertise in mergers in the financial industry has resulted in numerous speaking engagements. She has been a featured speaker at several industry conferences and has had articles published in *Finance Today* and *Professional Women in Banking*. She has also published articles in the *Hampton Roads Business News.*

The Southern Virginia Chapter of Women in Banking named Ms. Hutchison Loan Officer of the Year in 2000 in recognition of her "outstanding and innovative work in maximizing opportunities for women in banking." She has served as a board member for her local Kiwanis, where she recently led the strategic planning effort. She is presently serving her second term on the Alumni Board at Old Dominion University and is a member of the Institute of Management Consultants and national ASTD.

Ms. Hutchison focuses on the financial industry, facilitating team-building sessions and providing training in customer service, business ethics, mentoring, and strategic planning.

Ms. Hutchison has a bachelor's degree from Old Dominion University in business and education consulting and a master's degree in human resource development.

OTHER IMAGE BUILDERS

Sometimes the littlest things can make a big difference in what someone might think of you and your business.

Telephones

Purchase the best telephone equipment you can. If you are working out of your home, a second line is a basic requirement. Nothing can ruin your reputation faster that having your children start to squabble just as you get on the phone with a new client or to have your three-year-old answer the phone when the vice president of sales calls you about some work she would like you to do.

Staff should be trained to answer the phone cheerfully and professionally. Establish a standard greeting and then ensure that everyone uses it. Ours is, "Good morning, ebb associates, this is Emma." Establish telephone guidelines as well, including such things as no eating while on the phone, using the hold button, and using good listening and note-taking skills. I recently hired, then quickly fired, someone who could not understand the rule, "Do not eat while talking on the telephone." Listen carefully when you call your office. Your clients hear the same greeting and tone of voice. Is it what you want them to hear?

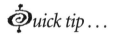uick tip . . .

> Develop a ten-minute training program for your staff for how to answer the telephone in your office. Ask your staff for ideas to improve your telephone image to your clients.

Answering Machines

If you do not have office staff, ensure that your answering machine is equally high quality. Use your answering machine like voice mail. And be certain to change your message regularly. Three times a day is not too much if you need to. What do you say three different times? "Hello, this is Kim. It's Tuesday, October 30th. I am in the office today, but have stepped away from my desk. Please leave a message and I will call you when I return." Later in the day, use the same opening (this lets callers know that the message they hear is current) and add, "I'm out of the office and will return at 3 o'clock. Please let me know that you have called and I will return your call at that time." Finally, at the end of the day use the same opening and add, "Our office is closed at this time and will reopen tomorrow morning at 8 o'clock."

Why all of this? First, it shows that you care enough about your clients to keep them informed about your whereabouts. Second, anyone who heard your messages will know exactly when to call you. Third, it adds credibility to your professional image. One last thing, refer to your message system as "voice mail," not "answering machine." And please don't refer to the signal to start speaking as a "beep"; use the word "tone" or don't use anything at all. Most people know when to start talking.

Websites

You need a website. Most of my new clients assume we have one and ask if they can obtain certain information off of it. If you can't create a website yourself, hire it out. If well done, it could be a great substitute for a brochure. Keep your website up-to-date and refresh it with something new at least monthly. A later chapter discusses websites in more depth.

Forms

Personalize your forms. Yes, you can print a fax sheet and an invoice off your computer program, but it isn't the same as displaying your logo and using your corporate font. You don't even need to hire a designer to do it. Get a black and white of your logo or use the one the designer has provided for your desktop. Use your favorite graphics program to design both forms. We have a master fax sheet from which we make copies (see Exhibit 4.2). The invoice form resides on the desktop ready and waiting to bill clients.

Quick tip . . .

Enhance your image by sending handwritten thank-you notes. Don't even bother with a thank-you e-mail. If someone has done something that deserves a thank you, a minute on e-mail is not enough.

Exhibit 4.2. Sample FAX Form

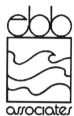

ebb associates inc
box 657
portage, wi 53901
608-742-5005
608-742-8657/FAX

ebb associates inc
box 8349
norfolk, va 23503
757-588-3939
757-480-1311/FAX

Fax To: _____   Location: _____

From: _____   Location: ❑ WI Office ❑ VA Office

Date: _____   Total Pages: _____

(Including Cover)

From E. Biech, *The Business of Consulting* (San Francisco: Jossey-Bass/Pfeiffer, 1998).

Little Touches

Find something that is uniquely you, that adds to your image, and that will increase your chances of being remembered. I use gold paperclips on all documents. Most recently I have purchased uniquely shaped paperclips: spirals and @ symbols. I also include a small card that can be opened to reveal a quote. I have different categories for different people: service, quality, teamwork, and women's quotes.

MARKETING: TAKE ACTION

1. Think about the image you project. Is it the one you want your clients to have? If not what can you do about it?

2. Take a look at your business card. Does it say what you want it to say? Does it send the message you want it to send? Do you love it?

3. Review your paper products. Do they project the professional image you desire? What do you need to change?

4. Read your bio sketch. Does it sell you from the client's perspective? Does it show the breadth and depth of your expertise?

part TWO

Build a Potential Client Base

Tools of the Trade

What Works; What Doesn't?

You have assessed your consulting company's marketing success, your competition's position, your client's needs, and your company's image. It is now time to move to the second phase of the marketing ABCs. Phase B is Build a Potential Client Base. In this phase we will begin by introducing all the marketing tools and what works in consulting.

In an effort to make this the most practical book about marketing possible for consultants, I am *not* going to lecture you on the difference between marketing and advertising, philosophize about your promotional mix, nor will I defend my definition of "promotional." I won't even entertain a discussion about whether these are actually tools, tactics, or strategies.

Remember, I promised practical.

WORD OF MOUTH

Are you tempted to skip this chapter because you think that all your marketing is done by word of mouth? I might have a few years ago. But word of mouth must come from some place. Perhaps someone has used your services, you have written dozens of personal notes, or you have spoken at conferences. Yes, your name is passed around by past, current, and potential clients. But you must have completed some marketing activities that fed the word of mouth. And you must continue to feed the word of mouth.

I remember reading a quote that said, "It's funny, the harder I work the luckier I become!"

Marketing is like that as well. The more you market, the more work comes your way. A few years ago I dealt with a personal tragedy. I did not conduct the marketing activities that I usually did for over twelve months. In a year's time when I normally sent about eighty articles, I sent no more than two; when I normally sent 350 handwritten notes, I sent about two dozen; when I normally sent fifty books, I sent fewer than five; when I normally attended about eighteen conference days, I attended about six; when I normally initiated hundreds of phone calls, I returned only those that I had to. The result was that the phone stopped ringing during that year and the word-of-mouth marketing dried up. It was quite dramatic! My clients had not forgotten about me, but without the regular reminders, they turned to other consultants who kept themselves in front of my clients.

Word-of-mouth marketing is the most effective. But it must be fed with the marketing tools and techniques you will find in this chapter. Don't delude yourself into believing that word of mouth is a standalone marketing technique. It is not. You must feed it with other marketing techniques.

MARKETING TOOLS

In his book *Guerrilla Marketing, Secrets for Making Big Profits from Your Small Business,* Jay Conrad Levinson, states, "A great deal of marketing isn't merely poorly executed these days; it's not executed at all! I'd venture a bold guess that fewer than 10 percent of the new and small business owners in America have explored most of the marketing methods available to them." It is with this spirit that I present any and all marketing tools that have a possibility of making it into your marketing plan—even blimps.

I present an exhaustive list of marketing tools. Some, like prospecting letters, slide into the selling arena. Don't worry about that. Now—before you develop your marketing plan—is when you should be thinking about all the tools. As you go through this list, check off the ones that you think are the most practical for your clients and the most comfortable for you to use. Note also that some will provide an immediate response and others will require time to produce results. Take that into consideration.

The marketing tools are divided into two categories. The categories I have chosen are Personal Marketing Tools and Promotional Marketing Tools. The personal tools are those that put you in direct contact with potential and current clients. The opportunity for one-to-one communication is greater and the impact is generally stronger, but you reach fewer people at one time. The promotional tools generally reach a larger number of people efficiently, but the impact is usually not as great and the cost is higher. The things for you to consider will help you make the decision about which tools may be best for you. Exhibit 5.1 provides you an overview of the differences.

Exhibit 5.1. Comparing Marketing Tools		
Characteristics	**Personal Tools**	**Promotional Tools**
Client Contact	Direct Contact	Indirect Contact
One-on-One Communication	Great Opportunity	Little Opportunity
Reach	Fewer People	Large Number of People
Impact	High	Low to Medium
Cost	Low	High

Personal Marketing Tools

Over three dozen marketing tools are presented in Exhibit 5.2 and described below. They are not always the traditional marketing list. They are the ones, however, that consultants could use to market their organizations.

Exhibit 5.2. Marketing Tools

PERSONAL MARKETING TOOLS	PROMOTIONAL MARKETING TOOLS
• Paper Products	• Direct Mail
• Deliver Conference Presentations or Speeches	• Brochures, Fliers, and Catalogs
• Demonstrations or Showcases	• Newsletters
• Networking	• Website
• Maintain Client Relationships	• Send an E-mail or an Electronic Newsletter
• Join Organizations	• Publish
• Teach a Class or Conduct a Seminar or Workshop	• Publicity
• Send Greetings	• Promotional Packages
• Send Information	• Advertising
• Send Congratulations	• Directories
• Send or Give Gifts	• Phone Hold Messages
• Accept Pro Bono Work	• Trade Shows
• Novelty Items, Geegaws, and Gadgets	• Sponsorships
• Shirts, Briefcases, and Portfolios	• Radio
• Go to Lunch	• Television
• Make a Telephone Call	• Balloons, Billboards, and Blimps
• Customer Appreciation Programs	
• Prospecting Letters	
• Telemarketing	
• Obtain Referrals	
• Obtain Endorsements and Testimonials	
• Respond to Requests for Proposals	

Paper Products Your paper products (stationery, business cards, envelopes, labels, note cards) are listed first because this is usually the first thing consultants think about as they start their businesses. And you should, too. Your business cards and other paper products often project the first image to your clients, so they may also be the most important marketing tool you have. With this level of importance to your business, do not skimp on quality or design. Since we covered this in Chapter Four, you know how important this marketing tool is to your image.

Considerations:

- Hire a professional designer to help you.
- Order twice as many cards as you think you will need and hand them out to everyone.
- Remember that your envelope is as important as your business card; carry the design through.
- Have cards printed for all of your staff, including your receptionist, and encourage them to hand them out to everyone they meet.

Deliver Conference Presentations or Speeches Organizations and associations frequently need interesting, educational, motivational, or entertaining speakers to address their employees or members at conferences or special events. This is one way to establish yourself as an expert in your field. You can register with speakers bureaus, who will charge a booking fee, to help get your name and your special area of expertise in front of organizations. Speeches are typically thirty to ninety minutes in length.

Considerations:

- Contact the National Speakers Association to learn more about speaking opportunities and to get expert advice.
- This is a great opportunity to put yourself in front of a large audience to demonstrate your talent.
- It requires considerable skill to develop and deliver a speech; speaking is not the same as training.
- Plan a significant amount of time for developing and practicing your speech.

Demonstrations or Showcases Demonstrations at conferences or showcases that may be by invitation only provide a way for you to display your expertise to a select group of people. This is a popular way for consultants to demonstrate what they can do. It is usually reserved for large clients or those who will provide repeat business over a long period of time.

Considerations:

- It may be costly to rent a hotel suite and food for the showcase.

- A showcase needs to impress and hook clients quickly to cover expenses.

- It is great to generate leads for later follow-up.

- It provides high visibility and creates the impression that you are a leader in the field.

Networking Network with other professionals, colleagues, your banker, your accountant, community leaders, mentors, and your competition. Attend professional meetings where you will meet them. Join teams and get involved in social events to have fun together. Network during conferences. You could set a goal to gather and give out one hundred business cards at your next professional conference.

Considerations:

- Keep a list of colleagues in other cities and set up dinners with them.

- To be most successful, networking must be about caring for and helping people.

- Networking is as much about giving as getting, giving leads to others as well as gathering them when they come your way.

- Be selective about whom you network with.

Maintain Client Relationships Chapter Nine focuses on this topic very thoroughly. Remember that it takes ten times the money and energy to land a new client as to retain a former client.

Considerations:

- Develop the relationship as early as you can.

- Read Harvey Mackay's books about building client relationships.

- Personalize every relationship.

- If maintaining a relationship is only about marketing, don't do it; sincerity is critical.

Join Organizations Joining civic, social, service, religious, or professional organizations helps to put the name of your business out there. They will offer you an opportunity to discuss your business with people who may not otherwise know about you. Some organizations such as Kiwanis, Rotary, or Optimists even provide an opportunity for you to speak about a topic related to your business. Even though you will be mixing with your competition, there may be an opportunity to refer or be referred when time is limited or a match is absent between the client and your competitor.

Considerations:

- Membership enables you to become knowledgeable about other professions that may lead to joint ventures.
- It provides visibility and a source of referrals.
- It helps you stay well-rounded and informed, besides giving something back to society and your community.
- Prepare yourself for how to handle volunteer activities unrelated to marketing.
- Take on a leadership role to have the most effect.

Teach a Class or Conduct a Seminar or Workshop These are opportunities to educate potential clients. You may provide information, offer hands-on experience, or build skills. Even though you may charge a fee, this is also an opportunity to market your consulting practice. A typical situation would be an accountant who teaches how to use a computer accounting program who may actually be marketing her services at tax time.

Considerations:

- Use the face-to-face time to subtly promote your consulting services by having brochures and business cards available.
- The fee should at least cover all your expenses, including design time, materials, and travel expenses.
- This is an opportunity to enhance your professional reputation.

- Once your basic presentation and marketing plan have been developed, it is easy to repeat.

Send Greetings Aha! One of my favorite personal marketing tools is sending letters, notes, birthday cards, and holiday greetings to clients, colleagues, and friends. I found a wonderful card designer in Minnesota who designs and hand makes special cards for me. Everyone should have a Janah designing cards for clients. Many of my clients keep the cards or even frame them!

Considerations:

- Find your own comfort zone on this one.
- Postcards are an alternative.
- Keep cards available so that you don't need to rush out to buy one for every event.
- Keep a list of client, employee, and colleague birthdays; add to it regularly.

✐uick tip . . .

Check out your local card shop. You will be amazed at how many celebration cards are available besides birthdays, for example, congratulations on your new grandchild and congratulations on your new position.

Send Information Send articles, books, or tapes. If you present at a conference, purchase copies of the tape to send to your clients. If an article is written about you in a magazine or newspaper, purchase reprints to send. If you come across books or articles that would be appropriate for special clients, buy the book or the magazine and send to the clients.

Considerations:

- Take care to follow all copyright laws.
- Purchasing reprints of a good article in bulk is less expensive than you think, has a professional look to it, and will impress your clients.
- Write notes to your clients in the books you give them; they will always remember who gave them the books.

Send Congratulations Watch the newspapers and keep your ears open for opportunities to congratulate your clients and colleagues. Many newspapers have a daily or weekly column featuring people who received promotions or other recognition. Cut out the article and place it in a card with a congratulations note from you. I usually do not write on the article in case the person needs one more copy to send to Aunt June. We also have a supply of chocolate stars and glass stars that accompany a "You're a real star!" message.

Considerations:

• Create your own ideas for congratulations.

• Never, never pass up an opportunity to congratulate someone; often it's more important than remembering a birthday.

• Tuck some star-shaped glitter in a congratulations card to create a mini celebration.

• Try something other than stars, such as miniature champagne bottles filled with bubbles or a party horn with a message like "You should toot your horn!"

Send or Give Gifts Gifts are always fun for everyone to receive. Stay alert for ideas. I tend to shop all year long for everyone. If I find something for someone, I buy it on the spot. This saves time (since I'm right there) and I rarely need to scramble at the last minute.

Considerations:

• Be sure to include money in your advertising budget for gifts.

• Choose carefully for whom and for what occasion you will present gifts.

• Toy stores are great places to search for adult gifts.

Accept Pro Bono Work Providing work for clients who cannot afford your services is a way to give back to society and also market your services. We should all do these things because they are good for us and the world, but if one of your reasons is to enhance your marketing, choose your projects well. They should be noncontroversial to the clients you are trying to attract. I've done pro bono work for the Women Marine Association, American Society for Training and Development, a small college in Virginia, and a battered women's shelter. In each case I received one referral as well as that warm feeling of having done something good.

Considerations:

- Select a cause you support and can rally behind.
- Ask for a letter outlining your out-of-pocket expenses for tax purposes.
- Take this on only if you will do your best and stick with it to the end.
- Stay in touch with the people for whom you did the work.

Novelty Items, Geegaws, and Gadgets Sending a lumpy envelope to my clients is my favorite marketing tool. I rely on little things that are memorable, unique, mailable, and useful. A number of catalogs provide these items. The items are basically a memory reinforcer, so personalize them to help your clients remember you. Exhibit 5.3 provides you with a list of catalog suppliers for interesting items to send to your clients. See the end of this chapter for tips on selecting a "keeper," something your clients will keep and that will remind them of you.

Exhibit 5.3. Get Your Geegaws and Gadgets Here

- 4imprint
  101 Commerce St.
  P.O. Box 320
  Oshkosh, WI 54903-0320
  877-446-7746
  www. 4imprint.com

- Best Impressions Catalog Company
  345 N. Lewis Ave.
  Oglesby, IL 61348
  800-635-2378
  www.bestimpressions.com

- Crestline Company, Inc.
  P.O. Box 1810
  33 Omni Circle
  Auburn, ME 04211
  800-221-7797
  www.crestline.com

- Genesis Productions, Inc.
  1672 Barclay Blvd.
  Buffalo Grove, IL 60089
  847-291-7263
  www.logomall.com/genesis

- M&N International
  Bright Idea Book
  P.O. Box 64784
  St. Paul, MN 55164-0784
  800-479-2043
  www.mninternational.com

- Oriental Trading Company
  P.O. Box 2659
  Omaha, NE 68103-2659
  800-228-7450
  www.orientaltrading.com

Considerations:

- Pick a theme, then pick an item. If that doesn't work, do the opposite. Ensure that the theme matches the item and create a message. Send a hat with a congratulatory note that says, "My hat's off to you . . ."
- Determine the number of recipients and the budgeted amount for each.
- Select something that will stay on your clients' desks. Fruit is nice, but will they remember you and that orange next May?
- Take a risk, be a little crazy, have some fun with this one.

Quick tip . . .

Never assume your mailing will meet postal requirements. Always check with the post office before printing. Always double-check the weight.

Shirts, Briefcases, and Portfolios Have your name printed on items that others will see. Briefcases and portfolios that you carry with you become an excellent marketing tool. Shirts with an embroidered corporate logo worn by your team to a conference or other event keeps your name in front of other attendees.

Considerations:

- High quality is key.
- Shop around; prices vary greatly.
- A first-time set-up charge may be expensive.
- Have enough items personalized so that you can give some away to your clients.

Go to Lunch Lunch, dinner, breakfast, a cup of coffee, whatever the occasion, these are a great opportunity to share a meal and complete a bit of business. As Americans we tend to plan lots of things around meals. Business is no exception. Meals tend to break down barriers and add a personal touch to the work at hand.

Considerations:

- Have your credit card ready so that you can easily pick up the bill without discussion.

- Select something that is easy to eat while doing business.
- If you select the restaurant, call ahead for reservations; even request a table in a quiet, out-of-the-way spot.
- If you are familiar with the restaurant, make suggestions to your guests.

Make a Telephone Call Like the movie *E.T.,* call home. It is critical to stay in touch with clients, colleagues, potential clients, friends, competitors, vendors, suppliers, and a host of others. Keep a list of who you need to call and then stay on top of your calls.

Considerations:

- Stay in touch with others and you will have a natural network.
- Keep updated telephone numbers in your Day-Timer or your PDA so that you can call while waiting in an airport or on a long taxi ride.

Customer Appreciation Programs Have a plan to specifically thank your customers and tell them how much you appreciate their business. It can be tied to some of the other ideas on this list, such as gifts at various holidays. It could also be a standalone event where you invite your top customers to a dinner party, or you could tie it to business and invite them to the rollout of a new program you will introduce to the public in the near future.

Considerations:

- You could develop a customer-of-the-month award, providing an engraved plaque to each one.
- Keep programs simple and measurable.
- Do it with class.

Prospecting Letters This is a letter that introduces you to your client and tells your client how you think you could work together. I recommend personalized letters for each organization. Any letter that tries to address a large number of potential clients will be tossed in the trash. If you are going in that direction, I suggest you use a flier, as described in the promotional marketing tools. Prospecting letters are detailed in Chapter Seven; when used as a complete process these can have dramatic results.

Considerations:

- Letters provide an opportunity for you to impress a client by demonstrating your knowledge of the organization.
- Be sure to target the recipient carefully.
- Take time to research the organization if you are going to customize.
- These usually provide you with an entrée into an organization.
- The p.s. is the most-read portion of any letter.

Quick tip ...

For every one hundred words you write, seventy-five should be five letters or fewer.

Telemarketing I know few small consulting firms who use telemarketing, although many large firms have an entire department dedicated to telemarketing. It is an efficient way to reach large numbers of potential clients on a personal level and should not be discarded as a possibility.

Considerations:

- Contact a large consulting firm to see if they will share telemarketing tips with you.
- Your local telephone company may offer training on telemarketing.
- Use it to quickly build a client base.
- Remember that it may be considered intrusive by potential clients.

Obtain Referrals Friends, current and past clients, colleagues, and even your competition can be a source of referrals for business. You need to ask. Remember, the referral alone will not get you new business; you will need to follow up on it, but it is a great foot-in-the-door technique. To encourage referrals in some consulting professions it is appropriate to pay a referral fee. Consult with your professional association to determine the etiquette in your field.

Considerations:

- Be sure to ask whether you can use the individual's name. This quadruples the value of the referral.

- Always, always, always follow up the referral immediately with a thank-you note; later let the person know what happened.

- There is minimal work and no expense to set a meeting with a potential client.

- Early on this may be a quick survival technique to get business started.

Obtain Endorsements and Testimonials Asking current and past clients for endorsements and testimonials should be a regular part of your marketing plan. This powerful tool can be sprinkled in catalogs, brochures, or other written marketing materials, as references in proposals, or to vouch for your skills and abilities as a speaker for a conference. They might appear on the outside of a direct mail envelope or on your website.

Considerations:

- Immediate thank-you notes are a requirement.

- Get over the tendency to avoid doing this because you don't want to "bother" someone.

- Keep a file and update it regularly. Store the original letters in plastic sleeves in a binder.

- Collect both endorsement letters as well as short quotes to use in a variety of situations.

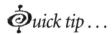

Quick tip . . .

There are four types of testimonials: customer, expert, celebrity, and groups of experts. The fourth group gets the best results.

Respond to Requests for Proposals Requests for proposals (RFPs) or quotes (RFQs) are offered as a way for consultants to bid on a project. The RFP is the formal written description of a project's scope. An RFQ provides the same statement of work, but it requires less in the form of a proposal. Both require a price quote. The process is competitive, and usually the client is looking for best value.

Considerations:

- Use the clients' language; they will understand your proposal better.
- Be clear, concise, and complete.
- Give the requesters exactly what they ask for and in the format they ask for it.

Promotional Marketing Tools

Direct Mail You touch direct mail every day that you go through your mail, the brochures, letters, or samples that are sent to you by companies hoping to obtain your business. Specialized mailing lists are used so that the piece is targeted to the most likely buyer. Direct mail pieces usually describe a client's needs and how you will satisfy those needs. A good strategy is to pair direct mail with telemarketing. The direct mail piece breaks the ice and the follow-up phone call adds a personal touch and an opportunity to schedule a meeting. Note that a recent survey I conducted showed that 60 percent of the training managers interviewed received over 150 pieces of direct mail each month; 8 percent received five hundred or more pieces each month. Your direct mail piece will need to stand out to compete with that kind of volume. You should begin your own corporate mailing list of contacts, clients, and potential clients from the first day you are in business. Update it at least twice each year and use it to send announcements, greetings, and information.

Considerations:

- Direct mail is usually not successful alone when selling a product or service that is valued over $1,000.
- Contact your local chapter of the Direct Marketing Association to locate a firm that can assist you.
- Purchase the most specific mailing list you can by identifying geographic locations, industry types, job categories and levels, and organizational departments.
- Develop a thorough and detailed budget for the project so that you are not caught off guard about the expense and involvement.
- Realize that the response rate is usually less than 2 percent.

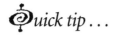*uick tip . . .*

> Three of the most response-generating words in direct mail are "you,"
> "free," and "guarantee."

Brochures, Fliers, and Catalogs Your brochure embodies the image and position you hold in the consulting field. They are a serious purchase and require the assistance and advice of a professional designer. You may need both a graphic designer as well as a copy writer. Don't try to do it yourself. It will hurt your image and your business. Brochures serve as a great leave-behind when you pay a visit to potential clients. A well-designed brochure gives the appearance of a well-established firm.

Fliers are an inexpensive alternative to a brochure. Discussed in the last chapter, they are an inexpensive way to inform potential clients about your business. They can be created to describe your business in general or you can create special fliers for special occasions, such as introducing a conference presentation or a new product, or announcing that you published a book. Exhibit 5.4 provides you with a list of places to obtain interesting papers for printing fliers.

Exhibit 5.4. Paper Places

- Baudville
  5380 52nd Street, S.E.
  Grand Rapids, MI 49512-9765
  800-728-0888
  www.baudville.com

- Flax Art & Design
  240 Valley Drive
  Brisbane, CA 94005-1206
  888-727-3763
  www.flaxart.com

- Idea Art
  P.O. Box 291505
  Nashville, TN 37229-1505
  800-433-2278
  www.ideaart.com

- Paper Direct
  P.O. Box 2970
  Colorado Springs, CO 80901-2970
  800-272-7377
  www.paperdirect.com

Catalogs are useful if you offer numerous products that you sell in addition to your consulting. Be sure the descriptions are complete and accurate. Your buyers will expect to see prices as well.

Considerations:

- Design brochures so that they are timeless or easily updated.

- Use clip art, graphics, or clear black-and-white photos to add appeal.

- Design fliers for their specific use, for example, flat to hang on bulletin boards or post in prominent places; tri-folded to mail to your clients, as doorknob hangers for hotel doors at conferences; or on colorful paper if you want potential clients to pick one up at a trade show.

- Have several people check the details from different perspectives before your catalog is printed.

Quick tip . . .

Avoid putting dates on any promotional material to ensure its shelf life is as long as possible.

Newsletters Writing a newsletter can be a lot of fun. You do need to recognize the responsibility you incur by sending out your first issue of a "monthly" newsletter. No matter what happens that month, your readers will expect your newsletter to arrive on time. Newsletters can be one to twelve pages long and usually contain short articles that will interest your readers. It is also an opportunity for you to keep your readers informed about your organization: new clients, new services, new employees, new products. However, it must contain something beyond what's happening with you. That's why it is called a NEWS-letter.

Considerations:

- Check into bulk mail rates and postal regulations for mailing; for example, you can no longer staple a fold-over newsletter.

- Plan for articles that are short, practical, and helpful to your readers.

- Include quizzes, self-assessments, interviews, and checklists to keep interest high.

- Some organizations publish newsletters that can be income-producing. Subscribers pay for the information they receive in the newsletter.

Website Your website should be state of the art. I find that my website is similar to my brochure twenty years ago. Everyone expected me to have one, but few really use it for anything beyond the first visit. Realize that your website does not replace your brochure—not yet anyway. Your website should be easy to maneuver and exciting to visit. Use a professional to help you design it.

Considerations:

- Your home page should be appealing and easy to understand.
- Provide immediate value with downloads of quizzes, articles, and tools that will appeal to potential clients.
- Have a process that makes it easy to contact you.
- Print your website address on your business cards, brochures, and other paper products.

Send an E-mail or an Electronic Newsletter E-mail promotions and electronic newsletters are different. While an e-mail is usually used to promote a seminar or your book, an e-newsletter should be non-promotional. Make your electronic campaigns successful by obtaining permission to send them first and identifying the kind of information potential clients want. Also give users the option to remove their names each time (this is required by law).

Considerations:

- Keep the message short; you have three to six seconds to grab and keep their attention; even e-newsletters should be no more than one screen long.
- Keep promotion separate from news.
- Use an informative subject line.
- Be prepared to reply within twelve to twenty-four hours.
- Ask current subscribers for referrals.

Publish Articles, books, a newspaper column, letters to the editor, and book reviews are all ways to put your name in front of potential clients. This is a great way to share your knowledge repeatedly. When submitting articles, always include a cover letter. Writing a book is a huge undertaking, but earns you instant respect and high visibility. Once you have written any of the above, you can reprint the information and use in a variety of ways. See Exhibit 5.5 for some suggestions to please editors.

Exhibit 5.5. Get Your Article Published

Comply with all submission guidelines and follow these suggestions for the article and the cover letter you submit.

Article

- Select a catchy title
- Leave wide margins
- Include your last name and article title on all pages
- Number the pages
- Use a paper clip, not staples
- Provide word count on the last page
- Liven up the narration with pull quotes, charts, checklists, photos, or sidebars

Cover Letter

- Specify why the article is relevant to the readers
- State whether the article is exclusive to the publication
- Briefly describe the article
- Provide a brief author bio similar to those in the publication

---

Considerations:

- Don't write unless you enjoy writing; there are other marketing tools and you do not need to put yourself in agony, as writing can do to those who do not like to write.
- Always check for guidelines with the publisher before beginning to write.

- Be sure to check the copyright with the publisher before you sign away your rights to the document.
- Cost is low, but time involvement is high.

Publicity Savvy marketers know that the press needs them as much as they need the media. You can create your own public relations plan by developing a series of public interest stories. The free publicity can be worth thousands of dollars in advertising. The topics can be anything from announcements about your business to insight into a newsworthy topic. If the announcement is of interest to an identifiable segment of the public, it will be accepted. Publicity can be a press release, an appearance on a radio or TV talk show, or a reference to your activities in a journal article. When each of my books is first published, I hire a publicist, Celia Rocks (I think she is the best), who helps with the book's publicity campaign. See Exhibit 5.6 for ideas.

Exhibit 5.6. Top Ten Press Release Topics

1. Related to national news
2. Related to community events
3. Solving a problem
4. Giving an award or scholarship
5. Staging an event, like a Guinness World Record
6. Reporting a special event
7. Giving away anything
8. Success story
9. Overcoming adversity
10. Celebrating an opening or anniversary

Considerations:

- For best results, know the media your prospective clients use; then target your efforts.
- Try a couple of press releases on your own; you have nothing to lose. Be sure they are accurate and timely.

- You control the content, so it becomes an inexpensive way to bolster your image and visibility; however, don't ignore the journalists' needs.
- A press release has the potential to reach thousands of people.

Promotional Packages Originally these kits were used to give to the press when they covered an event. Now they can be useful in many other ways; for example, you can pass them out at trade shows, provide information for your bank's loan officer, or list information for your clients. They are usually a two-pocket folder with information about you and your company inside. I like to use the shiny Duo-Tang® folders available at office supply stores. I have purchased self-sticking metallic logo stamps that I apply to the lower right-hand corner of the folders. Inside you can put information about your firm, your bio sketch, your picture, press releases, a background sheet, facts and history about your company, and price lists if appropriate.
Considerations:

- For real class, you may have the folders printed with your logo, name, and contact information.
- Keep the kit up-to-date and keep the masters in plastic sleeves in a binder.
- The kit can be used to introduce new employees to your company.
- Add endorsement letters and testimonials when appropriate.

Advertising Card decks, magazines, yellow pages, television, and radio are just a few places to advertise. Before embarking on any of these, contact a mass media specialist who will help guide you through the advertising jungle. Discuss costs early. Some may be shockingly high, while others may be much lower than you expected.
Considerations:

- Realize that the time or the space you purchase is just one piece of the cost; you will still need someone to script, direct, and read a radio spot or design, write copy, and create a magazine ad.
- When done right, high advertising costs may be balanced with quick responses and an abundance of work.

- Be aware of the many variables that are out of your control.

- Once a successful ad is designed it can be repeated.

- Only you can decide whether or not a yellow pages ad will help you to sell your services. A study showed that people go to the yellow pages with an open mind and the most effective ads are those that show a benefit in the headline and build trust by announcing the number of years in business.

Directories Directories are a way to list your business so that people can locate you. Industry-related or professional directories are abundant, and most are now accessible by computer. When you place your ad there will most likely be a small fee. When you develop your ad think about all the ways it could be cross-referenced: consultant, management consultant, change agent, team building, and so forth.
  Considerations:

- Don't fall for the direct mail ads that congratulate you for being selected as one of the world's greatest, youngest, best of anything. There is usually a fee connected with very little promotional opportunity.

- If you are going to place an ad, include your logo and picture for more impact.

- Determine who the directory's audience is and who will see your ad.

- Check with your local librarian, the Internet, your professional organization, and others to identify all the directories available to you before signing on with one.

Phone Hold Messages If you absolutely must put your clients on hold, a little light music helps to pass the time. You can also include some information about your company.
  Considerations:

- Avoid using radios; you can never be sure what the music or the ad will be when your most important client calls.

- If you do not take advantage of messages, it may be best to avoid doing this at all.

Trade Shows You may rent a booth at trade shows or expositions that are often connected to conferences. Remember, you will most likely pay for the space as well as rent for everything else you need, such as electrical hookups, carpeting, tables, table covers, backdrops, and even the wastebasket. It's a great way to interact with potential clients, to collect a list of names, and to display your wares. Check SETON's website at www.events.seton.com to view some basic trade show accessories.

Considerations:

- Booth space can be very expensive.
- You will need to design and purchase or build an exhibit.
- Be sure to have something that will encourage people to come to your booth, something interactive or something you can give away.
- Attend potential trade shows before registering for a booth. Each one will be different.

Sponsorships You can sponsor a conference or an event at a conference and have your name placed in the program or on the backdrop of the stage. Conference planners are frequently looking for someone to sponsor breaks, entertainment, or keynote speakers. We have sponsored the briefcases for two conferences. The first was as a gift to the speakers. For the second it was for all attendees. In both cases we had our logo and the association's logo embroidered on the cases. You could also sponsor community events, a youth sports team, races, or fund raisers.

Considerations:

- Price can be all over, from a couple hundred dollars to several thousand, depending on the event and the number of attendees.
- If you are required to provide something, like bags for attendees, be sure they are the highest quality you can afford.
- Sponsor events that will provide you with the kind of visibility you want.
- If the sponsorship is too costly, find another firm to partner with you.

Radio Talk shows, radio programs, or radio ads are all possible. If you have just written a book or released some new information, you should be able to schedule time on one of your local talk radio shows. You could also host your own radio program. Either of these gives you instant credibility and the ability to reach a very large audience.

Considerations:

- Identify the time that the majority of your potential clients will be listening.

- Know when and how to promote your own business during the show.

- Use professionals to assist you with writing an ad.

Television You could do a presentation, host your own show, or do an infomercial. Sound crazy? Not necessarily. Television is a mass medium, so your service or program or infomercial should have mass appeal. Many television programs are not broadcast live, but are taped at times that may be more convenient for you. As an advertiser you could purchase one half-hour time slot to sell your services on an infomercial. Just in case you are curious, the cost is about $500,000 per month, plus $250,000 to produce the show, plus another $40,000 for a media test market run and other incidentals.
Considerations:

- Be sure that your audience will watch the station you choose.

- Use the unique selling power of television—sight, sound, and motion—to create emotional appeal.

- Check into the cost before you nix television as an idea. You might be surprised at how low the costs have become.

- Infomercials provide a balance between entertainment and information; use lots of testimonials.

Balloons, Billboards, and Blimps While these are probably not practical for marketing a consulting firm, they should push you to think creatively about how you might use them. No way, you say? How about sending a balloon printed with your logo to your clients with a message such as, "We're so proud we're about to burst about . . ." How about using mini billboards at the entrance to a seminar. How about flying a miniature blimp-shaped balloon filled with helium above your booth at a trade show so attendees can find your booth. The point of this last example is to suggest that, with a little creativity, you can market in ways that others may never have considered.

Entire books are written about each of these tools. Once you have selected a couple that interest you, pay a visit to your local bookstore to find more information about what you should consider before embarking on any of these journeys.

Several of the marketing tools require you to contact people. If a long time has passed, it may be uncomfortable to call or write. Sometimes we need a good excuse to make the call.

NEED AN EXCUSE TO STAY IN TOUCH?

At the end of a successful project, most good-byes include assurances such as "Let's stay in touch" or "We'll get together for lunch." But time passes, everyone gets wrapped up in other activities, and staying in touch becomes a vague memory. A couple of months later it may even be uncomfortable to pick up the phone and contact the individuals with whom you spent a huge amount of time. You may feel like a pest.

The best thing to do, of course, is to prevent the passage of time from occurring. That means you need to plan time to follow up. When that doesn't happen, you may feel better if you have an excuse to make the call: "I ran across this article and thought of you" or "I need some advice and you are the best person to help."

The worst thing that can happen—but what happens most often—is that you come across these opportunities and you pass them by. If reports to me from my own clients are correct, I believe that people pass up on these opportunities over 90 percent of the time. Almost every time I contact someone whom I have not seen or heard from in some time, I get a response such as, "I was just thinking about you" or "I was reading the newspaper last week and meant to cut out an article for you" or "I was going to call you last month, but I got sucked into another project." The message? Don't hesitate to contact the other person, either by mail, by e-mail, by phone, or in person.

In Chapter Nine, I make a strong case for the reason to maintain relationships and retain clients for marketing your services. But common sense should tell you the importance of this for both personal and professional reasons. For those of you who need an excuse to stay in touch and to maintain the relationship, I present some practical ideas.

Giving Information

- Inform your client of an upcoming vendor fair.
- Provide free tickets to your client for an industry expo.

Obtaining Information

- Request the name of a supplier.

Staying Current with Business Changes

- Inform your client that you moved.
- Announce a new employee.
- Send a newspaper clipping in which your business is featured.

Recognition

- Thank your client for a referral.
- Deliver congratulations about a promotion or new job.
- Congratulate the client's company for being mentioned in a magazine article.

Personal Support

- Provide your client with data for an upcoming speech.
- Send a magazine article about a favorite vacation spot.
- Provide a contact at a child's desired college.
- Send an article about something of personal interest.

Professional Support

- Refer potential job candidates to your client.
- Offer assistance on an association project.
- Provide information on potential customers.
- Send articles related to an employee situation.
- Offer a contact for a job search.

Free Service

- Offer consulting.
- Provide information about something you just learned.

Asking for Help

- Request advice about a book or an article content.
- Ask for coaching about a possible new client.

Each of these ideas will give you a great excuse to connect with someone you haven't been in touch with for a long time. Once you hear that person's voice on the other end of the line, you will wonder why it took you so long to call.

TIPS FOR SENDING A KEEPER

A "keeper" is a novelty item that you send your clients. You have done such a great job of selecting it that your client wants to "keep" it. In our office we call these items "geegaws" and they can range anywhere from animal-shaped paper clips and coffee mugs filled with coffee beans to xylophones and ZIP code directories.

Getting Started

If you would like to send a keeper, these nine steps will get you started.

1. Decide the purpose of the novelty item. Will it be given away at a trade show or sent as a thank you to your clients for Thanksgiving?

2. Decide who will receive the mailing. Will everyone on your mailing list receive the item or will it be sent to a select number of people? For example, you might want something special if a couple dozen of your clients wrote endorsements for a book you recently published. How many items do you need?

3. Determine the budget for your mailing. How much will you invest in this marketing tool? Divide that amount by the number of people and you will have an approximate cost per item. Note: Remember that if you have the items personalized (which I HIGHLY recommend), there will be an additional personalization and set-up fee charged.

4. Select a novelty-item catalog and page through it looking for items in your price range. Several companies that we have used were identified in Exhibit 5.3. They will be happy to send you their catalogs or you can check them out on the web.

5. Once you have selected an item or two, brainstorm a few catchy messages that you would like to deliver to your clients with the item. For example, perhaps you have decided to send your clients a questionnaire, as suggested in Chapter Three. You have selected a round tape measure as one of your items. Your phrases might include things like, "We're checking to see how we measure up,"

"We're getting 'around' to asking our clients about our performance," "We believe improvement can be measured," "We're 'inching' to improve our service to you," or many others. Allow a couple of days for these ideas to simmer before you finalize them. We usually try to work several into our message.

6. Contact the supplier and be ready with all your questions about turnaround time, cost, special charges for logo, camera-ready art, and so on.

7. Decide what the card will look like. You may purchase specialty paper or design your own. Exhibit 5.4 lists specialty-paper catalog companies. You should get on their mailing lists; their catalogs are great creativity joggers on their own. If you decide to print your own, the easy way to design it is a full sheet of paper folded twice to one-fourth the size. That way you only need to print on one side and your office printer can do it easily. For example, the outside of your card might have a clip-art picture of a tape measure with the question, "How do we measure up?" Inside you would explain the purpose of the questionnaire you are sending.

8. If the item will be sent, you will need to determine how: in a padded envelope, a box, or something else. You will need to purchase enough supplies for the mailing. Be sure that you take a sample of the item, card, and packing material to the post office for weighing. If you attach stamps, be sure you do that before you have it weighed. Believe it or not, once we did not add the stamps. When we returned to the post office with nine hundred filled boxes, the weight of the stamps pushed the package into the next ounce and we had to return to the office again to add another stamp!

9. I suggest that you complete the previous three steps (ordering the item, creating the card, and organizing your mailing supplies) simultaneously. This will save you time. You can usually get a sample item from the supplier so that you can determine dimensions and weight for the mailing supplies.

The MUMU Measure

How can you be certain that you have chosen an item wisely? I have created the MUMU Measure (see Figure 5.1). It measures whether the item is memorable, unique, mailable, and useful. If your answer to all four is a resounding "yes," you have probably selected wisely. What should you look for in each?

Figure 5.1. The MUMU Measure

M Memorable

U Unique

M Mailable

U Useful

Memorable How do you ensure that it is memorable? Make sure the item has your corporate name and logo imprinted on it. If you cannot personalize it, it is almost not worth sending. I believe food items fall into this category, unless you can imprint the container. Once the food is eaten, your gift is gone. No matter how delicious those big Florida oranges were, there will be nothing for your client to remember two months from now.

Unique You know what makes a unique item—something you would never expect to receive in the mail. It might be a toy such as a jump rope or jacks. It might be some new gizmo or gadget like the new flat flashlights or a digital tire gauge. You could mail golf tees, emery boards, sponges, puzzles, recipes, light bulbs, flat glass candy, or hundreds of things. Keep your eyes open for ideas. Unique does not mean sending a pen.

Mailable This simply means that you can mail it easily. The items I prefer are flat and can slip into a padded envelope. It also means they are not perishable. We had a creative idea using lucky bamboo, but quickly gave it up when we thought about the logistics of mailing the bamboo! Even if the item does not fit in an envelope, boxes are easily ordered from shipping suppliers. And don't forget the packing material if it is fragile.

Useful If you want your clients to keep the item on their desks, it should have some utility or reason to stay on their desks, credenzas, or other place nearby. The reason is so that they will see what you gave them daily and think of you. A paper-clip holder filled with gold paper clips, a very special mug, a staple remover, a PDA cover, a computer gadget, a bottle opener, a unique paperweight, a Post-it dispenser, a Rolodex® punch, or you name it.

Apply the MUMU Measure

Once you have selected your item, run it through the MUMU check. If you can answer yes to all four, you've chosen a winner.

Now it's time for you to practice. Exhibit 5.7 offers you some situations when you might need to provide a "keeper." Select one or two of the situations and find at least one item you could send for the occasion. Determine the message that would go with it. Apply the MUMU Measure. And remember to have fun.

Exhibit 5.7. Select a Situation

Imagine that you are in one of the following situations and you need to select a "keeper" for the occasion. Identify at least one item you could purchase and determine the message that would go with it. Apply the MUMU Measure. Have fun!

1. Hosting an open house for 200 and want to provide a memento for the event that will remain on guests' desks. Your budget is $10 per person.
2. Identifying something your sales staff will leave at a client's office after introducing them to your newest customer service program. Your budget is $5 per item.
3. Providing the "take away" for a professional association's leadership conference for 350 chapter leaders. Your budget is $3 per person.
4. Creating a Thanksgiving "thank you" for 2,000 of your top clients that will be mailed to them. Your budget is $.50 per person plus printing, paper, and postage.
5. Sending a lumpy envelope that entices recipients to request information about your new sales training package to 10,000 sales managers. You can spend $3,000 plus printing and mailing costs.
6. Creating a give-away from your newly formed executive coaching company for a trade show that will be attended by 5,000 people. Your budget is $7,000.

The tools of the trade must work. Only you can determine that based on the kind of consulting you do and the kind of consultant you are. In the next chapter you will create a marketing plan and determine which of these tools you will use.

─────────

MARKETING: TAKE ACTION

1. Examine the characteristics of the personal and promotional marketing tools. Which are the most important to you?

2. Based on your response to the first question, select at least six potential marketing tools for consideration in your marketing plan. Be prepared to explain why you selected each one.

3. Identify one of the marketing tools that you will most likely never use. Now, however, create an argument for why it will be your first choice one year from today.

4. Identify two clients with whom you have built relationships in the past. Find excuses to call them today.

5. If you skipped the "select a situation" project in the last section, go back and do it now in preparation for the next chapter.

Your Marketing Plan

Can You Market on a Shoestring Budget?

As a consultant, you are most likely not on the Fortune 500 list. You are not a large business, but most likely a small entrepreneurial firm facing cash flow concerns, limited time availability, and a lack of marketing moxie. These issues can be viewed as insurmountable and the reason you cannot create a marketing plan or they can be viewed as the very impetus to create a marketing plan. Problem or opportunity? It's all in how you view it. If you have given up, don't read any further. Get back to the grindstone. If you see this as an opportunity, let's begin to plan for what you can do to keep sales flowing and growing.

MARKETING PLAN PRELIMINARIES

Let's first alleviate your concerns of a lack of money, time, and marketing expertise. Then let's examine the advantages you have as a small consulting organization. Then we will discuss a marketing plan that works. Finally, let's identify some ideas that will make your marketing work for you.

But I'm Not a Large Business

Not being a large business is not all that bad. What do you think you lack that large companies have? Well, money, time, and expertise for starters. Let's consider each.

Money Money is relative. The larger you are, the more money your company needs for everything, including marketing. Are you aware that there are many marketing things you can do with no money? Yes, that's right—$00.00. You may not be able to afford a thirty-second ad on Super Bowl Sunday, but you can probably afford a stamp to send a prospecting letter.

It costs very little to write an article and send it to a magazine. It costs a few cents to make prospecting phone calls. It costs nothing but the overnight package to respond to requests for proposals. It is free to call a satisfied client and request an endorsement. Newsletters can be designed, written, copied, and sent for less than a dollar each. It is free to clip articles from your local newspaper or business journal about local businesspeople and send them.

Time We all have the same amount, yet none of us thinks there is enough. If you have read the first five chapters of this book and have completed all the exercises, you will breeze through developing a marketing plan. After that you simply need to be disciplined enough to complete each item when you are supposed to. Remember to delegate portions to others. My staff has always helped with brainstorming ideas for our holiday mailing and the theme that would accompany it.

Many marketing activities do not take much time—especially if you have a marketing calendar to follow. It can act as a to-do list and you can check off items as they are completed. For example, you will probably read your business journals anyway—why not read them keeping in mind which clients would appreciate receiving a copy of one of the articles? If you have greeting cards available, it takes very little time to dash off a note and send it to a client. You need to eat lunch anyway; why not eat it with a client?

There are other things you can do to save time. For example, when you are developing your plan, one thing you can do is to stick with a narrow niche by targeting just one industry at a time. For example, you might focus on the banking industry this year and then add the communications industry next year. This allows you to concentrate on one area of research, one area of networking, and one area for submitting proposals to speak at conferences.

You could also save time by finding multiple uses of marketing tools. For example, you could deliver the same speech to different groups. You could use that same speech for the basis of an article, you could tailor the article for different publications, and you could use the article as the basis of a press release. Once they are published, you could use the article and the press release as direct mail pieces. If you intend to attend a conference to network, you could submit a speaking proposal to the same conference. You could conduct a survey at the conference and use that as a basis for an article, a direct mail piece, or a prospecting letter. Start thinking about how you could get multiple uses from the marketing tools you choose.

Expertise You may not have your own marketing department to develop slick television commercials, but there are ad agencies that can give you a fresh perspective on your logo or your new brochure. You may be surprised at how much you can do without hiring a graphic designer or a copy writer.

Desktop publishing plus a little creativity gives you your own mini marketing department. And this book will help you start creating ideas of your own. The chapter on creativity at the end of this book will teach you creativity tools and give you examples of how others have been creative.

In addition, this chapter features additional support for small businesses like yours. The *ebbvice* inserts are select, sure-fire marketing techniques. Each is a nugget of advice guaranteed to blow away your competition. *ebbvice* for your marketing plan—just when you need it the most!

The Marketing Advantages of Being a Small Consulting Firm

Flexibility is the greatest advantage you have as a small firm. You do not have a large board of directors to please. You can concentrate on your customers. You do not have a management group that expects things to be "the way we've always done it before." You have the flexibility to react to market changes quickly, to adjust your marketing plans as needed. You do not have a large marketing and sales force that have been indoctrinated in a corporate marketing style. You have just your desire to be as creative as you choose. Although flexibility is an advantage, there are still a couple of minimum expectations that you must adhere to for maximum marketing success.

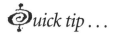*uick tip* . . .

> Flexibility is an advantage you have as a small business. It is important that you have a plan. It is equally important to build in flexibility that allows you to work around the projects you accept. For example, a project at the opposite end of the country affords you the opportunity to market to other companies in that area.

The Three Cs of Marketing: Minimums You Should Consider

You are about to put a marketing plan together, and there are a few things you should think about before you begin. These will also be important as you implement your plan. To achieve the maximum marketing success you must be committed, deliver a consistent message, and highlight it all with your creative touch. Consider these Three Cs to be a minimum to start.

Commitment You must be committed to your plan. Commitment begins with ensuring that you have established time and set aside a budget to implement your plan. Most important, however, is your personal commitment to continue with the plan. There is little instant gratification in marketing. You will need to be persistent. Calvin Coolidge said, "Press on. Nothing in the world can take the place of persistence. Talent will not; nothing is more common than unsuccessful men with talent. Genius will not; unrewarded genius is almost a proverb. Education alone will not; the world is full of educated derelicts. Persistence and determination alone are omnipotent."

An annual marketing plan ensures commitment. It will keep you organized. There will be days when you walk into your office after spending a day with a client and see forty-three e-mails and four telephone messages that need to be answered, six bills that need to be paid, two invoices that must be created, and a semi-developed plan for next week all screaming for your attention. At this time your marketing plan will also scream for your attention. You can do two things. You can add it to the stack of things that are weighting you down with their need for attention, or you can be buoyed up by the fact that you took the time to develop your plan six months ago. Indeed, probably the results of that marketing plan are keeping you busy! Perhaps it's time to think about hiring someone to keep your desk cleared of the administrative items.

Commitment also means that you continue to market even after the sale, even after the work has been completed. Remember, the only time to market is all the time!

Consistency You must be consistent in delivering your plan. The reason you invested time in Chapters Two, Three, and Four is to ensure that you knew what services you wanted to deliver to your clients, as well knowing what niche you would fill. If you have developed this with care and trust your assessment, you need to use it to develop a clear message for your clients. They need to understand what you have to offer them. Don't confuse them by changing messages or media. Don't disappear for long; put your marketing message out regularly.

Consistency also requires that your materials be consistent throughout. Besides a consistent message, maintain consistency through the colors you use and the designs you choose. Consistency helps to send the message that you are established, and this will raise the confidence level of your clients. Their confidence will lead to sales, and that's the reason you are marketing your services.

Creativity You must add your creative touch to your plan. Just as you found your niche in the services that you provide, you must find your "creativity niche" in what you will do to attract your clients' attention. That creativity might be translated in many different ways. It might be in a "wow" factor, or in the practicality, or the beauty. What does this mean?

Your marketing must stand out from the rest. Your clients receive hundreds of direct mail pieces each week. You are competing against hundreds of other consultants for the same consulting dollars. You need to grab potential clients' attention. How do you do that?

Let's consider the "wow," practicality, or beauty marketing possibilities. Remember, you are going to be consistent as well. A "wow" factor might be that you offer a 100 percent money-back guarantee if your clients are not satisfied. Won't that get their attention? We made this offer right from the start. After a successful project, one of our first clients, Bill Williams from NASA, said, "We decided that either she was very, very good or crazy, but with a money-back guarantee, what did we have to lose?"

A practicality twist might be that every marketing opportunity is a chance for the recipient to benefit in some way. It might be that the memorable gifts you send are useful items with a twist, such as staple removers that are actually desk art, paper clips that happen to be gold, or pens that happen to light up in the night.

Your direct mail might send a list of "ten tips to . . ." and your newsletter may be filled with time-saving ideas or suggestions for improvement.

Using beauty as your creative focus means your marketing materials will have a certain aura about them because you have taken care in choosing perfect paper with lovely ink and beautiful graphics. Your messages will be soft and will never shout (like those car dealers on the radio!). Your marketing may send a stress-relieving message. Flowers, clouds, and other items from nature will make their way into your messages and provide a serene backdrop.

Remember that even though we are focused on creativity, your marketing must send a message of benefit to your potential client. "Wow" probably sends the message: "We're going to knock your socks off with service!" Practicality probably sends the message: "We're going to solve your problems." And the beauty theme might send a message that says, "We're going to ensure a pleasant, productive experience."

"But I'm not creative," you may be wailing. We will provide you with some ideas in this chapter. In addition, Chapter Eleven focuses completely on creativity and making marketing fun.

WHY A MARKETING PLAN?

Consultants must be marketing-oriented. In the beginning you may need to market yourself tirelessly using every tactic that's at your disposal. If the term "marketing" scares you, think in terms of simply getting the word out that you are in business. You must get the word out. You must promote yourself. Companies need to know you are here. You must make sales. Or . . . you will be out of business.

You may argue that preparing a marketing plan and putting it on paper is a waste of time. But there are several reasons why it is the best use of your time.

- It can help you focus on what's important.
- Establishing deadlines will help you pace yourself and achieve your goals.
- Setting goals allows you a way to measure progress.
- A marketing plan is a good financial tool to show how you intend to build your business.

What's the Minimum I Need to Know About Marketing?

There must be more volumes written about marketing than about any other business topic. At times marketing appears to be glitzy and glamorous. On the other hand marketing can be complicated and mysterious. You may find yourself reading about marketing goals, objectives, strategies, tactics, promotional mix, segmentation, targeted audiences, niche, product lifecycles, and media scheduling. Some marketing experts discuss the four Ps of the marketing mix: product, price, place, and promotion. Other experts discuss the eight Ps and an S: product, price, place, promotion, positioning, people, profits, politics, and service. In addition you will read about advertising, public relations, and media. Then there are discussions about personal versus impersonal promotion or direct versus indirect marketing. You can read about personal selling, client-centered marketing, leveraging your clients—well, you get the idea. There are lots of words published about marketing. But what do you really need to know?

At this point you don't need a degree in marketing. You need to know how to get the word out that you have consulting services to offer. This may seem like a daunting task, and one you'd rather skip. But don't be tempted. Developing a marketing plan is critical if you are to stay in business. You can make it as useful and as simple as you like.

Your marketing plan will convert your ideas and intentions into commitment and action. Your marketing plan will guide you through the year so that the important task of marketing is never pushed to the back burner. Putting your plan in writing puts discipline into your ideas, enables you to measure success, and provides data for future use. Implementing your marketing plan will keep you in front of your clients. Done correctly, it helps you plan your most efficient and effective networking activities.

All of the time you spent in the first five chapters comes to fruition now. As you begin to think about your marketing plan, recognize that it should be a very natural part of your business. Let's look at how natural marketing can be.

Marketing Naturally

Phone clients regularly. When I telephone clients, I am amazed again and again by those who say, "I was just thinking about you" or "We have a situation and perhaps you're the one who . . ." or "I just got out of a meeting in which I was tasked to . . ."

Once you cease contact you will be forgotten and they will be answering the competition's calls instead with, "I was just thinking about you. . . ." Clients are more important to you than you will ever be to them.

Listen.

Use the mail system to send . . . everything! Congratulatory notes, magazine articles, newspaper stories, conference tapes, books, recipes, cards, letters, information about a problem the client is solving, a lunch invitation, bubbles, crayons, rulers, pie, umbrellas, even information about our competitors if it will help the client.

Listen.

Accept public speaking engagements for civic functions, conferences, after-dinner meetings, associations, universities, political organizations.

Listen.

Focus on class, not mass. Develop a few wonderful clients rather than a multitude of problem clients. Your goal is to serve your clients above and beyond their wildest dreams so that you create a client with such high expectations no one else will be able to achieve them. If your goal is to work fewer hours at a higher level of quality, think profit, not volume.

Listen.

Make any training so successful that those who attend will sell it to the next group and to the person paying the bill. How? Be genuinely interested in participants as individuals, keep things participative, and help them grow. Talk to people between tasks. Go to lunch with them at noon. Stay in touch after sessions. Follow up with additional materials and a personally written note. The best marketing tactic is a satisfied client.

Listen.

Create work for yourself. Go out of your way to locate information about whatever a client or potential client needs. Then send it with a personal note from you. And follow up again with a phone call—just to see if it arrived. And then start the process all over again with the same client or a new one. People seldom have time to conduct their own research. Do it for them.

Listen.

Listen for what? Hints about birth dates or special anniversaries. Honors. Favorite sports, topics, food, teams, hobbies, authors—even children's interests—favorite anything. Problems, concerns, corporate changes, challenges, needs. Perhaps you'll even hear about a new service or product you can provide!

Listen.

Listen to whom? Everyone. The president, CEO, CIO, CO, receptionist, administrative staff, training director. Listen to the participants. You'll learn how you can better serve them, things you need to know about the organization, and tidbits that you probably shouldn't know. You'll also hear information that will give you an excuse to talk to the person who hired you or people who should hire you. Listen to secretaries. They often know more about the organization than anyone else. They'll remember the thank-you note you sent the next time you're having trouble tracking down their bosses.

And finally, don't depend on your brain. Keep records, to-do lists, files, tickler files, notes, note cards, Post-its, and calendars.

Marketing can be this natural. But you must do it.

A MARKETING PLAN FORMAT

A marketing plan can become quite complex, using marketing jargon, formulas, and lots of analysis. Some of the ones I've seen have a heavy emphasis on the word "plan" and little emphasis on "implement." If you are a small consulting firm, you know that it is important to plan, but you must also not become paralyzed by planning.

The eight easy steps to a marketing plan displayed in Exhibit 6.1 are somewhat unconventional, but they are realistic. They require that you do some assessment and analysis. They require that you know some of the jargon. But marketing is a combination of intuition and logic. This process forces you to complete the assessment and analysis and then encourages you to be creative and to trust your intuition.

The eight-step format will move you through the process comfortably. It will ensure that your final marketing plan does what it is supposed to do—get your name out there! Let's examine what you might include in each step.

The eight-step plan is expanded here to help you with the actual writing. I suggest that you pull out your notes from the first five chapters, put the outline on your desktop computer, and begin filling in the words as you read each step. Don't get hung up on wording, spelling, and grammar. You will become discouraged. Just move quickly through the steps, filling in thoughts and ideas as you read the next few pages.

Exhibit 6.1. Your Marketing Plan

1. **Executive Summary**

2. **Assess the Situation**

   Assess Your Consulting Company
   - Define your business
   - Define your management plan
   - Define your company's customer base
   - Define your financial situation
   - Declare your strengths and weaknesses

   Assess Your Competition
   - Define who they are
   - Define how they differ from you

   Assess Your Clients
   - Identify their needs
   - Identify their level of satisfaction

3. **Build a Potential Client Base**

   Clarify Your Strategy
   - Identify your competitive position
   - Identify your niche
   - Describe your targeted client base
   - Describe what you will offer these clients
   - Identify what you will tell your clients about these services

4. **Set Measurable Six- to Twelve-Month Goals**

   Set Measurable Goals to Build Your Business
   - Goals should focus on the niche you have described
   - Goals should be measurable
   - Goals should be time bound

Exhibit 6.1. Your Marketing Plan, Cont'd

5. Select Marketing Tools to Accomplish Your Goals

Identify Tools You Will Use to Reach
- New clients
- Current clients
- Past clients

Identify Tools You Will Use to Ensure a Fit for Your
- Clients
- Budget
- Personality

6. Identify Resources

Identify Resources Required
- Person responsible
- Time required
- Cost

7. Develop an Annual Marketing Planning Calendar

- Lay out your plan for the year

8. Implement and Monitor Your Plan

- Identify how you will track results

- Identify how you will know if you need to adjust your plans

- Identify how you will reward yourself for completion

1. Executive Summary

Your executive summary provides an overview of your plan in about two minutes. You should not assume that everyone who reads your plan will know your business well. Therefore this summary gives the reader that background. The opening sentence lists your business name, what it does, where it is located, and your target audience. For example, "Write for Results is a Madison, Wisconsin, consulting firm that focuses on enhancing writing skills for employees of Fortune 500 companies." If more description is needed, add another sentence that might include sales growth or marketing strategy over the past year or two

Add a sentence or two about the changing situation with regard to your competitors and your customers. Discuss expansion into new markets and expansion of current business as well as what opportunities and threats this poses. Then add an explanation of how you intend to address these opportunities and threats.

Close with your positioning plan and your sales objectives. For example, "Write for Results will maintain its position as the premier writing skills firm that guarantees fast results. The company plans to increase sales by 15 percent and add five new clients during the year."

2. Assess the Situation

Return to Chapters Two and Three to obtain information for this section. You should be able to summarize all the assessing and exploring you did about your organization, your competition, and your clients.

Assess Your Consulting Company Define your business by going into more depth than you did in the executive summary. Add how long you have been in business and why you started your consulting firm. Discuss the kind of work you conduct, your specialty, and the reputation you have earned. Include your mission statement and your vision as well.

Add the information about your management plan, who is in your organization, and what marketing responsibilities they have. If you subcontract, briefly discuss these arrangements. Briefly discuss your customer base, the size, the industries that are represented, and changes you anticipate that may affect your business. Explain your financial situation and provide your projections. Summarize your strengths and weaknesses.

Assess Your Competition Rely on your assessment in Chapter Three to complete this section. Define who your competitors are and how they differ from you in products and services, position, pricing, marketing strategy, strengths, and weaknesses. Add any statistics about your kind of consulting and add an industry profile if you completed one.

Keep an eye on your competition. As a consultant, being alone and outside the employment loop can be psychologically difficult. But it can be financially devastating if you do not keep up with what's going on in your field. What's your competition doing? You must be aware of the trends around you. Changes in the economy, technology, management fads, and others will all affect your business.

To keep up with your competition, read your professional journals: Who's advertising? What are they selling? Who's writing articles? Attend conferences: Who's presenting? What are they expounding? What's the buzz in the hallways? Visit bookstores: Who's writing? What topics are being published? Even if you will not lead the profession, you must at least stay in touch. You owe it to your clients.

ebbvice   Wallow in Your Junk Mail

Junk mail is a marketing research gift. Read it! You can spend thousands to find out what your competition is doing. Or you can acknowledge the free research delivered to your door every day. Consultants often complain about the piles of advertising they receive, especially in conjunction with conferences they've attended. Instead, welcome your junk mail as the gift it is.

Why wallow in your junk mail? You can get a sense of the trends in the field. Trends are ever-changing. Is stress management in this year or out? Junk mail can spark ideas for your own marketing. Notice I said spark ideas—not steal them. Junk mail can keep you informed of new organizations that have entered the field.

Don't bemoan your junk mail delivery. Instead, be grateful for all the competitive information that has just been dumped in your lap. Don't throw it away! Read it. Study it. Wallow in your junk mail.

Assess Your Clients   Identify your clients' needs and their level of satisfaction in this section. Whether you conducted a survey, completed interviews, or hired an external source to conduct your research, this is where you will summarize it. You certainly might guess at what they would say if you had asked them, but it seems to me that if you do not ask, you are missing an essential opportunity to get yourself in front of them again—and that's marketing.

When you discuss their needs, summarize needs of today and anticipated needs of the future. Also add what criteria they use to select a consultant. When you discuss their level of satisfaction, identify the aspects of service that are important to them and how well they are met. Add any suggestions for improving the quality of service. This sets you up for the next section to discuss how you might meet these needs.

Quick tip . . .

> A fast strategy for marketing is to determine where your last five clients came from. Were they referrals? From advertising? Someone who purchased your book? Think about whether it would be worth your while to invest additional time and money in the areas that resulted in clients or perhaps to eliminate those that did not.

3. Build a Potential Client Base

In this section you will clarify your strategy. Return to Chapter Three and review what you have written with regard to your position and your niche.

Clarify Your Strategy First, of course, you need to be certain that you have one. Clarify your position and how it differs from your competition. Clearly state the niche that you have selected. You must have a strategy for several reasons. The first is so that you know where to focus your energy. If you have decided to focus on large businesses as your niche and you continue to work with the federal government, you may work the same number of days but may not reach the financial goals you set. Even with a strategy, many consultants stray from it and lead their business into trouble. So it's not enough to have a strategy; you must also pay attention to it. Besides, if you don't have a strategy, how will you know when you stray from it?

Determine the targeted client base on which you will focus, what size companies, what type of organizations, and in what industry. What skills will you promote? What services will you provide? And in response to the previous section, describe what you will offer these clients and identify what you will tell your clients about these services.

You need to determine whether you will target your current clients or new clients and whether you will market current services or new services. That means four combinations. Figure 6.1 shows you the risk, cost, and growth potential of each combination. Obviously, marketing the same services to the same clients is little or no risk or cost, but also results in little growth. Marketing new services to new clients is the highest risk and cost and results in slow growth. Marketing current services to new clients is a moderate risk and cost that results in moderate growth. Marketing new services to current clients is a low risk and moderate cost with significant growth potential. These decisions should fall out of the research you completed in Chapters Two and Three.

Figure 6.1. Client Strategy Choices

	Current	New
New	Risk: Little Cost: Moderate Result: Significant Growth Potential	Risk: High Cost: High Result: Probable Slow Growth
Current	Risk: Little Cost: Little Result: Little Growth	Risk: Moderate Cost: Moderate Result: Moderate Growth

Services (vertical axis) — Clients (horizontal axis)

What increases the risk in two of the four combinations? It is the potential of new clients. In general, new clients also require more marketing dollars and result in slower growth. It may take months—even years—of marketing to acquire a new client. That is why a client in hand is worth ten in your marketing plan.

ebbvice Go for the Big Fish; You'll Spend the Same Time Baiting the Hook

If you are going after new clients, don't let the size of the organization scare you. The people who manage large organizations need good consulting just like those who run the smaller ones. You will invest the same amount of time marketing your services to a large organization as a small one. Your payoff, however, may be much greater.

Many new consultants focus on small businesses first, perhaps because large organizations are more intimidating. However, when you realize that small businesses have smaller training and consulting budgets and that the decision to hire a consultant may be the one and only budgeted consulting expense for the year, you realize the problems you face.

On the other hand, large businesses make numerous training and consulting purchases in a year. They often feel more comfortable taking a risk on a new consultant. In addition, if you did a great job, you will have a better chance at repeat business with a larger organization. Small organizations may want to have you return, but may not be able to with this year's budget.

4. Set Measurable Six- to Twelve-Month Goals

You will set measurable goals to build your business. You know how important goal setting is. Be specific. These goals should focus on the niche you have described. In addition, your goals should be measurable and time-bound. Think of them this way. Exactly what will you do by when? I like to suggest a six- to twelve-month time frame. That means you have a few that you plan to achieve soon and some that require the entire year. You can set goals for two years out if you wish; however, with the marketplace changing as rapidly as it does, they may be more visionary. Do go ahead and establish longer-range goals if you choose. No matter what your timeline is, make certain that you believe all are achievable.

Here are a few examples of measurable goals:

- Generate $80,000 in repeat business from 1/1 to 5/31.
- Generate $70,000 in new business from 1/1 to 5/31.
- Retain all current clients.
- Expand services to current clients.
- Acquire two new clients with billable hours valued at $45,000 by 12/31.
- Acquire four new clients in the tri-state area by 2/28.
- Acquire one new client in the pharmaceutical industry by 2/28.
- Acquire three new clients in the Seattle area by October 31.
- Secure two major clients to occupy 40 percent of my time.
- Generate four prospective client leads within sixty days.
- Ask present clients for six referrals within thirty days.
- Acquire two new referral clients by mid-May.
- Acquire two contracts to install personnel tracking systems within six months.
- Select one new industry before the end of the year.
- Identify three new trade associations to support the newly selected industry.
- Increase client inquiries by 15 percent by next year.
- Present at one new conference in the next calendar year.
- Make twenty-five contacts in the banking industry by the end of April.
- Sell Communication Styles program to five current clients by June 30.
- Submit proposals to at least three new conferences within nine months.
- Offer to write another ASTD *Info-Line*.
- Teach one technical course at the local community college each semester.

- Improve relationship with current clients.
- Improve customer satisfaction by 10 percentage points over last year.

Notice that these goals all fall into two categories. They are a mix of promotional activities (such as presenting at conferences) that lead to an ultimate growth goal, as well as the ultimate growth goals. I generally establish at least one financial goal for repeat business and one financial goal for new business. I also establish a specific number of new clients with whom I would like to work. In addition I add one more goal that is industry or geographic specific and one goal related to promotional activities such as writing or speaking. It depends on my business goals for the year, but generally I have five to seven goals each year.

I post my sales goals on my bulletin board next to my desk. I still have some faded copies of those from 1985 and 1986. There is a huge amount of value in writing your goals down and keeping them in front of you. It helps keep you focused on where you are going.

There are many things that you have a choice of whether to include in your marketing plan. Establishing measurable marketing goals, however, is not something that you can choose. You must have goals. Once you set your goals, you can get as wild and crazy as you like in choosing the tools and tactics you will use to put your message out to potential clients. The next section of your marketing plan is the most fun.

5. Select Marketing Tools to Accomplish Your Goals

This step is the best part of the entire process. It's time to identify the tools you will use to reach your current and past clients. Examine your goals and determine which tools listed in Chapter Five are the most likely to achieve them. Your first decision is to determine whether you believe you should focus on personal or professional marketing tools. You may decide to use a mix. As you examine your goals, select tools that will do double duty for you. For example, if two of your goals are to "acquire three clients in the Seattle area" and to "generate four prospective client leads in the manufacturing industry," you may decide to speak at the Greater Northwest Manufacturing Association's fall conference.

You will also want to check around with your colleagues to determine what seems to be the most effective. I have found that, in general, advertising and direct mail do not work very well for promoting small consulting practices. Trade shows and newsletters seem to work if they are paired with a personal follow-up phone call. My friends in larger consulting firms use all four of these tools and claim that the success is in the marketing mix.

You will also want to ensure that the tools you select are a fit in several ways. First, they should fit comfortably with your clients' expectations; second, they should fit your budget and what you have decided to invest in marketing; and last, they should be a comfortable fit for your personality.

Client Fit The marketing tools you select should have your client in mind first and foremost. Where does your client expect to see your name? In what medium will your client expect to see your services? The marketing climate is changing for professionals, so don't be too conservative. Only a short time ago it was unethical and/or unprofessional for attorneys to purchase display ads in the yellow pages. Now it is considered quite normal to see billboards ablaze or television spots shouting the reason you should hire a specific lawyer.

Also remember to think beyond the obvious to the "what if?" I worked with some folks who owned motivational tourist shops called "Last Flight Out." The shops were somewhat related to aviation, but mostly geared to positive thinking and doing what you love. One of the shop owners wanted to advertise on the fuselage of one of the stunt planes. Initially this sounded like a great idea until one of the owners thought about how the Last Flight Out logo might appear in a picture of a crumpled plane should a mishap occur. They decided not to advertise in that way.

Your client would certainly expect to see you advertise in industry-related directories, journals, trade shows, or direct mail card decks. However, it might be unusual to see your services on television or on a billboard. A sponsorship for the printed program at a professional conference would be expected; sponsorship of a racecar might be questionable. Bottles of wine customized with your name on the label is creative, but may not be a wise choice if your clients disapprove of the subtle message it may send. Does the fact that something is unusual mean you should not do it? Of course not. If you believe a prospective client will see, recognize, and continue to respect your consulting name, it should be a consideration. Just remember to think about your clients' expectations.

ebbvice Mail a Lumpy Envelope

Direct mail can have a big payoff. You must get the recipient's attention so that the envelope is opened. You certainly don't want to think that your envelopes could be placed in someone's junk mail stack!

Over the years we have mailed dozens of lumpy envelopes. We've mailed typical things such as pens, staple removers, and holiday ornaments, but we've mailed the unusual, too:

- Tree-shaped pasta in January to send greetings for a "tree-mendous" new year with many "pasta-bilities."

- Polished stones to thank someone who has been a "real gem."

- Glass stars to congratulate champions and tell them they are "real stars."

- Miniature books that contained quotes for business, for people, or for life.

- Tape measures asking the recipients how they "measure up."

- Crayons to complete an interactive creativity brochure.

- Pumpkin pokes (black wire in the shape of bats that you "poke" into pumpkins) in October.

And when there is nothing to make a large lump, we may add confetti to celebrate a business success or tiny stars to say congratulations. We have acquired a reputation for our lumpy envelopes. Some clients open our envelopes over a wastebasket—just in case. We have gained a reputation for mailing things that brighten people's days.

Budget Fit It might seem like a blinding flash of the obvious, but you do need to remember your budget and what you are trying to accomplish with it. A rule of thumb is to invest 10 percent of your gross in marketing. Estimate how much you will sell next year and build your marketing plan around one-tenth of that amount. You will establish a specific budget in the next step. For now think in terms of whether you will be using tools that require large outlays of money, such as magazine advertising or sponsorships, or whether you will be selecting tools that are free or cost very little, such as telephone calls or publishing a book.

As you think through the questions about the budget, you will want to determine whether your budget will affect the image you project to your customers and, if so, whether it is the one you wish to project.

Personality Fit Finally, you will want to ensure that the tools you select are ones that enhance the image you wish to project. You will first need to examine the various marketing tools available to you and determine which will match your personality and the image you have chosen to project for your company. Do the personal marketing tools seem to be a match? Or are the promotional tools a better match?

Will the technical tools such as a website and an electronic newsletter project what you want? Or will a paper newsletter with tear-out tips be more like you? Is sending birthday cards with a handwritten greeting something you wish to do? Or do you prefer to send a brochure with a typed cover letter? Will you be comfortable sending a box of shamrock cookies on St. Patrick's Day? Or will you prefer the tried-and-true holiday card in December? Only you can answer these questions. Typically, consultants shy away from the more personalized tools available. (For additional thoughts on this issue, see the *ebbvice* section that addresses personalizing your marketing.)

When you begin to select tools, also think about whether they will be consistent with your corporate image.

Idea Jump-Start Need a quick start on things you can do once you select the tools? Here are three things you can do. First, you can examine lists that are already created. Two that I recommend are 113 ideas in *The Business of Consulting* and 105 ideas in *Marketing Your Services: For People Who Hate to Sell.* Both books are listed in the reading list at the back. The ideas will encompass everything from a hot new theme to cold calls.

Second, you can go to the actions listed at the end of the chapter and work through several of these. If you need stimulation, invite friends over to brainstorm with you. Third, you can skip ahead to Chapter Eleven and use several of the creativity techniques to begin to develop ideas for how you will use your marketing tools.

ebbvice Personalize Your Marketing

I am a strong proponent of personalized marketing tools. When I first started my business most of my exchanges with clients were very informal and personal. I claimed that we did no marketing, until Ian, one of my clients, asked what I thought I was doing when I sent him a hand-made thank-you card. Whether it's marketing or not, I do believe it built a strong relationship with my clients and potential clients. I suggest that you conduct more personalized marketing than you might originally consider. It can be fun, and it does work. It can be serious or hokey, but one thing's for sure: Few people do it, and you will stand out. What have we done?

Probably the most unusual thing I did was to send a pie to a bank vice president (usually a conservative industry) based on a personal discussion we had about how to coach employees. It worked. I was invited for a sales call and landed some work with them. Certainly this is not something I would have done with everyone. In fact it's the only time I used it. I believe, however, that most of you have opportunities like that and that 99 percent of the time they are not completed. One of three things happens:

1. The opportunity floats right over your head and you miss it. *ebbvice*: keep your ears and eyes open for those unique opportunities and write them down so you don't forget. Right now I have three items on my to-do list that are like this: Send flowers to a client's mother in the hospital, call a colleague who is writing a book to offer my publicist's name, and purchase and send a book about fly fishing to a client.

2. You recognize the opportunity, have a creative idea, perhaps even share it with someone. Then for some reason you discard the idea as either too foolish, too expensive, too risky, or for some other reason that seems perfectly plausible. *ebbvice*: do it anyway. Get it on your to-do list. Ask one other person (not too conservative) and if the individual gives you a thumbs up, put it in your A priorities.

3. You recognize the opportunity, perhaps you even write it on your to-do list, but you run out of time and do not follow up. It eventually becomes too late to be effective and you remove it from your actions. *ebbvice*: establish a

process that ensures you can complete these actions with minimal effort. If you have an assistant, determine how that person can help. Establish an easy place to list these items. For ease in mailing, purchase a label maker and have a designated area for all your mailing supplies. For telephone calls, have all phone numbers in one location and update the list regularly. Develop templates so that you do not need to reinvent a note each time. Use your downtime effectively, for example, take note cards with you to write while you are on a plane.

What else do we do that constitutes personalized marketing? We send cards filled with confetti to congratulate clients on job promotions. We send birthday cards. We send custom-designed cards to celebrate graduations, births, engagements, weddings, anniversaries, new cars, trips, a new life focus, a new house, a move. We send articles of interest about a favorite subject, hobby, child's college, vacation site, competitor, mutual friend. We may send items that have a special meaning such as Georgia O'Keeffe stamps, job ads, special coffee, music CDs, books (lots of books), pens, photos, good-luck tokens, stones.

We send many notes to follow up on conversations. Sometimes items are added. I once had a discussion with Kathleen Dolan Davies, my editor, in which we both marveled at the magic of television. I followed up by sending her a children's book, *How Things Work,* including the magic of television.

I do these things because I like people and I enjoy a personalized marketing focus. Personal marketing tools have been more powerful for me than the promotional marketing tools. While the personal tools are marketing tactics, I see them as relationship-building tools. If it's not comfortable for you (a fit to your personality), don't do it. If it's not sincere, it could backfire. If you are doing it "just to market your services," don't do it.

---

6. Identify Resources

Now you need to identify the resources you require to complete the marketing plans you have identified. There is a cost to marketing. Whether you speak at a local service organization meeting, complete prospecting calls, send a public relations letter to a newspaper, display at a tradeshow, publish an online newsletter, or advertise in your industry journal, there is a cost. As stated in the section above, you will need to determine the return on investment. You will need to compare the cost and the results to determine whether you will continue to use a marketing tool you have selected.

Of course, resources mean more than just your cash outlay. Resources include the cost, the time required, and the person who will actually complete the task. If one of your marketing goals is to target a specific industry, you could do several different things. You could purchase booth space at the industry trade show, purchase an ad in the industry's directory, submit an article to their journal, or take someone to lunch to identify ways to introduce your services to specific organizations within the industry.

The first two cost more money than the last two. The booth and the article will both take several days of your time. The booth and the lunch provide more personal contact. Submitting an article and purchasing an ad are indirect, but you could follow each with a copy and a personalized letter. The ad will probably require you to hire an expert to assist you. You may decide to do all, some, or none of these ideas.

In the last step we suggested that you use about 10 percent of your sales to expend on marketing. Use that information as a starting point. You will also need to determine how much the marketing activities you have developed will cost.

Obtain prices for the various marketing tools you expect to use. This may require that you speak to some of the specific vendors of these services. For example, if you decide to advertise in directories or journals, you will want to call them directly. You can usually find their phone numbers in the publication. Realize that you will be speaking to sales folks (account reps) and they will push to get your name and contact information. Ask them to send you their advertising package with spec sheets. In addition, you can expect them to follow up with you. Instead of thinking of these follow-up contacts as a nuisance, listen carefully and learn something from their sales techniques.

As you make plans, take care that you do not commit yourself to one medium too soon. Most print media (newspapers, yellow pages, magazines), for example, will sign you up for a series of ads. You might commit to a year of advertising in the yellow pages at $250 per month, only to find out that the ad does not garner one phone call after five months. You are still committed to the last seven months and the payments that equal another $1,750. Try to maintain as much flexibility as possible in your plans.

Compare what you know about your budget to what you have learned about the cost of marketing. Don't be surprised if you have identified more activities than you have budget. That is a typical situation. So now the difficulty comes in deciding what to cut.

The most important message here is that you must have a budget. It is easy to spend more than you intended. Some consultants run a couple of ads and, as business (and budget) is acquired, they run a few more. This does not create a reliable plan. It will be hard to determine the right mix and the right investment. A successful business wants to find the right marketing plan—enough to ensure the business thrives, but not so much that you waste money. A budget gives you one of the data pieces you need to determine your return on this marketing investment. Make informed decisions about your marketing tools based on the cost of each.

7. Develop an Annual Marketing Planning Calendar

This is the step where it all comes together on several pages. You will lay out your plan for the year on an annual marketing planning calendar like the one in Exhibit 6.2. Each of your goals will be broken down into substeps using the activities you chose and listed on the calendar. Notice that this format also tracks estimated costs. You will of course need more detail for some of the activities, but this format will help you see everything at a glance: how time will be expended each month and the anticipated marketing cost for the month.

Suppose that one of your marketing goals is to "have two new clients in the banking industry by the end of the year." In addition you have decided that you will use mostly personal marketing tools that will include conference attendance, presentations, referrals, and personal contacts. Your marketing activities for the first couple of months might look something like this:

Contact my banker for ideas   January 15

Speak at banking conference   February 8

Make twenty-five contacts at conference	February 7–9
Conduct additional research on contacts	February 10–11
Follow up all conference contacts	February 14
Brainstorm special mailing to contacts	February 16
Send special mailing to contacts	March 1
Follow-up calls to contacts	March 8
Include banking contacts in spring mailing	March 21
Submit article (presentation) to *Banking Today*	March 28
Send brochures to twenty-five contacts with personal note	April 22

This format allows you to track the dates and the expected cost of each month. You can tell at a glance what you intend to do each month, where your focus is, and which months are heavy or light in activities. You can look ahead to see what is coming up.

Use another format if you have one. The key is that you do need to put your plan on paper. This keeps it in front of you at all times. You will find three actual marketing plans in the last chapter. Each plan uses a different format, but they are all short, focused, and practical.

Quick tip ...

Have your marketing plan developed free. Most business schools require their marketing majors to develop a marketing plan. Students usually write plans for the school itself or non-profit agencies connected to it. Most would rather write a marketing plan for a real business. Allow enough time. Writing the plan will probably be a long process occurring over a full semester. Speak with the professor the semester before. Also, stay involved. You will need to provide the correct data so the plan is based on accurate assumptions. Even if the plan is less than perfect due to the students' inexperience, you may get good advice from the professor.

Exhibit 6.2. Annual Marketing Planning Calendar

Marketing Activity for (year)	Jan	Feb	Mar	April	May	June	July	Aug	Sept	Oct	Nov	Dec
Dates / Cost												
Total Budgeted Costs												

From E. Biech, *The Business of Consulting* (San Francisco: Jossey-Bass/Pfeiffer, 1998).

ebbvice The Time to Market Is All the Time

A calendar of marketing activities suggests that you will market on only certain days of the month. The truth is you are marketing all the time. Every experience with every client, every conversation with a colleague, every visit to a professional meeting, every comment to a friend is a marketing event. You are selling you. As a consultant, you represent your product or service. The people you meet are making decisions about whether they will use your services or recommend you to someone else.

"The time to market is all the time" also means that you must complete the activities on your marketing calendar (for example, call a friend who was just hired by Microsoft or begin the article for the technology magazine). At times you may feel too busy with a current project to market. Of course you must complete the project. If you tell yourself that you are too busy to also complete the marketing, you will come to the end of the current project and not have another project lined up. Yes, the time to market is all the time. And the most important time to market is when you are too busy to market!

8. Implement and Monitor Your Plan

This step is really the reason you put the plan together in the first place. You are ready to implement what you decided to do. Stay on top of your marketing activities. Your marketing may not yield any results for six months. Start now. Stay on top of your plan.

The monitoring portion means that you will track your progress as well as results. How do you do that? I do not believe that more paperwork will help you. I track my progress by simply checking off the items as I complete them. How about tracking results?

Typically each quarter I sit down to examine the marketing plan. Just because you have completed everything on your list doesn't mean it's over. You need to determine whether your marketing is having an effect on new business. You can do that by recording how many new clients, new work with former clients, and new potential clients you have. I identify these in a running list on my computer by quarter. Contract amount is also listed. I then determine how the connection was made. If clients initiate the contact, they will usually tell you how the work came about. And if you initiate the contact you will know. So this part is easier than you might imagine.

This information tells you whether you need to adjust your plans. For example, if the ad in *Training* magazine has not yielded any inquiries the first month, you may want to talk to your account rep to determine whether placement might be a problem. Perhaps it doesn't sell the benefits as it should. It may not appeal to this audience. If the ad still doesn't provide any activity after another month or two, you may want to reconsider its value.

You may also need to adjust your marketing plans due to your business. Have you targeted one market but learned that it was a mistake? For example, you may have targeted Fortune 500 companies only to discover that their projects were too large for you to manage. If you decide to change your target audience, you will need to change your marketing plans.

How do you know whether or not your marketing plan is working? Your clients are your best barometer. Ask them how they found you, then track their responses. As a consultant you will usually know immediately. It is still important to gather the data so that at the end of the year you will be able to review it and determine what is paying off.

Finally, you need to identify how you will reward yourself for completion. You have planned and implemented your marketing effort—just like any large company would do. Congratulations.

ebbvice Keep Yourself in Front of Your Clients

The bottom line is to keep yourself in front of your clients. You can accomplish this in three ways. First, you can physically be in their presence. When working on-site, be sure that you stop in to visit those with whom you've worked in the past or the person who hired you for this project. I stop in unannounced; you may need to schedule meetings. Whatever is comfortable, make the time. If you travel to the city of former clients, call to schedule time to meet with them while you are there.

Second, keep yourself in front of your clients with permanent, practical year-end gifts. We always look for something unique, something special. We have gained a reputation for creative gifts. For example, one year we sent miniature mugs filled with gold paper clips. They were high quality, useful, and had our logo sitting on everyone's desk every day. In 2001 we sent yo-yos that lit up and our card read, "It's been a year of ups and downs, but we want to help light up your new year."

Third, keep yourself in front of your clients by ensuring that things go across their desks throughout the year, for example, articles, notes of interest, books, announcements, cards, seasonal greetings, candy, or even cartoons! Find a reason. When someone joins our firm, we send a special announcement. For example, when Garland joined our firm, we sent a miniature chalkboard and chalk with the message, "Chalk another one up for ebb associates. . . ."

CAN YOU REALLY MARKET ON A SHOESTRING BUDGET?

Let's face it. You need business or you will go out of business. Marketing leads to business. You want to promote yourself and build a positive reputation. Marketing can do this as well. Marketing costs money, and that's one thing you may not have. Can you really market on a shoestring budget? Let's wrap this chapter up with some things you can do that require a small financial investment. Many of these are things you may have thought of in the past. But thinking doesn't get them done. Select a few of these and do them now—even if you have not completed your marketing plan. Remember: "The time to market is all the time."

Ten Ideas to Market on a Shoestring Budget

1. Call your college roommate and ask for a referral.

2. Call a dormant client and renew the relationship.

3. Slip an envelope stuffer in with your invoice to mention a new service or product.

4. Write a press release for your local newspaper.

5. Write an article to send to your clients.

6. List your company in free directories.

7. Submit a proposal to speak to an industry conference.

8. Begin to pass out two business cards to everyone you meet: one to keep and one to pass on.

9. Be a guest on a local talk show.

10. Do such a great job for your clients that they will want to market for you.

The next chapter introduces prospecting for new clients: the transition from your marketing plan in this chapter to selling your services.

———

MARKETING: TAKE ACTION

1. Review the three Cs of marketing: Commitment, Consistency, and Creativity. Identify three things you need to remember about each as you develop your marketing plan.

2. Your marketing plan should be fun to develop. To generate some ideas of what you can do, use this list of nouns to get your creative juices flowing: business cards, letters, seminars, television, speeches, brochures, conferences, articles, clubs, postcards, network, lunch, e-mail, Internet, directories, mailings, trade show, ads, news releases, friends, past bosses, books, phone calls, associations, journals, direct mail, newsletter, stunts, greeting cards, telemarketing, logo, competitors, church, community college, parties, civic organizations, radio, newspapers, free presentation, press release, celebrations, congratulations notes, holidays, pictures, charity, rumors, awards, testimonials, audiotapes, interviews.

Select a noun and brainstorm a list of marketing actions you could conduct. Each has many possibilities. For example for "newspapers," you could:

- Survey twenty industry leaders and publish the results in a newspaper.

- Interview a well-respected person at a conference and submit the article to the newspaper's business section.

- Be interviewed by a newspaper about your specialty.

- Submit a public relations release.

- Take an ad out in the newspaper.

- Submit a review of your book to a newspaper.

- Complete a publicity stunt (the largest team-building group) and submit a picture.

Now it's your turn. Use the nouns to create at least fifteen actions that you could complete that will get your name in front of the potential clients you've targeted.

3. Establish a budget for your marketing plan. How much can you invest in putting the word out that you exist? It may be anywhere from $0 to thousands of dollars. Examine your budget to determine what that amount is today. Now determine some contingencies. If some of the projects come through that you have in the works, what percent of the profits for each of those can be added to your marketing budget?

Prospecting in All the Right Places

How Do You Find Clients?

You've written your marketing plan. In your plan you have completed the assessment of your company, your competitors, and your clients. You have clarified your strategy by describing your competitive position, your niche, and your clients. You have even considered whether you will market new or current services to potential or current clients. You have established goals and have selected tools. Your resources are in place and your calendar is ready to keep you focused and moving.

But how do you find the clients? Who are they? Do you throw darts at the yellow pages to select them? Do you just start dialing the phone? Well, no. The process for prospecting for clients is one that I have used for twenty years. I presented it in *The Business of Consulting* and will present it here with more detail and additional tips.

We will also examine the dreaded cold call and how it can be fun when you warm it up and refocus your attitude.

PROSPECTING IS A TRANSITION

Prospecting is the transition between developing your market plan and selling your services. It's a transition for a couple of reasons.

First, it is the transition between marketing and selling. When you read marketing books you will find prospecting covered; when you read books about selling you will find prospecting covered. Some authors do not differentiate between marketing and selling and, quite honestly (remember that stack of eighty-seven books I mentioned in the preface?), I'm not so sure I can either. I do know that you need a marketing plan and you need to sell. Where the two divide is less important to me than what you need to do to move from one to the other (Remember, I promised practical), and that's where prospecting comes in.

Second, I consider prospecting a transition because it is this process that at times leads to changes in your marketing plan. You have a plan now. Once you begin to implement the promotional and personal marketing tools, you may find that you need to tweak the marketing plan. Perhaps you targeted small local businesses, but once you started prospecting you found that they had less to invest than you expected. Perhaps you targeted state government agencies and found that their process was too slow. Perhaps you targeted an industry that is now going through a difficult financial time. You will want to adjust your marketing plan on paper, but it is the prospecting process that helped you discover the issue. The change to your marketing plan will be implemented in future prospecting actions.

This chapter will focus on a prospecting process for targeting, identifying, and locating specific clients: the right clients, in the right industry, for the right consultant—you.

Take the Chill Out of Cold Calls

I've made very few cold calls as a consultant. I prefer to make warm calls. Making warm calls takes more preparation time. Cold calls take more execution time. In the end, I think that it takes the same amount of time to land a client. I enjoy the warm call process more.

What's the greatest fear about making cold calls? Rejection. And what can positively be guaranteed about making cold calls? Rejection. So create a positive cold call attitude. So what if someone says "no"? Hangs up? Or is rude? Don't let it bother you. You must refocus your attitude. You were not rejected; your services were rejected. The person did not need your services at this time. When you run into someone who frankly cannot use your services and cuts the phone call short, you should silently thank him or her for not wasting your valuable time. So rather than feeling rejected, you can feel thankful. And what do you say? "Thank you for your candor and have a great day!" Create your own cold call attitude.

In addition to creating your own cold call attitude, you can build a process to take the chill out of your cold calls. To start the process, I warm up the client with a letter. Not just any old letter, but one that I have written specifically to the client. In most cases the client reacts positively right from the start. With cold calls, the client is frequently negative initially. And the rejection, quite frankly, is not fun—and yes, I know I should not take it personally!

Cold calls, warm calls. The choice is yours. This chapter addresses prospecting for specific clients and then identifies a process to warm up your cold calls. Chapter Eight will take the process to the next step—selling. In that chapter we will cover more about what to do to open and close your sale, whether it is a warm call or a cold call.

FIND NEW CLIENTS

You have clarified your niche. Now it's time to specify the organizations by name. Who will be your first clients? To some extent it will depend on your marketing plan. If you intend to sell only to your current clients, you can skip this chapter. However, I am guessing that you are reading this book because you are looking for new clients.

Your new clients may come from referrals, networking, or prospecting. The referral work may come through your friends, family, colleagues, or even a past employer. Your networking may come your way through people you meet at professional meetings, conferences, or volunteer work. You have little control over the kind of work that comes from referrals or networking.

Some of the referral or network clients may be related to the niche you identified, but many of them may not. As these come your way, however, you will most likely not turn any of the work down. As you take on new work, your marketing plans may need to change. You will not likely turn down a great opportunity just because it is not in the geographical area you targeted. You may need to change the targeted area to coincide with your new client if all else is equal. It is more efficient to travel to the same area for several clients than to travel in opposite directions. Bottom line? Keep your marketing plans flexible.

The advantage of prospecting is that you have more control over the organizations with whom you will explore business opportunities.

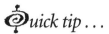*uick tip . . .*

> Set aside one full day each month for researching potential new clients. Make a date with yourself on your calendar, just as if you were working with a client. Accept no phone calls; and if you are at the library, do not call in for messages. You will find it easier to stay focused and will be surprised at how much you accomplish.

Who Ya Gonna Call?

How will you decide whom to call? You may have already decided to contact specific organizations that meet your criteria and with whom you would like to do business. List those organizations. Remember what I said in the last chapter about going after large organizations. This is not the time to be shy, timid, or modest. Go for it. Are you thinking that Microsoft is too large? Perhaps Harvard is too prestigious? Or General Motors is too impenetrable? Don't let size, prestige, or reputation scare you. The people who manage organizations need good consulting, no matter what the size. You will invest the same amount of time marketing to large organizations as small. However, the payoff may be much greater.

As I stated in the last chapter, larger organizations have larger consulting budgets, they generally have a greater need, they are more likely to hire for repeat work, and they are often willing to take a risk with new consultants. Don't be intimidated by the size. To whom do you want to provide consulting services? If you hope that your image is respected by larger organizations, this may be a great opportunity to test it.

It's unlikely that you will be able to easily identify a large number of clients and even more unlikely that you will have adequate knowledge about them. How do you do this? Let's examine a five-step prospecting process, which is shown in Exhibit 7.1 and described below.

PROSPECTING PROCESS

The five-step prospecting process in Exhibit 7.1 is the one I have used for over twenty years.

> ### Exhibit 7.1. Five-Step Prospecting Process
>
> ---
>
> **Step 1.** Identify twenty candidates
>
> **Step 2.** Assign one company profile for each organization you have targeted
>
> **Step 3.** Gather information about each organization electronically and at libraries
>
> **Step 4.** Compose a letter to each of the organizations
>
> **Step 5.** Mail your letter and follow up as promised

Step 1. Identify Twenty Candidates

List organizations that are potential clients for you. Perhaps you do not have specific organizations identified. You may have an industry or a geographical area targeted. This is where you may need to complete some investigation. You most likely have some experience in the targeted area or you would not have chosen to market to the "Norfolk, Virginia, area" or to the "fast food industry."

Start by identifying twenty or thirty organizations you wish to target. You will begin with that many because some may drop out along the way. You may have difficulty locating information about them or, in some cases, you may change your mind about wanting to work with them based on information your learn. Starting with twenty or more gives you some flexibility. If you cannot identify thirty organizations, check Exhibit 7.2 for ideas of whom to ask.

If you are identifying companies in your area, your banker, insurance provider, accountant, and attorney are all good places to start. As you continue to compile your list, remember to ask others in your network for suggestions. Ask people in your professional organizations as well. Even if they are competitors, you may receive suggestions that you may not have otherwise considered. Others you could ask include your mentors or those you have mentored, college contacts, members of organizations to which you belong, current or former clients, anyone you have referred, former coworkers, and other family or friends.

If you are identifying organizations in a specific industry, you can check out trade or professional directories that you will find online or in your library.

Exhibit 7.2. Where Can You Find New Clients?

- Present Clients
- Former Employers
- Business Directories
- Local Magazines
- Newspapers (check local business page)
- Professional Colleagues
- Church
- Yellow Pages
- Relatives
- Suppliers
- Friends
- High School Mates
- College Contacts
- Chamber of Commerce
- Professional Organizations
- Social Organizations
- Political Contacts
- Storekeepers
- Past Clients
- Volunteer Affiliations
- Industries in Which You're an Expert
- Service Organizations
- Internet
- Organizations That Need a Sponsor
- Conventions
- Trade Shows
- Neighbors
- Health Professionals (Your Dentist, Doctor)
- Your Accountant, Attorney, and Broker
-
-
-

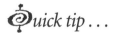

Quick tip . . .

> Examine your mailing list at least every six weeks. This action alone
> will remind you of people you should contact. Start at the beginning
> sometimes. At other times start at the end or in the middle so you see
> the entire list throughout the year.

If you do not have a list of companies, move to Steps 2 and 3 with an open mind. The research in Step 3 will open you to more potential companies than you can imagine. Conduct preliminary research, then return to Step 1 to regroup.

Step 2. Assign One Company Profile for Each Organization You Have Targeted

Make fifty copies of the company profile shown in Exhibit 7.3. You will want one copy for each organization you have targeted. You will also want extras to capture information about other interesting companies you discover during your research. The company profile will keep you organized during your research. It will help you focus on finding all the pieces of information you need to write a prospecting letter to potential clients. You will capture logistics such as the telephone number, address, and website; corporate information about locations and management; and other background about products and services, history, finances, and philosophy. It also allows a place for you to note relationships to your consulting services so that you can begin to build bridges between yourself and the potential new client. Organizing your research on the profile will make it a breeze to write your prospecting letter.

Complete whatever information you know about the companies you have targeted. If you know their website address or some of the key players, begin to fill in the blanks.

What if you start and for some reason determine that you need to select another industry? Perhaps you had not selected one and once you started researching you decided it would be easier to have an industry focus. Perhaps your research is revealing that you selected an industry that is not as strong as you thought it was.

Exhibit 7.3. Company Profile

Company Name _____

Address _____

_____

Telephone _____   Website _____

Employees _____

Management Positions

_____   _____

_____   _____

_____   _____

_____   _____

_____   _____

Products and Services _____

_____

History _____

_____

_____

_____

Financial Information _____

_____

Organizational Philosophy _____

_____

_____

Relationship to My Consulting Services _____

_____

Additional Relevant Information _____

_____

Resources Used _____

_____

How can you select another industry? These questions should help you make decisions about one industry over another:

- Is the industry growing or shrinking?
- How strong financially are individual companies in this industry?
- Can you reach this industry in a cost-effective way?
- How does geographic location affect your work with this industry?
- Will this industry embrace your services?
- Do you have a competitive advantage within this industry?
- How strong is your competition in this industry?
- Do you have referrals to this industry?
- Do you have the experience and reputation necessary to work within this industry?

Step 3. Gather Information About Each Organization Electronically and at Libraries

Electronically Begin by spending half a day in front of your computer. Check out the organization's website. Capture all the information that might be pertinent to services you could offer the organization. You are trying to gather enough information for two reasons: First, to learn as much as you can about the organization, and, second, to have enough information to compose a unique, personalized letter that will grab the reader's attention. Synthesize the information you uncover on the company profile. In addition, you will want to copy articles about the organization that you find. You can often pull quotes or statistics from articles to personalize the letters.

If the organization is publicly traded, you should be able to obtain its annual report. Continue to add information to the company profile. You probably will not find all that you need from the website. Therefore, you will continue your research at other sites. First, conduct a general search on the Internet. This may uncover a wide variety of information—some useful, some not. Continue searching through it looking for what you need.

As you are looking for information about companies you have targeted, you may come across other companies that you did not think of earlier. I highly recommend that you start a company profile for each of them as well. Remember, this is round one of a continuous process. Even if you do not continue to gather information about every company this time, having new candidates will give you a jump-start on round two.

At the Library You will probably not find all the information you need on the web. You may be able to find additional information at your libraries. Yes, that is plural. Your public library is a good start. You should also check out Department of Commerce libraries and university business libraries.

⏻*uick tip . . .*

Become good friends with your local librarians. They can lead you to resources you never knew existed.

If you are looking for a local company, check the local business magazines, journals and periodicals, local business newsletters, local newspaper, the city directory, manufacturer and business directories, and any other resources available. Each of these has an index that makes it easy to research a list of clients in a couple of hours. Several specific sources you may wish to ask for by name include:

- *The Advertising Red Book*—provides a considerable amount of information, including key executive names, company size, subsidiaries, and nature of the business.
- *Thomas Register*—indexed by industry, provides detailed information about each company to categorize companies within an industry.
- *The Over the Counter 1000*—published by Monitor Publishing, a directory of the people who manage the one thousand younger growth companies in the United States. Check other directories published by Monitor.

If you have not conducted this kind of research in the past, expect to be pleasantly surprised at the wealth of knowledge housed in your library. If you can't find what you are looking for, ask your friendly local librarians. They are sure to assist.

In Other Places There is no shortage of data sources. You could contact the trade or professional associations that serve a particular industry. Most associations will provide a membership list either free or for a small fee. The amount of information will vary, but if you have targeted a specific industry, this is a good reference tool. Gather information whenever you attend a trade show or a conference. Speak with your best clients and ask them directly for referrals or ask about the kind of publications they read.

If you have a specific city in mind, be sure to check the business development department and the city's Chamber of Commerce. You could gather lists of companies as well as specific information about the companies you have targeted. Both probably have newsletters and you should ask to be added to their mailing lists. If you anticipate having lots of work in a particular city, you may even want to join their Chamber of Commerce.

Remember your personal network. Do you know anyone who works in the company? Do you know anyone who knows someone who works in the company? Anyone who is a customer or vendor of the company? Any of these individuals may be able to give you some inside information that is not available in print.

Now use the company profile to organize all the information you found.

By the way, at this point you may not have all twenty of the candidates you started with. You may have dropped some because you found out they had filed for Chapter 11 or that they were in some other turmoil that was not conducive to the kind of consulting services you offer. On the other hand, perhaps restructuring organizations is your specialty and that is exactly the kind of work you desire. You may have dropped some organizations because you could not find enough information about them. I would not toss their company profiles just yet for lack of information. Place them in a pending file and try again during round two. I only toss ideas once I am absolutely certain that I will not want to research in the future.

You also may have added organizations. As you read interesting articles or conduct searches on the web, other names will pop up that interest you. You may as well at least start profiles for them. I encourage you to focus on fewer than twenty companies—especially this first round. Trying to keep track of more than twenty can become confusing and frustrating—which is why you have the profiles to summarize the information. Therefore, continue to sift through the list of names, continuing to maintain fewer than twenty. In addition, if you begin to collect many magazine, newspaper, or web articles that you want to keep, begin a file for each company. I find these files handy later when I have an appointment to speak with someone or when I write a proposal for a project for the company. One last thing about your research—don't keep everything. Prioritize what you believe you may use and toss the rest.

Step 4. Compose a Letter to Each of the Organizations

You've researched your twenty top candidates. Now how do you reach them? You could just make a phone call and speak to someone. That's called cold calling and usually isn't much fun. Articles about selling suggest that you must make one hundred phone calls to find ten people who will speak to you. Of these ten, two will agree to meet with you, and one will purchase your service or product. Since consulting is an expensive service, I'd bet that the odds are even greater. That doesn't sound like fun to me. There is a way to warm up your sales calls. And that's why you have worked so hard at your research.

Once you have gathered all your information, you will compose a letter to each client. Each letter will be customized for each organization. A sample prospecting letter is included in this chapter (Exhibit 7.4). Be sure to read them to understand the flow of the content and to get a sense of the climate they are meant to establish. It may sound like a lot of work, but once you are in the rhythm the letters will flow off your pen (or out of your computer). If it still sounds like a huge amount of work, remember the one hundred cold calls to schedule two meetings. Besides, even if you do decide to go the cold call route, you will need to conduct some research before your meeting to have maximum success. The person you meet with will expect that you know something about the company. You will be able to rely on the folders you have created.

Letter Composition It will be most effective when the body of your letter addresses three different but connected content areas. As you compose your letter, think in terms of these three questions: What's important to them? What do they need that you can provide? And what can they expect next?

Exhibit 7.4. Sample Introductory Prospecting Letter

July 12, 20xx

Mr. Roger Brown, President
Rocky Rococo Corporation
333 West Mifflin Street
Madison, WI 53703

Dear Mr. Brown,

From Brown's Diner to fifteen units and franchising plans is a success story that could only be written by the best Chicago pan-style pizza. This exceptional product is a result of your high standard for consistency and quality. In addition, we know how highly Rocky Rococo values people. You do not want customers to wait, yet you want them to experience the best pan-style pizza in the nation. You want to offer variety yet consistency, thus your unique system of selling pizza by the slice. You want families to feel at home, thus your new Hostess Program.

We at ebb associates value people, too. In fact, staying in touch with the needs of a company and its employees is our specialty. We work with companies and organizations who are interested in improving their productivity through improved communications. Managers and supervisors who participate in our training programs have found as their communication and management skills improve, so do the quality and quantity of work. ebb associates presents workshops and seminars on supervisory training, management development, sales training, and customer relations. Our clients, including Land O' Lakes, Dorman-Roth Foods, Hershey Chocolate, and many others, recognize our commitment to meeting their needs, providing exceptional training, and getting results.

Opening eight new stores in the next year in such places as Oshkosh, La Crosse, and Milwaukee is not an easy task. We at ebb associates would like to show you how improved communications can result in a smoother expansion plan, and how it can reduce mistakes and continue to improve customer relations.

I will call you within the week to schedule an appointment to discuss how we can assist you to meet your goals at Rocky Rococo. I am enclosing a list of the course titles that we will individualize for your specific needs.

Sincerely,

Elaine Biech
ebb associates

The first paragraph should focus on the recipient's company. It should discuss what is important to the company. It depends on what your research uncovered. You might focus on the company's principles of doing business, service values, most recent challenge, corporate award or milestone, why the business was started, its growth rate, corporate goals, length of time in business, recent breakthrough, employee policies, or even something intriguing about their clients. Let your research guide your writing. As you are thinking about the most salient pieces of information, you should also be thinking ahead to the next section in your letter that alludes to why the company should hire you.

 *uick tip...*

> Start your letters with "you" to grab attention every time. End letters
> with a p.s. to get them to read the most important line.

The next one or two paragraphs connect the recipient to the need for your consulting services and establish your qualifications. You must customize these paragraphs as well. Your research should have uncovered something that the company needs or something that is challenging to them. Once you hone in on this, you will state how you could help. For example, you might refer to your expertise and how it relates to the recipient's need. You might mention your experience in the industry. You might mention a similar challenge you solved for another organization.

When referring to past clients, select those who are related to the recipient by industry, location, or size. If that's not possible, select a couple of your most impressive clients. Whatever you provide, be sure it clearly relates to the company's needs.

The final paragraph tells the person what to expect. You will want to maintain control of the process by saying, "I will call you within the week to schedule an appointment to . . ." Before you put that message in your letter, check your calendar to ensure that you can truly follow up as you promised. Make a note in your PDA or Day-Timer to make the call.

By the way, you will want to try to keep your letter to one page. Most of the people I speak with do not have time to read much more than that. You can find additional examples of this type of letter in *The Business of Consulting*.

Letter Mechanics The mechanics of this letter are not unlike any other important letter you write. It should be neat, organized, and on your best stationery. Be certain you are sending the letter to the right person. What a waste to go through all that you have, only to learn later that you sent the letter to someone who retired last week! It could be worse. The person you have targeted may have been promoted from assistant director of sales to the director last year. Your attention to detail may be questioned if you used an older reference and missed that change. So check your facts out. Call the corporate receptionist and ask to speak to someone in the department where your letter is headed. Double-check the person's title and spelling of the person's name. Check the address.

Before you send the letter have it proofed by two other people. Proof it for spelling and grammar, of course. You will also want to have it proofed for clarity and whether your message is coming across. Have you identified your area of expertise and how you could partner with the company? I try to have another consultant read my letters before they are sent.

Do not send brochures or business cards with this letter. If you are considering it, you have missed the entire point of this exercise. The letter should be a personal marketing tool that stands on its own.

I usually send these letters in my regular stationery envelopes. Some consultants send them flat in a priority envelope. Yes, it costs a couple of dollars as opposed to a few cents, but it might be worth it to grab a potential client's attention.

One last thing. I usually affix stamps to these letters, as opposed to putting them through our postage meter. Metered mail always sends me the message of mass mailings.

Step 5. Mail Your Letter and Follow Up as Promised

I find it best to call soon after I believe the individual has received my letter. I start early in case the person is traveling. If you have targeted someone at the top of the organization, you may encounter a gatekeeper, someone whose main job is to protect the person. If a gatekeeper prevents you from reaching the person, you can say, "I believe she is expecting my call." You might also ask, "Can you help me find a good time to call him?" When the gatekeeper specifies a time to call, keep that call time religiously. I have even had one gatekeeper prevent others from getting through when she knew that she had given a specific time to me. By the way, gatekeepers can often tell you whether the individual has received and read your letter. That's an important piece of information to have before talking to him or her.

Gatekeepers usually take their jobs very seriously. You will never get through if you come across as arrogant and short. Be polite, ask for help, say please and thank you, use the person's name. Manners work.

By the way, try calling during off-peak hours—before 9:00 A.M. and after 4:00 P.M. Think about it. You are probably trying to reach people with lots of responsibility, which means that they most likely come in early and stay late. You may find that you get through directly more often. I also seem to have good results on Friday afternoons.

You have the person on the phone. Now what? I use the person's name first, identify myself, and ask if the person received my letter. If the person has read the letter, he or she usually takes control of the conversation from that point, commenting on the letter or asking how I knew all that I did about the organization. By the way, don't forget to smile. Yes, I said smile. Your listener can hear you smile over the phone.

During the phone call the prospective clients will be listening to determine whether you live up to the expectations you presented in your letter. Will you come across as articulate, straightforward, knowledgeable, enthusiastic, intelligent, and caring as you did on paper?

What if the recipients have not read the letter? If they have not received or read the letter, I usually provide a brief statement from the letter and then ask a question, also based on the content of the letter. Don't, I repeat DON'T in capital letters, ask the obvious questions you have read in some script such as, "Would you like to increase your profitability?" or "Would you like to double sales?" Do you expect them to say "no"? This trick has been used before, and the listeners suspect that as soon as they say "yes" you will use it later in the conversation. Ask them real questions based on your research and what you learned about their companies.

Your key goal for these phone calls is to schedule appointments with the individuals. So keep the calls short. You are selling the appointment, not your services. If they are willing to meet, set a date and time. I usually ask if the individuals have their calendars handy or if I should make the appointment through the secretary, whom I call by name. I know others who insist that you should not ask open-ended questions when setting up the meeting. These consultants say something like, "I will be in your area next Tuesday or Wednesday. Will either of these days work?" or even, "How does next Tuesday at 3:00 sound?" I've never tried this, but it seems to me that you may eliminate other possible times if you use this strategy.

By the way, I usually try to schedule the meeting within seventy-two hours. This helps to maintain the client's enthusiasm.

If the individuals are not ready to meet with you at this time, ask if you can keep them on your contact list or if you could follow up with something. Send thank-you notes the same day. Thank them for the time they spent with you on the phone and say you look forward to meeting them in the future. Within the week send something pertinent to the conversation or something you uncovered in the research. The next chapter covers meeting with potential clients to sell your services. Here are some preliminary thoughts about the meeting:

1. Use the individuals' names when you meet them.

2. Remember to carry through the thread in your letters that connects you to the clients during the meetings.

3. Ask a question, such as, "How do you handle your needs for . . . ?"

4. Be a good listener.

5. I rarely take my business brochure with me for two reasons. First, it seems too sales-like for me. Second, it gives me a great excuse to follow up later.

*Q*uick tip . . .

> Most consultants obtain information about clients before meeting with them. Go one step further; learn something about your client's competition before the meeting.

This is the end of the prospecting process. You have made a contact. You will not want to lose track of this person. The client contact log in Exhibit 7.5 is a tool to track your prospecting list. Add your new contact to the log. Keep the log on the top of your desk as a reminder to stay in touch.

Exhibit 7.5. Client Contact Log

Organization/ Phone Number	Contact Person	First Contact			Second Contact			Third Contact		
		Date	First Contact	FU*	Date	Second Contact	FU*	Date	Third Contact	FU*

*FU = Follow-Up

From E. Biech, *The Business of Consulting* (San Francisco: Jossey-Bass/Pfeiffer, 1998).

How About Results?

I enjoy the process of ferreting out information about potential clients. I developed this process over twenty years ago and continue to use it with remarkable success. I usually find enough information for at least one-half the potential clients I target. Ninety-five percent of all recipients are interested enough to speak to me. More than half of them agree to meet me within the month. And of those half become clients within a year. The rest become contacts, resources, or clients in the future because I stay in touch with them.

These odds are much better than the success rates for cold calls and the process is more fun. I enjoy the challenge of the research and the creativity of the letter composition. And I particularly like beginning a relationship in this positive way.

I once read a formula that went something like this: Make five prospecting calls every week and send five prospecting letters every week for fifty weeks each year. That results in five hundred contacts every year. If you close just 2 percent, or ten projects, at an average project fee of $25,000, it equals $250,000 in revenue for the year.

You can have this same success rate. Although the process takes some investment up-front, the odds of an immediate sale are much greater than with cold calling, you will begin to build relationships for future sales, and it's much more fun.

And you too will find that this is a very positive way to begin a client-consultant relationship.

PROSPECTING IN OTHER WAYS AND PLACES

What About the Referrals You Receive?

You have a marketing plan and you have targeted specific companies or industries. Should you follow up on unsolicited referrals? Absolutely yes. Follow up with every referral you receive from friends, family, and colleagues. Even if the project is not quite right for you now, the meeting may lead to other work in the future. And you may also ask these new contacts if they can refer you to someone who might be able to use your services. This is networking at its finest.

In addition, if the project isn't right for you, you could pass it on to someone who could do it. Passing it on to another colleague will prompt that person to consider you for referrals too. Recognizing leads for others is critical to successful networking.

Besides, some of these may have originated with your prospecting. How do you know? Ask. Make it a practice to ask how clients found out about you.

Be alert for direct referrals, too. On occasion I have attended sales meetings as an observer. I am always amazed that individuals can become so involved in their goals of selling one service or product that they miss other sales opportunities zinging overhead. Comments about meeting someone else in the company or someone in another company should all be probed for more information.

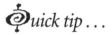 *uick tip . . .*

> Obtaining referrals is important. It is equally important to provide referrals to others. Think of someone you could refer today.

Should You Respond with Proposals?

Should you respond to a request for proposal (RFP)? You will have opportunities to write proposals. Proposals are often one of the steps in the prospecting process. You may be asked to write one at the beginning of the process as a part of a competitive bidding process. You may also be asked to write one at the end of the process summarizing how you have defined and clarified your prospective client's needs.

The secret to writing a good proposal is to listen carefully to the client, take good notes, and then use the client's words to write the proposal. Let me repeat that. *Use the client's words to write the proposal.* Even if you are the expert and you believe you have the correct phrase, use the client's phrase. For example, if the client asks for a "needs assessment," but you know the technical term is a "situational analysis," use the client's terminology. The client will not understand what you propose if you use your phrase. Use their words and you may be surprised about how often you hear new clients say, "That's exactly what we needed! How did you know?"

Your proposal should be similar to a newspaper article. It should tell the client who will do what, by when, and for how much. I recommend the following five steps to write your proposal:

1. Gather as much information as you can.

2. Design a structure that is easy for your clients to read and understand. I prefer categories that include a purpose statement, a description of the situa-

tion, a proposed approach, a timeline, your qualifications, and the investment (cost) required to complete the plan.

3. Write each section from your clients' perspective in their language. Follow their rules. If it says only two pages for resumes, do not submit more. You will most likely be penalized if you do not follow the directions.

4. Have someone read the proposal before you send it. Check for clarity, typos, accuracy, and understanding.

5. Print the proposal on the best paper you can buy. Attach supplemental material as allowed. Add a cover and have it professionally bound. Send the appropriate number of copies in an overnight package. This is your insurance against losing it.

One concern that consultants have is how much information to include in their proposals. I believe that the more you can show prospective clients, the more likely they will hire you. You probably do not have all the answers at the proposal-writing stage. If you do, it seems the problem is so simple that it doesn't require a consultant to solve it. My advice is to tell them what you know. In today's market, even if you give them the complete answer, they probably do not have the right people to implement it.

Prioritize Your Prospects

What if you do such a great job of prospecting that you have too many potential clients? Like many other things, you may want to prioritize your list. Ask these questions:

- Has the client defined a specific project?
- Has a budget been approved?
- Is the budget at least as large as the contracts you have targeted for your business?
- Will the job be assigned without a competitive process?

- Is there a possibility of repeat business?
- Do you have the credibility to be the final choice?

Potential clients who receive six "yes" responses should be your top priorities. Now arrange these prospects in order of placement in the sales cycle that could be like this:

1. Everything's a go except a signed contract.
2. High possibility of project approval within the month.
3. Solid lead, close to closing the deal.
4. Qualified prospect.
5. Initial contact.

How do you prioritize your time with these clients? I have created a half-of-halves priority. That means that I start out by assigning 50 percent of my marketing effort to the number-one clients. The next group gets half of that amount of time, or 25 percent. The next group gets half of that, or 13 percent, and so on to 7 percent, and 4 percent. This adds up to 99 percent.

Of course, once you have landed the projects for your top-priority clients, you reprioritize. If you have lots of clients, you may want to write your priorities and assign the percentage formula on paper. I tend to do this in my head. It is just a way to think about how you are expending your time. And remember, this is only necessary when you have too many potential clients.

Be a Realist—Prospect

I have an anonymous quote in my Day-Timer that says, "Consultants should be realists, not optimists. Optimists always look for the light at the end of the tunnel; realists look for the next tunnel" (see Figure 7.1). Prospecting is being a realist. Reality is that you have work. The work will end. You need more work. Prospecting is the way to obtain more work. You need to be looking for the next tunnel.

Figure 7.1. Prospecting Is Being a Realist

"Consultants should be realists, not optimists. Optimists always look for the light at the end of the tunnel; realists look for the next tunnel."

Figure 7.1. Prospecting Is Being a Realist

How do you find clients? Remember: "The only time to market is all the time." So chances are that you will find clients everywhere. It is nice to know, however, that you can find clients in all the right places—the clients you have pre-qualified as clients with whom you choose to work. In the next section we will examine how to contact these clients.

MARKETING: TAKE ACTION

1. Complete a trial run for the research you are about to begin. Select one company you would like to use your services. Spend about forty-five minutes in front of your computer gathering as much information as you can about the

company. Now compose a rough draft letter. Think about what you learned. How can this help you to market to this organization?

2. Select a referral that you have received recently. If you do not have one, contact someone off the "Where Can You Find New Clients?" list (Exhibit 7.2). Make an appointment to explore possibilities with the client. Consider this appointment a practice run. You will find this meeting helpful in several ways. First, you will understand what to expect when you visit a potential client on a cold call. Second, you will have an opportunity to practice selling your services when you are not sure what to expect. Third, you will have a better idea of the kind of information you may want to identify for each client during your investigations.

3. Visit your public library. Spend thirty minutes with the librarian. Explain what you are looking for and ask her to tell you how the library might be able to assist. Take good notes. This will help you immeasurably when you prepare to gather data about an organization. Send a thank-you card to the librarian after your visit.

4. Visit your library and locate a copy of the *Business Commerce Daily.* Identify at least one RFP that identifies your qualifications. Request a copy of the RFP and decide whether or not you will submit a proposal.

Contact Potential Clients

Selling Services

How Do You Sell You?

It's time to sell. You need to be face-to-face with a prospective client to make a sale. Oh, sure, some deals are closed through a proposal process and sometimes you will be called based on a referral. But normally you need to go eyeball-to-eyeball with a potential client in order to sell your services—sell you. The potential client most likely learned about your work from one of the marketing tools you have employed. That means your marketing mix is working. The next step is to meet the individual in person to discuss the company's needs. The sale is the ultimate marketing event.

This chapter will discuss the rainmaker concept—that is, how to create business. It will address using a value-added selling concept and introduce a selling process for consultants. Do you know how to prepare for a sales call? What should you do during the sales call? And how can you be more effective at marketing by following up your sales call? Like the other chapters, this one is filled with practical suggestions and tips for you to use on your next sales call.

RAINMAKER?

The term rainmaker comes from Native American traditions. Some tribes revered the rainmaker, whom it was believed had spiritual powers to bring rain during times of drought. This term is loosely used to describe individuals within organizations who bring revenue to an organization. Like the Native American rainmakers, today's organizational rainmakers bring a flow required for life, except instead of a flow of water, it is a flow of income-generating sales. The rainmaker title is usually bestowed upon the one or two top salespeople in an organization. They usually bring in a much greater proportion of the sales than others and usually close the largest deals.

The term has been around for some time, but not widely used outside the sales profession in several industries including consulting, advertising, accounting, investment banking, and other professional service industries.

Do rainmakers have magical powers? Not really. They most likely use the same skills and techniques we will discuss in this chapter. However, they may employ them with a greater amount of expertise and more confidence than most of us.

Selling—is it really just for a special few? The rainmakers of an organization? I think not. We could all perfect the art of selling and increase revenue flow—like the rainmakers.

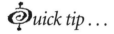 *uick tip . . .*

Read *How to Become a Rainmaker* by Jeffrey J. Fox.

VALUE-ADDED SELLING

You will find many definitions and many names for the value-added selling concept. The definition I prefer is to "be a resource, not a salesperson." You may also read about client-centered selling or relationship selling or consultative selling. Except for minor variations, the philosophy is the same. Be a resource. Be helpful. When clients need assistance, they will frequently call a (sales) person whom they trust the most; they call someone they believe will have an answer. They call a resource.

Harvey Mackay, author of *Swim with the Sharks Without Being Eaten Alive,* says that the mark of good salespeople is that clients don't think of them as salespeople, but as "trusted and indispensable advisors, auxiliary employees who, fortunately, are on someone else's payroll." It is important to recognize that, as the title of this chapter indicates, your clients buy you.

Selling has changed over the years. A value-driven relationship is taking over the old lists of tactics and techniques. It is more important to know the person than a list of closing techniques. And it is especially more important to ask questions than to tell.

An important aspect of value-added selling is availability. You need to keep yourself in front of your clients and prospective clients regularly. You need to be helpful and thoughtful if you want your clients to view you as a resource. We have discussed how to do that in other parts of this book. You will be seen as a resource when you send your clients pertinent articles or information about upcoming trade shows or whatever you do to keep them in the know. You are adding value to your clients when you take advantage of opportunities to exceed their expectations—being available and being of value.

Value-added selling goes outside the sales call. It means that you do whatever you can to help build their businesses as well. I continue to use and sell Land O' Lakes and Lands' End products everywhere I am, even though I have not done business with them for several years. It means that you put your client first with few unreasonable demands. It means that you continue to grow and learn so that you become more valuable to your clients.

What skills are required to be successful conducting value-added selling? First and foremost, excellent listening and questioning skills. Followed quickly behind that you need to be knowledgeable about your prospective client and know how to gather that information. This includes information about the potential client and the industry. You will need to be articulate about the services you provide and how you can add value for the client. Knowing how to respond to objections, close the sale, and follow up after the meeting are important to make the sale. And last but not least, building trust and relationships should be a natural skill.

What is your selling attitude? Do you send yourself messages such as, "I hate to sell!" or "I don't know how to sell"? If these are the messages you plant firmly in your brain, you will not be successful at selling. However, if you are in business, you must be selling. My guess is that your selling style is one of value added and that the definition of selling is not the one to which you subscribe. Selling is about building relationships and helping. It is about providing value, not taking your share of the consulting budget. It is about reaching agreement, not manipulation.

In summary, you will want to develop and impart your consulting philosophy. My philosophy is to build a relationship with my clients, add value in all situations, and to get up every day to have fun. If you do not have a philosophy to guide your work, it may be time to determine what it is.

YOU HAVE AN APPOINTMENT—NOW WHAT?

It will be easiest for you if you break your sales call into three parts: what you will do to prepare before the meeting; what you will do during the meeting; and what you will do to follow up the meeting.

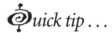 *uick tip ...*

Work with a colleague to do each other's cold calls for a week.

Before Your Sales Call

Okay, you have a meeting scheduled with a potential client. What do you need to know before you go? Be sure you know at least the following: meeting purpose, who will attend, how long the meeting will last, and exactly where it will be (office, conference room, or wherever). What do you do once you go in the door? If more than two people will attend the meeting, I generally ask for a list and their positions in the company. Commit that list to memory before going to the meeting.

Your initial meeting is critical. It sets a tone for the rest of your relationship. You may come prepared with a PowerPoint® presentation, materials in a bound folder, and a precisely worded presentation. My preference is to create a conversation with the client, learning as much about the client as possible. That means that my preparation includes reviewing the notes that I wrote during the research, making a copy of the letter I sent, and identifying a list of questions that I will ask to gather the information I need. I jot a few phrases, numbers, or other notes that will be pertinent to the meeting. These are things I want to remember to say or to ask about during the meeting.

Exhibit 8.1 provides examples of the kinds of questions you might ask. Notice they are divided into two categories. The "general" questions refer to a situation where no specific project has been identified. The "questions specific to a project" list can be used to gather more information about a clearly identified project. Even if you are meeting to discuss a specific project, you may still begin with some of the questions from the first list. Don't take the entire list to the meeting, but select the few questions that will be appropriate. Also note that you will need to rephrase them, since these are generically worded.

Exhibit 8.1. What to Ask Potential Clients

General Questions

1. What does your company (division, department) value most?

2. What are your company's (division's, department's) vision and mission?

3. What is your strategy to achieve your vision and mission?

4. What are your company's (division's, department's, leadership team's) strengths?

5. What's going well for your company (division, department, team)?

6. What are the greatest challenges you are facing?

7. What prevents you from achieving your goals (objectives, mission)?

8. Where is the greatest need for improvement?

9. What prevents you from making that improvement?

10. Describe the communication process. How well does it work?

11. What experience have you had working with consultants?

12. What kind of provisions do you have for training?

13. If you had one message to give your president (CEO, board, manager), what would it be?

14. What have you heard about our services?

15. Are you aware of the work we've completed with other organizations?

16. How would our services help your organization?

17. What past experiences have you had with other consultants?

18. Who usually makes scheduling decisions?

19. What should I have asked, but didn't?

(Continued)

Exhibit 8.1. What to Ask Potential Clients, Cont'd

Questions Specific to a Project

1. Has anything changed since we last spoke?

2. Why are you considering this project?

3. Can you define the scope of this project?

4. What is the situation (problem, issue, concern) you need to address?

5. Why do you think the situation exists?

6. How long has this been occurring?

7. What have you tried to resolve it?

8. How will you know that you have received a return on the investment for the money and time you will spend on this project?

9. What will be different as a result of this project?

10. What behavioral changes do you expect when this project is successful?

11. What is your goal? What measurable outcomes do you desire?

12. What specific improvements and changes would you like to see occur?

13. What obstacles to success can you predict?

14. What organizational barriers exist that might prevent success?

15. How will you be involved in this project?

16. Do you have any concerns about being involved in this project?

17. What is your timeline?

18. What is the budget for this project?

19. How will a decision be made about proceeding with this project? Who will make the decision?

20. What's the next step? Do you want a proposal?

Questions the Client Will Ask

If you have not attended many sales calls, you may want to prepare yourself for questions that may come from the client. Usually clients who have used consultants in the past ask many of the same questions. Most will want to know what you do. Know how to tell your story in a sixty-second sound-bite. I experience the following question variations:

- What are the deliverables? What will the final product look like?
- What are the critical milestones? At what point will progress, quality, quantity be checked? How?
- How much will this cost me? (Answer this one using the word *investment*. For example, "Your investment for completing this project will be $13,900.")
- What are your billing practices? How often will you invoice me?
- How can you help me with the kickoff of this project?
- Whom do I contact if there are problems or concerns?
- How can we stay in contact?
- How can you help me communicate with my boss?
- What is our responsibility at each phase? How will you involve our employees?
- How will you evaluate the success of this project?

Clarify Your Meeting Objective

Prior to the meeting, I clarify my meeting objective. Is it to gather more data or to close the sale, or something in between? You will probably have more than one objective. Your primary objective may be related to how close to making the sale you find yourself. But there are other objectives. Discover something about your client to use as follow-up material. Learn more about the organization. Identify how you could help the organization. Begin to build a partnership with the client. Define project goals and deliverables. Define the scope of the effort. Establish your credibility. These are all viable objectives for your meeting. Write your objectives on your notes and check them just before walking in the door.

I usually take a leather portfolio into these meetings with me in which I have tucked my notes and questions, a nice-looking pen, and a few business cards. As I previously mentioned, I rarely take my business brochure with me for two reasons.

First, it seems too sales-like for me. Second, it gives me a great excuse to follow up later. I usually leave my purse in the car (it's just a problem). I never take a pager or cell phone into the meeting either.

During Your Sales Call

In Chapter Seven I provided you with a few things to think about before your sales call. Let's review them. First, remember to use the individuals' names when you meet them. A firm handshake and a solid greeting will start you on the right foot. Again, forget the brochures and the business card. Focus only on your client.

Remember the letter you wrote in Chapter Seven? You connected your company with the client in that letter. Now weave that same thread during the meeting. Ask questions to learn as much as you can. You should spend twice as much time listening as talking. Be a good listener. Listen for understanding. Read between the lines. Does the client mean what was said? Remember that there are always two messages in every statement: the *content* and the *intent*. Also read the client. Take cues from what the client says and does to determine whether to make small talk or get right down to business.

Ask pertinent, thought-provoking questions. Use the list of prepared questions based on what you know about the situation. If others attend the meeting, greet and address them by name as well. Make a personal connection with each individual. If more than three people attend the meeting, I subtly make a seating chart with their names on my notes. This gives me an accurate reference without worrying about remembering everyone's names throughout the meeting.

Exude self-confidence without arrogance. Your firm handshake, appropriate attire, and high-quality materials will project a professional image when you arrive. You will continue to project self-confidence with your body language: good eye contact, a pleasant demeanor, and confident posture. The client will most likely ask you about your past experience. If you provide examples and relate similar situations rather than use a string of superlatives, your expertise will shine through. Be careful that you do not give too much detail or sound like you have a rehearsed speech. You do not want to use up your precious time.

I remember a sales call I made with a client whose office was over one thousand miles from our office. When I arrived, we started out with small talk. Bill told me about his kids, his wife, his headaches, his sailing, his dream to become a college professor, and many other things I would be able to follow up with later. But he didn't tell me about the project we were supposed to discuss. After an hour, he said thanks for coming in and that I would hear from him. I flew back home feeling dejected. I always knew I wasn't that good at closing a sale, but now I couldn't even open the discussion! I was sure it was a lost opportunity. A couple days later an acquaintance from inside the company called and said, "I don't know what you did to Bill, but he said it was the best darned sales call he'd ever had and that we would be doing lots of work with you!" What did I do? I listened. Although I do not recommend that you never open the discussion, I do want to point out how important listening is to building a relationship.

The real display of your professionalism will occur when you demonstrate a genuine interest in the client. You will begin by determining your client's communication style, that is, whether the client is more task-oriented or people-oriented and whether the client is more take-charge or easygoing. Knowing these dimensions of your client's style will help you to get into your client's comfort zone. You will learn the specifics about communication style in the next chapter.

Add Value Early

Show that you can add value early in the relationship. Ask the questions from the list you brought with you. Allow your potential client to answer them completely. As your client speaks, take notes—lots of them. If you are asked to write a proposal following this meeting, you have just been given the words to use. It's almost like being given the right answers before the test! In addition, you will impress your clients with the importance you are putting on their words.

Learn as much as you can about your client's business and its problems. Your earlier research should have given you some information to start with. And now you can talk intelligently about the situation. What are your client's goals and how can you link your services to those goals? Again, you started this process with the letter you wrote.

During your conversation you can begin to build a partnership with the client by offering suggestions based on your experience or something you've read. You could recommend a book or article, or even reference a contact who has had a similar experience. Be sure to ask questions for clarity and to acknowledge the person for what is working well or for trying something different. Recognize the individual for doing the best given the situation.

You Can Expect the Client to Ask Questions . . . and If the Client Doesn't Ask?

What if the client doesn't ask questions? Perhaps your client has little experience working with consultants. You will still want to ensure that certain basics have been covered in your discussion. If your client doesn't ask, you can introduce the topic by saying, "You probably want to know . . ." This gets the topic on the table in an efficient way.

You may also be meeting with someone who is more of a thinker than a talker. Chapter Nine, the next chapter, identifies a communication styles model. If you have a non-talker on your hands, you are dealing with either a controller or an analyzer. Since you will most likely read that chapter before you go off on your first sales call, I will not say much more here, but that chapter provides some ideas for addressing each style. Even more important, use the research you have about the client to start a conversation. Refer to the prospecting letter you sent.

How Do You Handle Objections and Other Challenges?

The most successful salespeople believe that an objection is simply the way clients identify their needs. An objection is a request to provide more information about why a client should buy from you. If a client says, "Your price is too high," it may simply be a desire to get full value for the project. If a client says, "There will be too much delay to start the project," the real issue might be a concern for completing it on time. If a client says, "We've used that approach and it's been unsuccessful," it may be a desire to for reassurance that you will provide success.

Your responses might be something like the following:

- Regarding price: "So you need information that ensures that you will receive maximum value for the price. Is that correct?"

- Regarding schedule: "Your objective is to ensure that the work is completed on time, correct?"

- Regarding the approach: "You would like some proof that this approach works. Is that right?"

If you have identified the desire or the need correctly, you can address the objection. The client's objection is really just a way to inform you about an objective that must be met.

If you are a small consulting firm, you may also want to prepare for these objections:

- Whether you have the required experience.
- Whether the client's employees would respect someone from a larger, more well-known firm than yours.
- Whether you will be available on-site often enough.
- Whether you have experience in the specific industry.
- And for me, the fact that I am a woman in a "man's" world (yes, this still occurs).

What if the client mentions your competition? You should state that your competition is good at what they do and ask whether the client wants to know how you differ. Your response will, of course, not criticize your competition, but will clarify the differences.

What if your client becomes obnoxious and demands a response, such as, "Why should we choose you?" or "Why do you think you can solve this?" or "What's this going to cost?" Diffuse the aggression by stating: "That's a good question, and I can't answer it yet. I will be able to with some additional information."

Contracting

If you've read Peter Block's *Flawless Consulting* (and you should have if you are considering a consulting career), you recognize that you are moving into the contracting phase of the consulting process. Contracting is ensuring that both you and your client are as explicit as possible about your needs, wants, and expectations of each other. The contracting discussion is an important link to writing a good proposal. Exhibit 8.2 provides several questions you may wish to ask yourself after the meeting. You may also want to pull that copy of *Flawless Consulting* off your bookshelf and review Peter's advice.

Exhibit 8.2. Contracting Checklist

Evaluate the contracting meeting with your client.

Did I: Yes

1. Do my homework before the meeting? .... ☐

2. Determine the primary client? .... ☐

3. Determine the secondary clients and stakeholders? .... ☐

4. Define the scope of the effort? .... ☐

5. Elicit the client's specific needs and expectations? .... ☐

6. Identify shared values and differences? .... ☐

7. Evaluate the client's expertise and abilities to support the effort? ...... ☐

8. Discuss my rates and consulting approach? .... ☐

9. Clearly state my needs and expectations? .... ☐

10. Obtain a sense of client commitment to the effort? .... ☐

11. Provide references? .... ☐

Ask About Money

During first meetings with prospective clients, the cost of your services should be discussed. If the client does not bring it up, you may want to. Some clients are uncomfortable talking about money. I generally take the lead by saying, "You are probably wondering how much a project like this will cost." I then answer my own question by stating when I will have a clear idea of the cost based on the scope of the project.

Many clients think that consulting fees are ridiculously expensive, so you need to be prepared to explain your fees. It is usually better to spend more time explaining the value of the benefits to the client. Firms that have studied this subject find that the benefits are about 10:1. In other words, the firm receives about $300,000 worth of tangible value for every $30,000 invested in a consultant. This is usually a better approach then trying to explain that as a consultant you are billable only 40 percent of the time, pay all your own taxes and insurance, have staff and office overhead, and so on.

If I think I have enough information to submit a proposal, I will usually tell them when they can expect the proposal (usually within a day or two). If we have not identified a specific proposal, I will talk about my pricing structure. I explain that I generally price by project, identifying the advantages. Don't quote your price before you are ready. Erring in either direction can be a disaster. And that's not the way you want to start a value-added relationship.

$\mathcal{Q}$uick tip . . .

> Never be forced to provide a price quote before you are ready—and especially while in the potential client's office. When pushed you can say, "Let me go back to my office and put a proposal together that will outline a work plan and cost. It will be on your desk tomorrow." Then do it.

Closing the Sale

Harvey Mackay, author of *Swim with the Sharks Without Being Eaten Alive,* says that he closes every sale—some just take him years of follow-through. That's an optimistic salesman! But it says a lot more. Harvey lives the value-added sales process. And he will stay with a client, continuing to add value and build a relationship until the prospect becomes a customer. What's the secret of closings?

Those in a professional sales position study and use specific closing techniques. A few of the most common include:

- *Direct close:* Ask if the client is ready to buy, place an order, or use your services.

- *Process close:* Take the client to the next step in the process, perhaps begin to create a schedule.

- *Analytical close:* Use an analysis such as identifying the pros and cons to lead to the sales conclusion.

- *Wrap-up close:* Summarize the client's needs and your services and show the relationship to reach a buying decision.
- *Trial close:* Suggest that the project be broken into smaller milestones and that the client use you for an initial step or two.

Do these techniques work? Sure. Salespeople have been using them for years. What I find, however, is that I am usually too busy building the relationship and adding value to have time to think about closing techniques.

Instead of closing techniques, think in terms of mutual problem solving. If you are solving a problem and truly communicating with the client, you will spot the closing signals, words, gestures, requests for more information, or even returning to earlier discussion. You may take the lead in the discussion at that point, but it may not be a contrived "close," but rather a natural flow into a discussion of next steps. A sale is not something you close; it closes itself while you are busy serving your client.

What If You Can't Help Them?

State clearly that you cannot help. If you believe they can solve the problem themselves, tell them so. If you do not have the skills the project requires and you know someone else who does, recommend that person. If you don't know, volunteer to find someone for them. Value-added selling approaches the problem of finding a solution, no matter what that might be.

Remember the movie *Miracle on 34th Street*? Macy's Santa Claus sent people to other department stores that had better toys than could be found in Macy's. This so impressed Macy's customers that their loyalty increased. If you know that another consultant offers a better solution, a better toy than you, tell your prospective client. Like Macy's, you will still win the relationship, build loyalty, and most likely will obtain work in the future.

Learn Something

You will most likely follow up with this prospective client, whether your call ends on a let's-do-business note or a never-no-way note. You should follow up. Whoa! Why would you follow up if the individual says, "No!" First, you want to thank the person for the time spent in the meeting and for sharing information with you. Second, a *no* today is not necessarily a *no* tomorrow. Remember Harvey Mackay's comment a few paragraphs back. Things change. Jobs change. Needs change. People change. I stay in touch with all the no's I have had in the past.

If you intend to follow up, you need to learn something new about the client. You will certainly learn from the questions you ask and the responses you receive. You can also pick up information by reading their walls. That is, looking around the office to check the client's bookshelves and walls. What books line the shelves? What diplomas and certificates grace the wall? What pictures smile back at you? What magazines lie waiting on the table? Trophies or memorabilia can tell you what's important. All of these are clues. Don't be so focused on closing the sale that you forget to learn something about the client as a person. You can use the clues to open discussion. You can also use these clues as information about the kind of meaningful follow-up you could complete. What could you do to add personal value to your relationship with this client?

Leave Behinds

As they wrap up a meeting, many consultants like to provide a "leave behind," some written material that the client will most likely keep. It could be your brochure or an article you've written. The purpose is to provide something to remind the client that you were there. Be sure it represents your image. You may also decide to just leave your business card. If you leave both a card and material, paper-clip the two together. A gold paper clip or one in an unusual shape is a nice touch.

The most important step at this point is to ensure that you have a next step. Next steps might be a meeting scheduled in the near future, information you will send to the client, some research you may do, or dozens of other things. Before you leave and after you thank the client for the meeting, briefly reiterate what you have agreed will happen next. It might sound like this: "Thanks for taking the time to help me better understand your situation. I look forward to meeting you next week, and you can expect that article in the mail in a day or two."

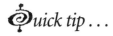 *uick tip . . .*

> When you make your first sales call, be sure to get the individual's e-mail address. Don't misuse it, but it does guarantee direct access to the person in the future.

After Your Sales Call
Follow Up Every Sales Call

Get in the habit of following up every meeting with a written note thanking prospects for their time. Even if you will submit a proposal, dash off a quick note to maintain the momentum of a positive meeting. This is not a common practice. You will stand out as someone who cares and appreciates the time investment. What do you say?

I usually begin each note with a "you" or a specific quote from the individual. I might say something like, "You certainly have a challenge with . . ." and then follow up by saying that I am looking forward to working on the project. I mention any deliverables that I have promised and thank the individual for taking time to meet with me, for agreeing to meet in the future, or for the business if we struck a deal. That's it. I try to mail it the same day, or the next day at the latest.

Review Your Meeting

Did you achieve your objectives? Were you as prepared as you needed to be? Did you get the information you need for the next step? Did you build rapport? Did you build credibility? Trust? Did you perform as you would expect a rainmaker to perform? Do you know what you will do better next time?

Four of the most common mistakes I witness during sales meetings is that the consultant talks too much, jumps in with a solution too early, fails to build a relationship, and is unprepared. Think back to the meeting. If you were talking more than one third of the time, it was probably too much. You can't learn anything while you are talking.

Which brings me to the second mistake. What were you talking about? You cannot solve a problem without knowing what the problem is. If you were talking about the effective process you use or the model you have created, you may still not know whether the client even needs them. One of the books on the stacks around my desk is entitled *Shut Up and Sell*. Although it doesn't present the concept I am relating to you, the title sums up my message.

The third mistake, failing to build a relationship, is a result of the first two. As a consultant you most likely build trust and work to solve your clients' problems. Selling is the same. You build the relationship and help the client solve a problem—who to hire. The only difference is that you may not be a part of the final solution—this time. However, you will have built a relationship for the next opportunity.

The fourth mistake, attending the meeting unprepared, may very well be the root cause for the other three mistakes. If you are well-prepared, you may not use 80 percent of the information you gathered. You may ask only half of the questions you chose. But you were prepared. Don't allow one meeting to fool you into thinking you can get by with less preparation next time.

Track Client Contacts

Once you begin to contact clients, you will want to track more of the detail: what they said, what you sent them, and when they have asked you to call again. The client contact log that was presented in the last chapter will keep this information organized for you.

Enter the information from your meeting on the client contact log. Sometimes I do this as soon as I get back to my car. I add a few words to the client contact log to help me remember critical information and next steps. I also add action items to my to-do list and sometimes even call my office and ask my staff to pull information, find something on the web, or print a label so I am ready to write my thank-you note as soon as I return. I generally keep a file for each prospect so that all my notes can be kept in one place.

OTHER MEETING PLACES

Meet at Your Place

Although most busy clients will prefer that you meet them in their offices, it is possible that the meeting may be held at your office. It may make the most sense if you have a demonstration such as software that will be important to the project. It really depends on your office. Do you have a real office or are you operating out of the den? If you are, you may want to meet at the client's office.

You might also consider meeting at a neutral location, a restaurant, or a gourmet coffeehouse. The location allows you to get away from the office turf. In my experience, however, I accomplish less in a social setting like this. Restaurants are noisy, it's difficult to take notes while juggling your soup and salad, and food always adds a disaster dimension.

Out-of-Town Clients

What if the client lives out of town—three thousand miles out of town? You will need to consider the benefits and compare them to the cost of going that far. How much will it cost? How long will it take? What are the chances you will get the work? Do you want the work? How will work on the other side of the country affect the work that you are now completing or work that you anticipate coming through? What are the chances that you might get another client in the same geographic area? How badly do you want this company as a client? There are other questions that you can ask as well. But only you will be able to make the final decision.

There was a time when I paid my own travel fees for sales calls like this one. Now, however, when asked to travel to a client's site, I ask, "Shall I talk to your staff about travel arrangements or would you like me to make them and bill you at cost?"

CONTRACTS

Contracts are legal documents that bind both parties to the content stated. I rarely require a contract, but my co-author (on a previous book, *The Consultant's Legal Guide*) and legal guru, Linda Byars Swindling, will advise you differently. I believe they start the relationship on a trust-questioning level. Contracts involve the legal department, and that may delay the project. Except for our government work, most of our work is conducted on the basis of a clarifying proposal or a handshake.

Linda on the other hand will tell you that a contract prevents misunderstandings later on in the relationship and it may actually be a relationship saver. So I guess from a marketing perspective, I would lean toward using a well-crafted contract.

I recommend that you allow the client's legal department to initiate the contract. It will save you a great deal of time and frustration. If you believe a contract will provide you with security or clarity, use it. And by all means use them when it makes the client feel more comfortable with the new relationship.

What should be included? Contracts usually cover the terms of the project: effective dates, project scope, deliverables, confidentiality, communication, staffing, supervision of the consultant, scheduling, payment schedule, incentives and penalties, termination terms, cancellation policy, arbitration arrangements, transfer of responsibilities, taxes, and modifications to the contract.

As I said, if a contract is required, let their attorney draw one up. Share it with your attorney and, unless something is truly awry, sign it and get on with business.

STAY IN BUSINESS

Selling You Many things can ensure that you stay in business. Only one thing will ensure that you go out of business—a lack of work. Staying in business is dependent on a steady flow of clients. Those clients will be there only if you sell your services. To succeed as a consultant, you must attain personal mastery in selling. You must be confident, professional, consistent, patient, committed, and excited about what you do. You are selling the best product in the world. You are selling you. So close a sale today. You will starve waiting for the phone to ring!

═══════

MARKETING: TAKE ACTION

1. Suspend any negative thoughts you have toward selling for four weeks. Contact four new prospects each day. Use a 4:1 ratio of four cold calls to each "warm" call described in Chapter Seven. (That's eighty calls total, sixty-four cold calls, and sixteen "warm" calls.) Track your calls and your appointments. How many phone calls does it take to find someone who will talk to you with each kind of call? How does this information affect your marketing plan?

2. Determine your consulting philosophy. How does this fit together with what you believe about selling?

3. Think back to your last sales call. What do you think you did well? What would you have changed if you could?

4. The last paragraph of this chapter states that entrepreneurial salespeople must be, "confident, professional, consistent, patient, committed, and excited" about what they do. Place these six adjectives in order of your assessment of yourself as a salesperson. Put them along a continuum from "great, no improvement necessary" to "needs lots of improvement." Now select the one that needs the most work. Identify something you can begin doing tomorrow that will improve that aspect of your selling attitude.

A Client in Hand Is Worth Ten in Your Plan

Will Your Clients Market for You?

Acquiring a new client requires ten times the effort that acquiring repeat business does. So what does that mean with regard to marketing? Up to this point we have:

- Determined your strengths and weaknesses;
- Established your competition;
- Identified the clients you want to serve;
- Examined the effect of your image on clients;
- Established a marketing plan;
- Discussed prospecting; and
- Designed a selling process.

After all that work to bring in new clients, it is easy to see why acquiring new clients requires ten times the effort as acquiring repeat business. That makes it easy to see why we ought to dedicate at least a chapter to how to retain clients in a book about marketing.

Gerald Weinberg, author of *The Secrets of Consulting*, states, "The best way to get clients is to have clients." It makes sense because satisfied clients will recommend you to other clients. In addition, your clients will invite you back for additional projects.

Retention is an ultimate goal. You can't simply say, "I will retain 100 percent of my clients this year." You need to determine what it is that will ultimately lead your customers to want to do business with you again. How do you hold on to your clients and ensure that they will want to use you again? Customer loyalty is an interesting topic.

CUSTOMER LOYALTY AND RETENTION

How's your customer loyalty quotient? Do you swear by a certain "quick lube" franchise? You have been taking your car there every 3,000 miles for a couple years. Service is fast and friendly. They seem to go the extra mile, washing your car's windows inside and out, vacuuming the floor and the dash, and thoroughly explaining the services they completed on your vehicle. They use a brand of oil you trust and always call you by name and thank you for your business. So why are you tempted by that 50 percent–off coupon that arrived in the mail yesterday from their competitor? Pretty tempting, isn't it, especially since you're going in that direction anyway.

Just as it is difficult for you to pass up a real deal when the coupon floats across your counter, it is equally difficult for your client to pass up a seemingly real deal offered by your competitor, especially since he is sitting across the desk from your client. Your quick lube owner is not there when you are facing that decision; you are not there when your client is facing your competitor. If your client has not heard from you in a while, it will be easier to make the decision in your competitor's favor. What can you do? How can you retain clients after the work has been completed?

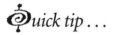 *uick tip* . . .

> Read any of Harvey Mackay's books. They will provide you with
> hundreds of ways to build relationships with your clients.

WHY RETAIN CLIENTS?

If you've been in business for a while, you know there are several strong arguments for why it makes sense to retain your clients—in addition to the fact that it takes ten times the effort, ten times the money, and perhaps one hundred times the amount of time to land a new client as to obtain repeat business. Let's consider why this is worth a chapter in this book.

Retaining clients for repeat business means you will be able to save time, money, and energy on marketing, as mentioned. In addition, there is less time delay from the time the client hires you to the time you can begin the work. This is good for the client because you will be able to start the project sooner than a new consultant could. And while I don't mean to sound crass, this is good for you, too, because it translates into less time before money can be deposited into your bank account.

Retaining clients means that you are aware of the idiosyncrasies of the organization. You will spend less time getting up-to-speed about the politics, an advantage for both you and your client. If there is a glitch, you will know how to resolve it faster than if you were working with a new client. For example, you may already know your way around the accounts payable department should there be a delay with your check.

Retaining clients means that you will become more and more valuable to the organization. The client will call you regularly to assist on many projects. Each assignment will build on past work. In addition, you can expect to be referred from department to department. This is good for your client because you will be able to get up-to-speed faster. It's good for you because you will not need to do as much research and background work.

Should work be presented for competitive bid, you will have an unspoken advantage both in what you know about the client and in what the client knows about you. And during difficult economic times, a client who know your work will not even second-guess the need to call on you for your assistance—without asking for bids.

Finally, you will have developed one of the most valuable marketing tools—far surpassing any we discussed in Chapter Five. A client's referral is gold in your marketing plan. A solid relationship with clients ensures that they will give you glowing referrals. In addition, they will refer you to others without you asking them to do so. The ebb associates vision states: "Our clients are so satisfied that they will market for us." It has taken a long time to achieve that vision, but it is a vision in action today. We can trace more than 80 percent of our business back to three of our original clients.

So why is it important to retain clients? I think it is quite clear there are benefits to both you and the client. Now how do you ensure that this occurs? To retain clients you need to build a relationship with the organization as well as the people who work there.

BUILD A RELATIONSHIP WITH THE ORGANIZATION

Every organization that you work with will be unique. What is not unique is the list of things you can do to build a relationship with each of them. You may already be involved in some of these activities. In addition, some of the things we discussed in Chapters Five and Six may be useful.

Know Where You Stand

There are four things: (1) Ask them if they are satisfied; (2) Find out what is important; (3) Gather data to determine how you compare to your competition regarding what is important; and (4) Develop an action plan. "Wait a minute," you might say, "that sounds suspiciously familiar." It should. It is the same thing we did in Chapters Two, Three, Four, and Six. Conduct a customer satisfaction audit. That might be as simple as a letter or a telephone call. You might also take them to lunch and ask how you are doing. Do you know where you stand with your clients? All of them?

Continue to Learn More About Them

Learn as much as you can about your clients while you are on the job. Interview employees throughout your project and gather data to add to what you may have learned at the beginning of the project. For example, after implementing a new software, conduct a mini survey to learn what skills employees still need in order to be successful. Always share your findings with management. Tour stores, plants, branch offices, and other locations to better understand the entire organization. Observe meetings to learn about communication, politics, meeting management, the culture, and other things that give an organization its personality.

Keep Yourself in Front of Your Clients

The key is to keep yourself in front of your clients. By that I don't mean you need to be in their faces or stop in for lunch on Wednesdays. There are other ways. Find reasons to connect with them. This might be anything from handwritten notes to telephone calls when you are in their cities. You might invite them out to lunch or send them copies of an article or book you have published. You can find excuses to connect with them, such as introducing a new client or congratulating someone on a recent personal or professional accomplishment. Include them on your holiday greeting list. Or send them information that you know would interest them. I can't begin to tell you how often I have done one of the things listed and two days later received a phone call from the individual saying, "We have this new project and I was wondering if you . . ." or "I got your note and it reminded me that I need someone who . . ." Out of sight, out of mind is a saying that covers it all. How do you stay in your clients' sight?

Be Unique

Chapters Two and Three helped you explore your niche. What do you offer clients that other consultants do not offer? What do clients want? Perhaps it is high-quality paper in your materials. Perhaps it is free graphic design. Perhaps it is free and continued follow-up. Perhaps it is a money-back guarantee. Whatever it is, be sure that it is something that your clients want and that they are aware of it. We stand out for all of the items listed here. In addition, many of our clients love the practical marketing items we send. Some claim that they would pay to be on our mailing list. We add fun to their lives. What makes you unique?

Make Your Customers Number One

Customers need to feel as if they are your number-one priority. Whenever I think of making customers number one, I remember a pizza company that I used in another city. Their motto was "Pizza delivered to your door, fast, hot, and friendly." They identified and intended to achieve everything their customers wanted: fast service, hot food, and a friendly exchange. This made the customers feel like they were number one. This is easier than you might think. Try some of these ideas. Always give your clients your undivided attention—do not accept or make phone calls to other clients while at a client's site. Be easy to work with—prima donnas are not successful for long as consultants. Communicate clearly and often—I've never heard a client complain that a consultant was over-communicating.

Do Good Work

Seems like this might go without saying. You might be surprised at how many consultants I work with who think that good work and marketing are not connected. No matter what you do in the way of marketing, you must do great work to earn repeat business. Determine how you can add value. You might be surprised at how easy it is to be above average. You might assist your clients to develop the specifications for a job before you submit a proposal. Most clients have little experience with that part of the job. You might also simply consider completing the job early or charging less than you originally bid.

Most of my clients tell tales of woe of consultants who request time extensions or additional money to complete a project. Unless there is scope creep (which, of course, you have discussed as it arises with your client), you should never miss a deadline or request additional money. If you are behind schedule, work overtime to complete it on time. If you underestimated the cost of the project, keep it to yourself and bid better next time. So if the majority of consultants are missing deadlines, simply complete the project earlier than you promised. You will be a hero. How you deliver your services is as critical as what you deliver. Always give a little more than you promised. See the list in Exhibit 9.1 for ideas. What can you do to add unexpected value to your projects?

What the Client Wants

A few years ago a huge consulting firm hired an expensive marketing firm to conduct research to determine what was most important to its clients. After interviewing the clients, the top three items included: Be honest about what you can do; take time to understand our needs; and be responsive to our schedule. That's Consulting 101. Reminders are good for us. Remember the basics when you are building a relationship with your clients.

Exhibit 9.1. How You Deliver Services

How you deliver consulting services is as important as the service you provide. Build your relationship with your client by providing superb service. These commonly accepted elements of service apply to all businesses, including your consulting practice.

1. *Time.* How much time are you spending on the project? Too little and your clients will wonder what they are paying for; too much and your clients will wonder if you have moved in! In addition, plan time to build the client relationship. It's a key element in delivering high-quality service.

2. *Timeliness.* Do you do what you say you are going to do when you say you will? Do you return your phone calls promptly?

3. *Completeness.* Do you do everything you say you will? Do you do everything you should do? Always?

4. *Courtesy.* Do you treat everyone in your client's firm respectfully, politely, and cheerfully? Do you greet the receptionist with the same positive attention with which you greet the CEO?

5. *Consistency.* Do you provide the same high-quality services to all clients?

6. *Convenience.* Are you easy to reach? Are you able to turn on a dime to meet special needs that may come up?

7. *Accuracy.* Is your service provided right the first time? Do you aim for "flawless consulting"? Do the results demonstrate the accuracy that was agreed on initially?

8. *Responsiveness.* How quickly do you respond if something goes awry? Do you accept the responsibility for problems?

In Closing

As you end your work with your client—don't. Yes, that's right. Don't end your work with your client. It may be a relief to end one project and move on to another because sometimes there is overlap between the two and you may have had difficulty balancing both projects. However, it is important that you build in time to finalize the project in a way that continues to build the relationship. First, be certain that you tie up all the loose ends; there's always a final report or something that needs to be completed. Second, build in time for the follow-up and you will reap the benefits for a long time. How can you follow up? Develop a system of continued communication before you leave. Follow up with a phone call to find out if there are any questions or problems you might be able to solve. Follow up with articles or a list of ideas that add value to the project. See the list in Exhibit 9.2 for ideas. What can you do to follow up after completing the project you are working on now?

Exhibit 9.2. How to Follow Up

- Purchase article reprints that will be interesting to your clients and send them on a regular basis.

- Stay in touch. Continue to send notes and cards. If you've learned a great deal about your client's likes, dislikes, pet peeves, hobbies, and interests, you may find items or reading materials about any of these.

- Find a reason to call them.

- If you are near a previous client's location, call the client and plan to have breakfast, lunch, dinner, or just a visit. Drop in and visit their business location when you can.

- Encourage your clients to call at any time. Help them find resources or materials or track down a bit of information or someone who could help them.

- When they call for information, respond immediately. It is a sign of a solid partnership to have requests coming your way regularly.

- Sell your clients to others. Find new customers for them. Recommend them to serve on boards. Sell their products.

- Call clients if you need help. Call them if you know of available jobs or good employees. Call them to serve as a resource for someone else. Call them to ask if you can use their names as references. Always ask permission before you use a client as a reference for another project. Even this continues to maintain the relationship.

BUILD A RELATIONSHIP WITH THE INDIVIDUALS

Although it is important to build a relationship with the organization, all organizations are made up of people. Although you are consulting for Microsoft, Ross actually decided to use you over other consultants. And although Hershey's pays your invoices, it is Jaquell with whom you communicate on a daily basis. So it is very important to build relationships on a more personal level and with the individuals. You might participate in the organization's social events to which you are invited, such as holiday parties and summer picnics. If possible, participate in fundraising or charity events. Attend on-site birthday parties and going-away parties for people you have worked with. Of course you are NOT charging for this time—right?

On a more personal level you might go to lunch with individuals. If you talk business, it is only appropriate business with the appropriate individuals. Otherwise just try to get to know people better. During a one-hour lunch you can see pictures of the grandchildren, hear about the latest vacation, and understand the person's views of the most recent political faux pas. All of this information is fodder for follow-ups. To be certain that I remember the detail, I jot notes in my Day-Timer immediately following lunch and transfer the notes to a note card for a permanent record. What do I capture? Things such as favorite sports team, spouse and children's names, golf handicap, favorite author, hobbies, hometown, alma mater, awards, career aspirations, and anything else I want to remember for our next visit.

Provide people with informal coaching. I frequently go to lunch with people who are considering a career move or retirement or who just want to brainstorm ideas for new projects (work-related and personal). I am sometimes asked for advice about difficult employees or bosses. I certainly do not consider myself an expert and dispense very little advice. However, I am good at asking questions and helping people find the answers that are within themselves.

Let people in on who you are. You don't have to spill any deep, dark secrets, but people are usually interested in your family, your hobbies, where you grew up, or where you attended college. This makes you human and allows people to connect with you on a personal level rather than just a consulting level.

Show how dependable you are. If you are there for a full day, arrive early and stay late. It doesn't matter what you were doing between 5:00 and 9:00 A.M.; if you waltz in at 10 o'clock, it will be perceived that you slept in.

One of the most important things you can do to build relationships in your professional as well as your personal life is to use information about their communication styles. You can attend a workshop or you can pick up a book about the subject. From the first time I learned about the information, it changed the way I view others and their behaviors. Let me whet your appetite about the subject by telling you a bit about communication styles.

Communication Styles Background

The communication style model is based on the work of Carl G. Jung. Jung believed that people form personality preferences early in life and that these preferences form the basis of an individual's behavior. Jung also believed that these preferences remained constant throughout life.

The communication style model measures observable aspects of your behavior to create a composite that explains how you come across to others—your style. Although everyone exhibits characteristics from all style types, it has been shown we prefer one style type (out of twenty-one) and that our behavior generally reflects this preference. No one style is better or worse than the others. Each style brings with it a unique set of strengths and weaknesses.

In general, your ability to move into others' comfort zones when working with them will set the stage for positive working relationships. Knowing your own style can help you be a better communicator, consultant, marketer, salesperson, as well as friend.

Why Communication Style?

We are all unique, all different. Because of this, our needs, goals, and desires may clash with those of others. Without a clear understanding that these differences are natural, we may label these differences negatively—"I'm right; you're wrong!" Understanding communication style provides the foundation for improving interpersonal relationships. It provides you with a clearer understanding of how you come across to others as well as why others do the things they do. How could this information be useful to you as you market to new clients, make sales calls, or retain present clients?

First, it will simply help you communicate better because you will better understand how you come across to others. You will be able to adapt how you deliver your message, whether you are working with a client or selling your services, so that it is easier for your client to hear, understand, and respond to your message.

Second, once you know individuals' styles, you will be able to predict how they will make decisions, what's important to them, how they use time, deal with stress, build trust, and act when they have bought into an idea. And you can predict this with at least 90 percent accuracy.

What Does It Measure?

The communication style model measures three observable aspects of your behavior: power, formality, and flexibility. To obtain this information, surveys are sent to five people who know you well—that is, individuals who have seen you in a variety of situations. The surveys are completed and returned anonymously. The power and formality characteristics are plotted on a grid to form your communication profile.

In addition, you also learn about your flexibility. Your flexibility rating tells you how easily you adapt to the needs of others and to changing situations.

First, let's look at the two scales that make up your communication style profile. As characteristics at each end of a continuum are described, think about how you see yourself. Perhaps you will not relate to all of the characteristics or to the extreme in which they are described, but you will probably get a good sense of which end of the continuum more accurately reflects your comfort zone. Also keep in mind that, while you could probably demonstrate characteristics at both ends of the continuum, you want to think about preferences, not abilities.

The Power Scale

Figure 9.1, the "Power Scale," identifies the horizontal continuum. The Power Scale reflects the amount of control we try to exert in our communication with others. The following characteristics will add meaning to the continuum. As you continue reading, you may wish to fill in some of your own ideas.

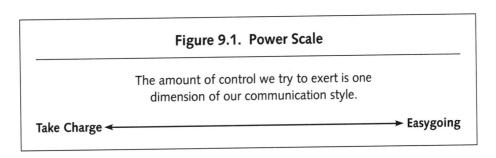

Figure 9.1. Power Scale

The amount of control we try to exert is one
dimension of our communication style.

Take Charge ←—————————————→ Easygoing

Individuals at the "take-charge" end (left) of the Power Scale:

- Dominate conversations, meetings, and most situations in which they participate;
- Are direct, outspoken communicators—you always know where you stand with them;
- Have thoughts about everything and always have an answer to a question;
- Get to the point quickly and offer an opinion early in conversation, even if it hasn't been requested;
- Are seen as risk takers;
- Talk fast and usually loudly;
- Make many decisions and make them quickly;
- Prefer working on multiple tasks;
- Appear intense, assertive;
- Prefer to focus on the big picture;
- Have a sense of urgency about everything they do and say; and
- Do everything fast . . . talk, walk, eat, sleep.

Individuals at the "easygoing" end (right) of the Power Scale:

- Go along with—the agenda, the group decision, the flow of the discussion;
- Are indirect, tentative communicators—they listen more often than they speak and ask questions more often than they make statements, even when a statement is required;
- Are cautious, calculated risk takers;
- Speak more softly;
- Make fewer decisions, deliberating carefully over them;
- Prefer working on consecutive tasks—taking one thing at a time through to completion when possible;
- Appear relaxed, calm, easygoing, patient, cooperative;
- Prefer to focus on the details; and
- Are cautious, reserved, slower-paced communicators.

Which is better? The answer is "neither." It depends on the situation and the person with whom you are communicating. In some cases you may need to take time making decisions; at other times you may be required to make a quick decision. In addition, consulting projects may require you to be detail-oriented at times; they may require you to focus on the big picture at other times.

The most successful people are flexible and able to easily move along the continuum depending on the situation. This is critical for you as a consultant. You will need to be able to move often depending on each client with whom you may be working.

While the most successful people are flexible, each of us has a favorite, most comfortable spot. Take a few moments to place an "x" at the point on the Power Continuum where you believe you are most comfortable.

Remember, this means where you would be when you are being yourself. We are all a combination of all of these characteristics. Yet when no one is asking us to be anything other than what we really are, we all have one favorite spot along the continuum that feels natural to us.

The Formality Scale

The "Formality Scale" in Figure 9.2 identifies the vertical continuum. While we all have emotions, the Formality Scale reflects how much of our emotions we exhibit to others. Let's take a look at the characteristics on the vertical continuum, the Formality Scale.

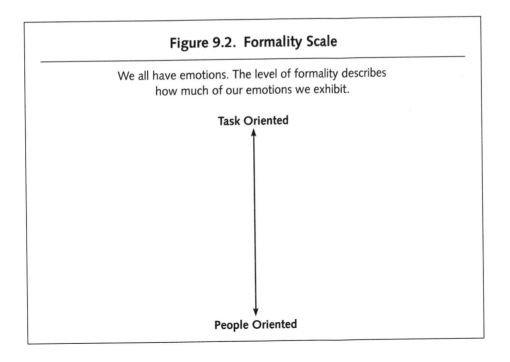

Figure 9.2. Formality Scale

We all have emotions. The level of formality describes
how much of our emotions we exhibit.

Task Oriented

People Oriented

Individuals at the "task-oriented" end (top) of the Formality Scale:

- Speak with efficiency and can say a lot in few words;
- Withhold feelings and are viewed as reserved;
- Appear cool and distant and may seem "hard to get to know";
- Exercise self-control in all they do and say;
- Prefer to make fact-based decisions;
- Work more comfortably with objective, fact-based data;
- Are structured and systematic in most of what they do, including how they think;
- Express their thoughts in flat, monotone voices;
- Appear unemotional, which leads others to believe that feelings, relationships, and people are irrelevant. (Note that this is not true. It only *appears* that way. We all have emotions, but do not display them in the same way.);
- Have difficulty making small talk;
- Are the efficiency experts of the world. Few squeeze as much into a day as these folks (or would want to). They manage their time themselves; and
- Create and follow rigid plans and schedules.

Individuals at the "people-oriented" end (bottom) of the Formality Scale:

- Speak with anecdotes or "side trips" and use many words to communicate a message (building a watch, when you've only asked for the time);
- Express feelings—verbally, nonverbally, or both; most often you will know exactly how they feel about a topic, a person, or a situation;
- Avoid being alone;
- Appear warm and friendly and are easy to talk with;
- Speak and take action with spontaneity, sometimes talking before they think;
- Prefer to make gut-feel decisions;
- Are more comfortable working with subjective, opinion-based data;

- Are unstructured in most of what they do and how they think;

- Use an expressive tone of voice;

- Appear highly emotional, which makes it seem that feelings drive all else;

- Are small-talk experts who like the personal side of communication;

- Often become physically and mentally close to people; and

- Like free-flowing communication and often digress during conversations.

Which end of the continuum do you believe is better? Of course, the answer again is, "Neither end is better." However, again recognize that the most successful people easily move along this continuum as needed by the individuals with whom they are communicating or by the demands of the situation. Again, this is critical to remember as a consultant.

Take a few moments to decide where you believe you are on the Formality Continuum. Where do you believe you fall most often when you are not being anyone but who you are? Place an "x" at the point on the Formality Continuum where you believe you are most comfortable.

Again, remember that we are all a combination of all of these characteristics. Yet when the situation calls for nothing more than for you to be yourself, you have one favorite spot along the continuum that feels most natural to you. Where is this comfortable spot for you?

You have probably guessed by this time that the two continuums are put together to form a grid. And your two "x's" will be a tentative placement for you on that grid. There are several other ways to identify your style as well, but this is the most we can accomplish in this chapter.

The Communication Style Grid

When you superimpose the Power Scale over the Formality Scale, you create a format to identify your own and others' styles. The communication style grid forms four quadrants, shown in Figure 9.3.

Individuals can be anywhere in those quadrants. Their position in a quadrant signifies the strength of the style. Someone near the center would be moderate, while someone near the outer edges would be considered strong in the defined style. Someone close to one of the lines or on a line is considered a combination

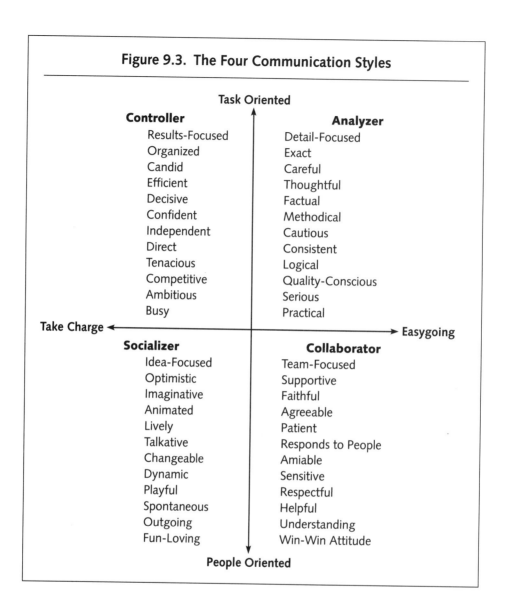

Figure 9.3. The Four Communication Styles

	Task Oriented	
Controller		Analyzer
Results-Focused		Detail-Focused
Organized		Exact
Candid		Careful
Efficient		Thoughtful
Decisive		Factual
Confident		Methodical
Independent		Cautious
Direct		Consistent
Tenacious		Logical
Competitive		Quality-Conscious
Ambitious		Serious
Busy		Practical

Take Charge ← → Easygoing

Socializer		Collaborator
Idea-Focused		Team-Focused
Optimistic		Supportive
Imaginative		Faithful
Animated		Agreeable
Lively		Patient
Talkative		Responds to People
Changeable		Amiable
Dynamic		Sensitive
Playful		Respectful
Spontaneous		Helpful
Outgoing		Understanding
Fun-Loving		Win-Win Attitude

People Oriented

of the styles on both sides of the lines. The figure presents some other words that describe individuals in each of the quadrants.

When you combine the task-oriented end of the scale with the take-charge end, you have people who prefer to be on top of things and in control of themselves, situations, and others. We call this style *the controller.*

The quadrant diagonally opposite the controller is the people-oriented, easygoing quadrant. These are people who are easy to be with, relationship-oriented, have a win-win attitude, and make time for others. They are accepting and prefer being with people who will accept them and work toward consensus. We call this style the *collaborator*.

The task-oriented, easygoing quadrant refers to people who have a "show me" attitude. They are inquisitive, persistent, detail-oriented, introspective, and prefer proven alternatives. Logical thinkers, they are quality conscious and prefer to analyze situations, others, and themselves. Therefore, we call this style the *analyzer*.

The people-oriented, take-charge quadrant describes people who thrive on change. They can easily change direction, change a plan, or change their minds. They are outgoing, fun-loving, expressive people and prefer to generate ideas, avoid the routine, and get involved in everything. They enjoy meeting people and are usually the first to introduce themselves. We call this style the *socializer*.

Grab a pen and circle the following words for each style in the figure. These key words will help you get a quick picture of each style. In the controller quadrant, circle the word "competitive." Controllers can make competition out of anything from mowing the lawn to being the first to arrive at the airport luggage carousel. This may manifest itself with one of your clients wanting to have the best department or taking a project over from you.

In the analyzer quadrant, circle "quality-conscious." Analyzers are first and foremost interested in quality. You will hear them say, "If you can't do it right, don't do it." An analytical-style client will want you to prove as much as possible that what you are about to do will certainly work.

In the collaborator quadrant, circle "win-win attitude." Collaborators want to ensure that everyone is happy. They work toward a true team spirit. You will see collaborators offering to help others at your client's place of work. They are often the ones who start collections for the employee who had a baby or initiate holiday parties.

And in the socializer quadrant, circle "outgoing." Socializers want and need people around them. You will see them in extended conversations at other colleagues' desks, on the phone regularly, or meeting and greeting people as they come to work. They may tend to be late in the morning or returning from lunch. It is usually because they have been chatting with someone—perhaps resolving a problem for someone they met coming in. They are enthusiastic and will provide the most creative energy for your projects.

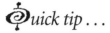uick tip . . .

> Sign up for a communication styles course. It will be the best investment you have ever made in yourself.

Most Important: Flexibility

Knowing styles is important to improve communication and increase your impact on others. However, the ability to adapt to others' styles and to be flexible in any given situation is even more important. This can't be stressed enough for consultants who regularly interact with many different styles. Flexibility is the invisible shield that lets you glide with influence from person to person.

Most successful people easily move along the two continuums. This is called flexibility. Flexibility is your ability and willingness to adapt to the situation, as well as to the individuals with whom you are communicating. You can be flexible or inflexible. Imagine a sheet of ice between you and another person. If you are highly flexible, the ice is smooth and slippery, making it easy to glide to another person's comfort zone. If you are not very flexible, the ice is rough, making it difficult to glide to another's comfort zone. Let's consider what it takes to be flexible.

There are many characteristics to consider when describing flexibility. We have selected ten of the most important. You will see that some of these may be more natural to some styles than others. For example, it would seem that analyzers and collaborators have a tendency to be better listeners because they do more asking. Of course, you realize that just because they aren't "talking," it doesn't mean that they are listening!

As you examine the list of flexibility characteristics that are described below, you will probably recognize that they are all skills required of consultants, whether or not they are using the communication styles model.

Listeners Flexible people are naturally good listeners. This is probably not due to learning and practicing listening skills, but because they genuinely like to listen to others. Flexible people ask questions and are interested in others' answers. In fact they are interested in many things, especially new things. They are attentive to others' needs, even when they are not spoken. They "listen" to body position and gestures, facial expression, eye movement, tone of voice, emotions, and other clues that come through all six senses.

Tolerant Flexible people have an open mind and readily accept differences in others. They like to be with people and allow others their space. They don't take things personally that were never meant to be personal, since they can tell the difference. Flexible people handle ambiguity well and can function within uncertainty. They use few judgmental words and allow others to have their thoughts.

Learners Flexible people like to learn about other things and about people. And they especially like to learn about themselves. They are confident enough to ask for feedback, listen to suggestions, evaluate themselves, and learn from their mistakes. They are willing to learn new communication skills and techniques and try out new behaviors. Generally, they are skilled and competent in a variety of interpersonal skills so they have many options at their disposal.

Resilient Flexible people bounce back readily. They do not worry, fret, and wring their hands over things that go wrong. They admit defeat (rather than placing blame), make new plans, and move on.

Sensitive and Caring Flexible people genuinely care about others. They are sensitive to their unique needs and attempt to go more than halfway to meet those needs. They change their behavior to match another's. They put others at ease. When communicating, they understand that another point of view is just that. It is not meant as a reason for conflict, attacks, or accusations.

Energetic Flexibility expends energy. Flexible people are willing to invest time and energy in meeting the needs of others. They are aware of what other people need and want and take that into consideration when making decisions. This does not mean, however, that they are only other-focused. They ensure that they meet both their own needs and the needs of others. Flexible people invest the energy to build relationships.

Positive Flexible people maintain a good outlook on life. When something goes wrong, they ask themselves, "What's good about it?" In general, their positive attitude gives them an upbeat focus on work, people, and everything around them. They think the best of everything and everyone first. When things go wrong, flexible people look first for what went wrong in the process, rather than placing blame on someone.

Creative and Open to Change Flexible people know that there is always a better way. They are willing to change their minds, change direction, and even change decisions. They believe there are always many options. They look for alternatives and will seek other opinions. They adjust plans easily and are not rigid. Flexible people are willing to negotiate and look for creative solutions. They are willing to compromise and will work toward resolving difficult situations. They are willing to take risks and will try out new ideas.

Respectful Flexible people appreciate the differences that others bring to the party. They accept that other people have preferences and choices that may or may not be similar to their own. They appreciate diversity and recognize that out of diversity comes the ability to work together to achieve more than individuals working alone could achieve. They appreciate others and respect what they have to contribute.

Trusting Flexible people trust others, until others are proven untrustworthy. This, of course, doesn't mean that they are gullible or that they take risks in dangerous situations. It does mean that they don't always go with first impressions.

These ten characteristics add up to individuals who are flexible and situational. These people can quickly sum up a situation and then adapt their behaviors to the situations and the people involved. Flexible people appreciate what all of the styles bring to the situation. They are not boxed in by one style and are able to see the uniqueness of each situation and person.

Recognizing, understanding, and valuing communication styles is important. Equally important is developing the flexibility to adapt your style to move into others' comfort zones when working with them. It's not easy. It takes much practice and planning about how to handle specific situations.

How to Adapt to Others' Styles

As you may have imagined, there are four basic ways you can move to be more flexible. You can adapt your style to take charge more, be more easygoing, be more task-oriented, or be more people-oriented.

To do any of these, first identify another person's style and compare it to yours. Are you more easygoing or do you take charge more than the other person? Are you more task-oriented or people-oriented as compared to the other person? Once you have answered these questions, you can decide which way you will need to move to get into that person's comfort zone.

For example, let's say that you are a collaborator and you are dealing with a controller client. That individual is more likely to take charge more and be more task-oriented than you. If you place yourself and the individual on a grid, you can easily see that to get into that person's comfort zone, you need to move toward the "take-charge" end and up to the "task-oriented" end.

Now let's translate all this into behaviors you can adjust to your client's preferences. Moving to the left means that you may want to speed up your discussion, be more decisive, and limit the details.

Moving up toward the task-oriented end means that you will want to get down to business sooner than you may normally prefer and provide more logical discussion. If you adapt to another's style, are you being a fake? A charlatan? Not at all. You are bending toward the other person, being flexible to ensure good communication. Without flexibility, you will be less effective and less likely to positively influence others.

Communicating with Style

You are your own best resource for learning specific ways to adapt your style to other colleagues,' clients,' or friends' styles.

How might this information help you as you continue to build relationships with your clients? Figure 9.4 gives you some ideas about how each style communicates, how each style makes decisions, what aspects of a project are important, and how to know when each has bought off on an idea. Determine your clients' styles, then begin to build your relations with clients one style at a time.

Figure 9.4. Adapt to Your Client's Style

Controller

Communicates:
Businesslike, fast, direct

Making Decisions:
Make many, quickly, fact-based

Project Aspects:
Complete on time and under budget

How to Know When They've Bought:
Take over discussion and begin to organize

Analyzer

Communicates:
Project focus, deliberate

Making Decisions:
Make few, deliberately, fact-based

Project Aspects:
Require data to support

How to Know When They've Bought:
Say "I'll think about it," or discuss pros and cons

(lower left quadrant — Socializer)

Communicates:
Informal, fast, spontaneous

Making Decisions:
Make many, quickly, gut feel

Project Aspects:
Desire creativity

How to Know When They've Bought:
Begin to talk about the ideas as their own

Socializer

(lower right quadrant — Collaborator)

Communicates:
People focus, casual, friendly

Making Decisions:
Make fewer, deliberately, opinion-based

Project Aspects:
Work as a team, collaborative effort

How to Know When They've Bought:
Begin to discuss who they wish to "run this past"

Collaborator

CUSTOMER SATISFACTION *IS* MARKETING

Customer satisfaction *is* marketing. Doing a good job *is* marketing. That is why the only time to market is all the time. You must stay in touch with your clients and know where you stand with them—how satisfied they are with your work, present and past. You should regularly ask yourself, "What can I do to maintain and improve customer satisfaction?" There is always room for improvement.

Do You Know Where You Stand?

In Chapter Three I provided a four-question letter that you could send to your clients to determine their level of satisfaction with your work. If you did not send it then, this is a great time to reconsider. In Chapter Three you sent it because it was a good market research tool. This time you would send it because it is a good client retention tool. Your clients will appreciate that you asked and usually will respond with good feedback. People like to be asked their opinions. The secondary message here is that you need to market all the time.

Do You Know What Satisfaction You Provide?

If your clients have a high level of satisfaction with your work and provide repeat work as well as referrals for you, you are obviously doing something right. But do you know what you are doing right? The list in Exhibit 9.3 provides some questions you may wish to ask yourself. Your responses will provide insight for you to ensure clarity and consistency in your marketing efforts. Your responses will also remind you of the things you may wish to continue to do to improve client satisfaction and to increase client retention.

Exhibit 9.3. Why Are Your Clients Satisfied?

1. Why do clients want to work with you?
2. What has changed the most for your clients at project's end?
3. What have prior clients said about your work?
4. Why have clients hired you for repeat work?
5. Why have clients referred you to others?
6. What product or service has gained you the greatest reputation?

How Much Time Can Referrals Save?

Many consultants suggest that you should regularly spend 25 to 40 percent of your time in marketing activities. During the first six to nine months of business, I spent about 35 hours each week in marketing activities. At first glance that appears to be over 80 percent of a normal work week. However, keep in mind that I was working 60 to 80 hours each week as well. That early investment in marketing resulted in new customers. During the mid-years, I personally spent a full day on marketing activities each week. In addition, other members of our team conducted marketing activities. Now I spend less than 10 percent of my time marketing, and most of that is of a very personal nature—personal notes, cards, or phone calls.

Why the decrease and should that be a goal? The decrease is because customer satisfaction has led to a large portion of repeat and referral work. Clients are satisfied and hire us back or refer us to another organization. Should it be a goal? It depends on the kind of consulting you do and the kind of work you want to do. Although I love to stay in touch with my clients, I don't see it as much marketing as trying to continue a positive relationship.

How Can You Measure Retention Success?

You might guess by this time that I am going to suggest that you measure your retention success by how much repeat work and how many referrals you receive.

Repeat Work Are your clients bringing you back for more work? The best measure of your marketing success may very well be how many clients you keep, not how many you acquire. I believe there is a fine line between trying to keep a client for life to line your own pockets and keeping a client for life because you continue to add value to their organization. For your own sake, know the difference. If it is new work, or continued work that no one else in the company can do, it is value-added. If it is repeat work that you should train someone internal to the organization to complete, it may not be value-added. Only you and the client can determine this. You should at least discuss it with your client.

Repeat work is a wonderful measure of the confidence your clients have in you and the satisfaction they have in your work. Examine your workload today. How much of it is repeat work from the same clients? Are you satisfied with that level?

Identify people to whom you are comfortable referring clients. Contact each of these people to be certain that you are on their referral lists as well.

Referrals Are your clients selling for you? Not a month goes by when I don't get a couple of calls from individuals who say something like, "Joe suggested I call you to see if you could . . ." I call these "referrals in action"—referrals from present or past clients who pass your name on to someone else. This is the best kind of marketing. They found you. They called you. They hire you. So in the end, one of the best measures of successful retention is whether your clients will market for you.

The ideal situation for any consultant is to find that clients speak highly of you and recommend you to other clients. Nothing, I repeat, *nothing* is more valuable to you than a client's recommendation. You earn that by exceeding your customers' expectations, adding value in everything you do, completing the highest quality work, building trusting relationships, and modeling the highest ethics. In other words, doing a good job.

Expanding the ABCs: Adding Four Rs It is time to expand the ABC model presented in Chapter One. It's clear at this point that marketing is much more than assessing the situation, building a potential client base, and contacting potential clients. There are other important spin-offs: Building Relationships, Reaping New Business and Repeat Business, and Receiving Referrals.

If the C of the ABCs is successful, it will result in reaping new business. Even if you do not obtain immediate business, you will most likely build relationships with potential clients. And these relationships will someday lead to more new business. The new business will spin off into either repeat business or, at the minimum, new referrals. And these new referrals will come back into the original ABC model as building your client base.

I hope this chapter has clearly shown you how critical it is to build relationships with your clients. And the model in Figure 9.5 is a picture of how it happens.

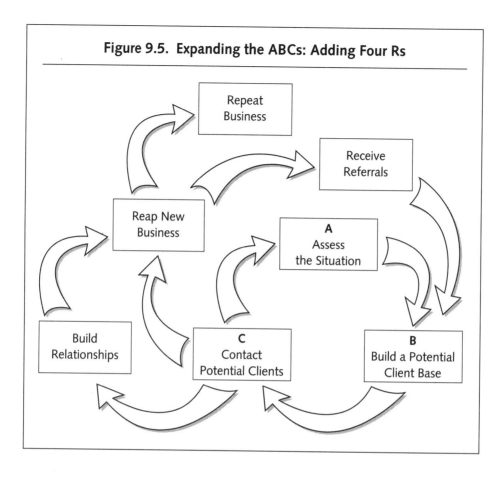

Figure 9.5. Expanding the ABCs: Adding Four Rs

Send Thanks Thank your referral sources!!! The least you can do is to acknowledge the referral. You can do this in hundreds of different ways. I always recommend a handwritten note on very nice stationery. You can certainly do more. Be aware, however, that some clients cannot ethically accept gifts or dinners or other gratuities because their corporate guidelines define this as unethical. Sometimes companies have dollar limits. Be sure that you follow them. You would not want to put a client in a difficult situation.

One Last Thing An effective marketing plan can't ensure that your current clients are your greatest fans. Only you can do that. Make that happen. Exhibit 9.4 shows you how you can continue to improve the relationship. Do good consulting. And your clients will market for you.

Exhibit 9.4. Continuously Improve the Relationship

What can you do so that your client will brag about you?

- Deliver more than you promise.
- Make opportunities to meet as many employees as possible.
- Request copies of the organization's newsletter and telephone directory.
- Learn something personal about your most frequent contacts.
- Keep everyone informed, publicize status as appropriate.
- Keep both company and individual information confidential.
- Arrive early, stay late.
- Adapt your work style to that of the organization.
- Meet all deadlines.
- Find ways to build trust.
- If you cannot meet a deadline, inform your clients as soon as you know and tell them why.
- Invite the client to shadow you when appropriate.
- Make the client feel like the "only" client.
- Send articles and share books that would be helpful to individuals.
- Be tough on the problem, but supportive of the person.
- Openly offer information about yourself.
- Explore a non-business-related topic you both enjoy discussing.
- Discover common acquaintances.
- Discover locations where you have both lived or visited.
- Discover common experiences you have both had.
- Write thank-you notes or how-are-you-doing notes.
- Call frequently when not on-site.

(Continued)

Exhibit 9.4. Continuously Improve the Relationship, Cont'd

- Be available when not on-site.
- Follow through on special requests from individuals.
- Provide donuts for special meetings or if it's not in the budget.
- Offer and provide resources.
- Assist with developing outlines for future needs that support the effort.
- Send surprises: puzzles, posters, cartoons, or special overhead transparencies.
- Be prepared to help your client deal with the stress of change.
- Support your client. Find positive aspects he or she may not see.
- Avoid internal politics.
- Discuss the organization's successes, but also discuss your objective thoughts about what they could do better.
- Discuss small problems before they become big problems.
- Be prepared to deal with unplanned delays—cheerfully.
- Openly discuss delays caused by the client that may prevent you from meeting deadlines; resolve them with the client.
- Plan and work as partners.
- Give the client credit for success.
- Attend the organization's social functions.
- Coach on an individual basis.
- Teach by example.
- Ask for feedback.
- Apologize.
- Smile.

MARKETING: TAKE ACTION

1. Think about your retention strategy. What percent of your work would you like to be repeat work and what percent would you like to be new work? Make a case for why you have chosen this breakdown.

2. List what you do to build relationships with organizations. Determine whether you need to do more. If so, select three things you will do over the next six months with specific clients. Now schedule these events with yourself in your Day-Timer or on your PDA.

3. Review the communication styles information. What do you think your style is? What do you think your most important client's communication style is? What do the similarities and differences tell you about what you should do to build that relationship? Do this same analysis with other clients.

4. Determine how many of your clients are referrals in action. Complete a client historical path. List all your clients, equally spaced, down the right side of a large sheet of paper. Next go through each client one-by-one. If the client was referred to you by anyone (colleague, another client, anyone), list that to the left of the present client in the next column. Draw a line connecting the referral source and your client. If someone referred more than one client, you do not need to list them again, but draw multiple lines from the referral source. Now examine this second column. Did anyone refer you to these clients? Complete the same process. What did you learn about referrals and where your business is today? What can you learn from this? What can you repeat? What can you do better?

5. Identify three clients you would like to be references for your business. Create a four-question letter that identifies their customer satisfaction level. Deliver it to them to determine what you need to improve.

Marketing Technology

What Will Work for You?

D omain name, hyperlinks, host, browser, search engines, URL.
The Internet introduced a foreign language to most of us. Yet
just as everyone expects a consultant to have a telephone number, people also expect us to have a website address. You won't be asked, "Do
you have a website?" You will be asked, "What is your website address?" with the assumption that you have one.

This chapter will discuss marketing on the web, electronic newsletters, e-mail
marketing, and a few other ideas about using technology in your marketing mix.

This chapter will be relatively short. Living up to my earlier promise to make
this practical, I will provide you with ideas and tips that I have learned. However,
I am not an expert in the technical arena. Therefore, I am short on practical!

Even so, I think you should consider technology and all that it has to offer. I
highly advise that you find your own consultant to help you through the cyberspace and technology issues and concerns.

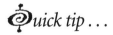uick tip . . .

Get your own domain—a .com is best.

ESTABLISH A WEBSITE

What can you put on your website? Start with a homepage that provides general information. The other information emanates from your homepage. You may publish client lists, samples of your materials, in-depth descriptions of some of your services, reviews of books you've written, an expert's column, articles written by guest consultants, or anything else you believe will interest the individuals you want to visit your website. Know the reason for your website. Then design it to meet that need.

What is the reason for your website? To create a place where you can sell your products and services? To build relationships with prospects? To provide clients and potential clients with information about you and your consulting? To provide a service where clients can go to find updated information (for example, if you conduct research for your clients, they could visit the site to respond or to find information)? Like almost everything you do as a business owner, you need to have a clear objective before you set out to establish a website. In many cases your objective may be a combination of the above four. You still need to determine the key reason.

Design Your Website

Like everything else you do, your website should project the image you desire. Therefore, hire a highly qualified web designer to assist you. Check out other sites that the individual has designed. You will want someone who has expertise, but like your paper product designer in Chapter Four, you will want someone who listens to your needs and meets them. Ask for references and establish costs for both the initial design and any annual or ongoing charges. The initial design will most likely cost somewhere in the neighborhood of $2,000 to $7,000. You won't need the most expensive designer, but, as with your brochures, this is not the time to cut corners.

Your website should be one that is effective but simple. Don't let the designer overload it so that it takes a long time to download. Most people will become frustrated—even if the cause is their slow modem. Ask potential designers how they will ensure that your website is easy to navigate. Ensure that visitors can easily e-mail you while visiting your site. And for marketing purposes, ask your designer how you could capture names of interested visitors for follow-up. You should also provide a way for individuals to contact you directly beyond e-mail, such as your mailing address, telephone number, and fax number.

Your designer should speak with you about selecting a provider and the kind of services you will want to have. Your designer should also discuss sending notices to Internet directories and search engines to attract visitors to your site. Contact your attorney if you intend to accept online credit card transactions or conduct contests. These raise legal issues for which you need an expert's advice.

The address you choose should be something that is easy to remember and that makes sense to your potential clients. Using your corporate name is the easiest. Ours was not available. One of our employees, Garland, came up with something that is almost as good. Our address is www.ebbweb.com. The advantage of our name is that it is easy to remember. However, it is not easy to say clearly. A clear domain name is necessary; a great domain name is a competitive tool. Leslie Charles' website is www.whyiseveryonesocranky.com, the name of her book. Very practical and clever. I highly recommend that you choose a .com address. It is an assumption in the world of business. Also keep it simple.

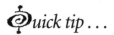

Unify your web address and e-mail address. For example, elaine@ebbweb.com.

Maintain Your Website

You will want to post new information to your website every month or two. This is a responsibility that can become a burden if you are not clear about it up-front. You want people to return to your site. Seeing the same thing after the second or third visit will not encourage them to return.

Visit your site regularly. Respond to e-mail and requests within twenty-four hours. If you have an order process, complete an order yourself to ensure that the process remains as smooth as you desire.

Ask your clients to visit your website and provide you with suggestions. What would they like to see more of, less off, deleted, changed, or added? Would they like how-to advice? Articles they could download for their own newsletters? More information about your services? You won't know until you ask.

Your visitors should learn enough about you and your firm from your website to gain confidence in your skills and abilities. Your website should not only exude the kind of image you desire, but also the credibility you have earned.

Your website is the only marketing tool that must be combined with other tools to work. It is not intended to broadcast information like your other marketing tools. It will not replace any other marketing tools. Instead, you will need to publish your website address in conjunction with your other marketing items so that potential clients can find you and your information.

Website Tips

There is so much to remember about websites! I think it is much better digested in little "bytes." The tips listed here are a few of the practical ideas I discovered as we put our website together. I think they will be helpful to you as well.

- Before you launch your site, test it with four or five colleagues who will give you candid feedback about the site.
- Keep your first paragraph short and grab your readers' attention immediately. Less than 5 percent of the readers will scroll beyond what they see on the screen.
- Keep your site up-to-date. Changes create interest and encourage repeat visits. So update yours every month or two.
- Promote your site through all of your other marketing tools. Your website should be listed on articles you publish, on your stationery, business cards, any ads or direct mail, and every other form of marketing you conduct.
- Ensure that your website continues to have the same look and project the same image as your other marketing materials. The message, the graphics, and the typeface should all be congruent.
- Give something away. The climate of the web is one of sharing. You may consider giving away an article you've written or tips for doing something.
- Make it interactive. Post quizzes, puzzles, self-assessments, or other activity-based materials that your visitors can have fun with or have scored.
- Be sure to link your site to others that share your philosophy or that provide information that will interest your visitors. Update your links as you discover others. Make these links a different color from the rest of the text.
- Finally, remember that the strength of the Internet is not in the technology, or the convenience, or even the speed. The strength lies in the message that you deliver. You must find a way to offer value to the visitors.

If after all this you still think you would like to take a shot at designing your own website, you will find a simple process with a CD-ROM for support in Alexander Hiam's book *Marketing Kit for Dummies.*

One last thing. Do you realize that launching your website is just one more reason to contact your clients? It is. So once it is up and running and all the bugs are worked out, determine how you can grab the attention of everyone on your mailing list. We conducted two direct mailings. One included an @-shaped flashlight and the other one was a giant silver @-shaped paper clip. The items were perfect for the launch and they met the MUMU Measure. They were memorable, unique, mailable, and useful.

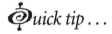 *uick tip . . .*

> Purchase and read *Permission Marketing* by Seth Godin, the founder of Yahoo.

E-MAIL MARKETING

Weigh the option to market by e-mail. It can backfire. All of us have felt the frustration when we begin to open e-mail and find eight of them from mortgage companies! E-mail marketing works best in two cases.

The first is to your present clients to inform them of something new that is going on with you. The second is to potential clients who have asked for something specific.

To be effective, you should follow the same guidelines that you do for any direct-mail piece. The e-mail should have a headline that grabs attention, a short message that emphasizes benefits, and a call to action. Check your spelling and grammar, personalize it if you can, and use a short, descriptive subject line. Include instructions for how readers can be removed from the list if they wish.

If you still think that you have a service or product you wish to promote via e-mail, I suggest that you use an organization that specializes in Internet mass mailings to help you. An e-mail mass mailing may cost as little as $29 or as much as $500. It is inexpensive, but the rate of return is very low. Since it is possible to e-mail to millions of potential clients in a matter of minutes, you need to zero in on the market you want to receive your e-mail. Ensure that the person you hire uses a list that targets the individuals and companies you wish.

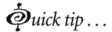

Quick tip...

If you have written a book, check into linking your website with www.Amazon.com. The website will tell you how to join their affiliate program.

ELECTRONIC NEWSLETTERS

Electronic newsletters are used frequently by consultants. They are easy to distribute, inexpensive, and good for building a relationship with your clients. Because they are inexpensive, it is easy to add individuals to your mailing list. Your electronic newsletter can do the same things your printed one does for your business. You can include the same kind of articles, tips, news, and updates.

The design that works the best is one that lists all the articles by title at the beginning. I especially appreciate the ones that number the articles. When I see the list, I can easily scroll down to the number of the article that I want to read. Keep the rest of the page as clean as possible. Use a font in a size and style that is easy to read, because most people will read it on the screen. Articles that are rated the highest by readers include workplace advice and book recommendations.

If you have a website, be sure you include a way for visitors to sign up for your newsletter. Be sure you offer the subscribers the opportunity to remove themselves from your mailing list.

OTHER TECHNOLOGIES TO EXPLORE

The Internet brings other marketing opportunities besides a website. You may find some of these helpful to your marketing efforts.

Learn About Bulletin Boards

Bulletin boards are a great way to network with other professionals. A wide variety of professionals "talk" to each other by posting messages to ask questions and to give and receive advice. Sometimes the desire is to get emotional support when going through a difficult situation, such as firing an employee. The major online services offer bulletin boards, but if you are not associated with one, you can still do the same thing through Internet newsgroups or mailing lists. Check into this one. It is definitely something you should consider for networking or marketing ideas.

Join a Consultant Referral Service

You may wish to join a service that has a presence on the Internet. If you belong to a professional organization such as the Association of Professional Consultants, www.consultapc.org, you may list your consulting firm on its referral service. You may also check into a listing on the Expert Marketplace, www.expert-market.com/em, which considers itself the resource for technical and consulting services. Expert Marketplace maintains a database of almost 300,000 consultants.

Personal Selling

Whatever you decide about technology, you must admit that it's here and it has its benefits. The Internet can help you do your job more effectively and efficiently, especially during prospecting. The internet, e-mail, and a laptop computer are almost a necessity if you travel a great deal.

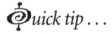 *uick tip . . .*

Internet interviews are an easy way to market on the web. These folks find your name as the author of journal articles, books, or public relations pieces you author.

What marketing technology will work for you? Only you can answer that. A website is a no-brainer. You most likely need to have one to be viewed as a viable consultant. Some estimate there are over six billion URLs in cyberspace. So the likelihood of you putting up your website, then sitting back and waiting for potential clients to stumble on your site, is not very likely. That means you will need to identify ways to bring visitors to your website. Also remember, you want them to return. Determine what you will do to ensure that it happens. The next section of the book, Marketing Support, will present ways for you to do just that.

MARKETING: TAKE ACTION

1. Visit five other consultants' websites. Identify all the things you like and do not like about their websites. What will you want your web designer to incorporate in your website?

2. Make a list of at least ten things that you have right now that you could put on your website. What could you develop for the website in the future?

3. If you have a website, visit it and identify how you might improve it. Contact five colleagues and ask them for recommendations for improvement.

4. Amazon.com is one of the most well-known websites. Visit the site at www.amazon.com and determine how they enhance their customers' buying experience. How could you translate some of the techniques that Amazon uses to add value to your website?

Marketing Support

Marketing

Can It Be Fun?

As a consultant, I have the most fun when I am involved with sales and marketing. That's a long way from my declaring to a potential client fifteen years ago that "I don't do sales and marketing!" But why? Why do I have the most fun by marketing?

Marketing is a combination of creativity and logic. Up to this point we have spent a great deal of time discussing the logic side, such as how to research your competition, how to write a marketing plan, how to retain clients, and how to warm up a sales call. While all of those are critical to successful marketing, it's really the creative side that is the most fun. Creativity makes marketing pop and gives selling a sizzle.

So how do you come up with creative ideas? How do you create that pop and sizzle? Let's have some fun.

PROVEN WAYS TO GENERATE MARKETING IDEAS

Where can you find creative ideas? How do you generate something that will grab people's attention and send your message as well? How do you turn them into marketing ideas? And how do you implement them? Can you use the MUMU

Measure (memorable, unique, mailable, useful) from Chapter Six and still be creative?

If you are interested in developing your own creative marketing ideas, you should probably read a couple of books about creativity or take a creativity class. You will learn creativity techniques, but in addition, you will learn what limits you and prevents you from being creative as well as tips to help your creativity flourish. In the meantime, try the ten creativity techniques listed here.

Ten Creativity Techniques

I have been teaching creativity techniques for over twenty years. I am still amazed at how often creativity is important in the various things we do every day. For example, I recently was in a hotel and realized that I forgot to pack a belt for the dress I was wearing to see a client. Sometimes this would not be a problem, but in this case, the dress reached almost to my ankles and I depended on the belt to shorten it a bit. I yanked the shoestring from my sneaker, tied it around my waist, pulled the dress up so that it overlapped the shoestring, put my jacket over the top, and was off to my first meeting. I am sure you have had the same kind of situation where you needed to be creative on the spot and you came through.

But can you always be creative on-demand? Wouldn't it be nice if there were a handful of techniques to jump-start the flow of creative ideas? To whet your creative juices? Well, there are techniques that can do just that.

The following ten creativity techniques are based on research and ideas from many sources, including Edward de Bono, Roger von Oech, and Michael Michalko. These creativity experts have helped to shape my creative thinking over the years and influenced my ability to compile a list of practical techniques. I have revised, reworked, and refined these ten techniques so that they can be easily implemented in almost any situation. They are easy to remember since the first letter of each technique spells CREATIVITY (see Exhibit 11.1). They are practical and fun to use. Because of all these reasons, they have become a natural way for me to approach problems requiring creative solutions.

You will find a challenge at the end of each of the creativity technique descriptions. I suggest you grab a note pad and work through each activity. If you do, I guarantee that at the end of reading this section you will have at least two dozen ideas for marketing your business: marketing themes, how to generate ideas, or places you could find ideas.

Exhibit 11.1. Creativity Techniques

Compare and Combine

Risk Taking

Expand and Shrink

Ask What's Good? And What If?

Transform Your Viewpoint

In Another Sequence

Visit Other Places

Incubate

Trigger Concepts

Youth's Advantage

---

1. Compare and Combine

The first technique is actually two-in-one. They are somewhat related, in that they involve putting together unrelated concepts. Both, however, are standalone ideas.

The first, Compare, conjures up analogies to determine how something is like or unlike something else. Consulting is like climbing a mountain because . . . Pringles® used this technique to create a new way to package potato chips. If you were a potato chip manufacturer, you would know that your greatest challenge would be packaging and shipping your product to avoid breakage. No one wants to buy a bag of chip crumbs. Pringles established an analogy that stated: potato chips are like leaves because . . . Because when they are dry they break. Because when they are moist they are pliable. The way that Pringles are shaped and packaged while still moist occurred due to exploring the similarities between two dissimilar items.

The second, Combine, is a technique in which your thrust two concepts together for a unique result. Once you force the two concepts together, you pretty much stand back and see what transpires. When Gutenberg combined a wine press and a coin punch, the printing press was invented. When Swift combined a refrigerator and a railroad car, the refrigerated railroad car was invented. When Bowerman combined rubber and a waffle iron, he discovered a sole for his Nike® shoe.

Your Challenges Complete this analogy to identify at least three ideas that could lead you to marketing ideas. My services are like a Monopoly™ Game because . . . For example, you might say, "because you collect money only when you pass go." You might then consider whether you could market a product that would complement your services and make money even when you were not passing go.

Your second challenge is to combine your marketing plan with anything that you see on your desk. For example, you see your telephone. Perhaps you could make four cold calls every Friday afternoon (the best time to make a phone call, by the way). Or you see the Post-its and wonder whether it's time you explored having your logos printed on them.

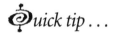*uick tip . . .*

> On your next business trip, purchase a magazine that you have never read. This will jog you out of your normal routine and make way for creativity to enter.

2. Risk Taking

Critical as it is, we sometimes forget to think about the relationship of risk taking to creativity. Creativity is virtually nothing unless you take a risk and do something with it. For example, when the creative designer, Kathy Armstrong, suggested that I use waves in my logo, my initial reaction was, "No way! Waves? I live in Wisconsin. The only waves Wisconsin is known for are at the football games in the university stadium!" She persisted, saying that the name ebb associates suggests waves and that it would be a marketing faux pas to ignore it. She was right. The risk paid off. Our logo is known among peers, clients, and the consulting field.

By the way, as soon as we decided to keep the waves on the logo we had some interesting water events occur: Kohler Company hired us to teach a creativity class, the Newport News Shipbuilding Company hired us, and we opened an office in Virginia on the Chesapeake Bay. Not long after that, our first Navy client hired us as well. It was just coincidental. Wasn't it?

The year Babe Ruth hit the most home runs, he also struck out the most often. Wayne Gretzky says you miss 100 percent of the shots you do not take. What are these two athletes telling us? Perhaps that if you really want to succeed you need to take a few more risks. Tom Peters states in his presentations that failure is a sign that someone is doing something. He also says that companies ought to fail faster—that is, take more risks. Some will fail, but get the failures out of the way, learn something from them, and move on to success.

Your Challenge Identify five risky things you could do to enhance your marketing plan. Need one for starters? The owners of Ben & Jerry's ice cream challenged their company to meet a goal. If the goal was reached, they promised to dance the hula on Wall Street. The company achieved the goal and owners danced away. Now it's your turn to think of five risky things you could do. Try these words to get you started: fire, mud, hot pink, jalapeño peppers. And remember James Bryant Conant's quote: "Behold the turtle. He makes progress only when he sticks his neck out."

3. Expand and Shrink
Again, a bonus of two related but different techniques. I am amazed at how often I have used this technique in its simplest form with great results. This technique suggests that you expand or shrink the problem, the marketing challenge, or the situation to another size to determine what you might do differently.

Have you ever plucked a chicken? Few of us have, so let me explain the process. First you plunge the beheaded chicken into scalding water to loosen the feathers. Next you pluck the feathers out, but you are left with hair on the chicken's skin. The best way to remove the hair is to singe it. But the chicken is wet and wet anything doesn't burn. Okay, how would you dry the chicken hair if you were in a hurry? Of course! A hair dryer. But that's a small problem. You have a huge problem if you are Frank Perdue with thousands of chickens to dry. If you expanded on the hair dryer idea, what might you use? Well, Frank used the expand technique and uses a jet engine to dry his birds.

I am presently working on new business cards to advertise my book, *The Business of Consulting*. In the past I had a very simple white card with a picture of the cover of the book, a quote from Peter Block, and my contact information. That's a very simple example of how you can use the "shrink" concept. I shrunk the cover to fit on a business card. I am now expanding that idea to make the entire front of the business card a replica of the book cover. The business card will be folded, opening on the side like a book, and the contact information will be located on the inside.

The advantages of this latest idea are that it is creative and looks like what it is meant to market. The drawbacks are that it will be costly to print and a pain for people who like the traditional business-card shape and size. The next step is whether I take the risk (see the second creativity technique above, risk taking) that people may complain that the business card is too far outside the box. The reason that I mention this example is that you can see that you can shrink and expand the same idea: shrink the picture of the book cover to fit on a business card, then expand it to be the entire business card.

Your Challenge Imagine that you want to do something that will be remembered by your clients for its size. It might be larger than life or it might be miniature. What could you do? In the first instance you might consider spending all your budget on a billboard advertisement. Or you might say, "What if my staff size expanded by fifty tomorrow. How would I market?"

In the second, you might consider going to a novelty shop to find miniature anything. For example, right now we have a box of miniature dice in our marketing idea box. We have no ideas for how we will use the ⅛-inch cubes. Perhaps to accompany a card that reads, "You won't be gambling when you use us. . . ." Your turn. Take something you are doing at this time in the marketing arena and expand it some way. Then take something else, perhaps a product or a client effort, and shrink it.

4. Ask What's Good? and What If?

Probably two of the most important questions you can ask to generate a bundle of ideas are "What's good about this situation?" and "What if we did something differently?"

In my workshops I like to ask the question: "What's good about being fired?" At first people look askance at me, but then the creative ideas start flowing: "I could get a job I really love" "I would have time to finish painting my house" "I would get away from the office politics" "I could sleep late every day" "I could move closer to my grandchildren." Although this example is wishful thinking, it can pay off. The engineers at Conoco asked, "What's good about toxic waste?" and discovered a substance in the water that could be turned into a lubricant.

Asking "What if?" can be just as much fun and with the same kind of payoff. What if your marketing problems were actually the solutions? DuPont Information Systems found themselves in a situation of needing to provide more training services that were increasing in cost with budgets that could not keep up. They were paying more and getting less. What if their problem was actually the solution? What if they paid more money? What if they paid more money to fewer vendors? DuPont asked the question and initially saved $400,000.

Our office headquarters recently moved to Virginia after being in Wisconsin for over twenty years. At first that looked like lots of problems: finding new support staff, changing telephone service, alerting people of address changes. It seemed like a never-ending list until we asked, "What's good about the move?" Well, in addition to that's what we really wanted to do, it gave us a great excuse to personally connect with clients and past clients we had not spoken with in a long time. What a great marketing opportunity!

Your Challenge Think of something that is not going the way you wish it would. Perhaps it is that you have fewer clients than you wish you had. First ask, "What's good about it?" Maybe you have clients that you need to get rid of because they are unethical, don't pay their bills, or are not profitable. Maybe this is an opportunity to select the clients you want to have.

Now ask, "What if?" What if the problem was the solution? What if having fewer clients gave you the time to develop some dynamite materials or write a book or develop a knock-their-socks-off marketing campaign? What if those few clients were actually the leads you needed to get your second tier of clients (because you asked them for help)? What if having too few clients forced you to examine the products and services you offered to identify others in greater demand? What would happen to those few clients if you changed your corporate values and/or philosophy? Create your own "what if" questions. And of course, answer them.

5. Transform Your Viewpoint

Seeing things from a different perspective is something we do daily and probably should do more often. If we always saw things from our adversary's perspective, there would be fewer disagreements. You can transform your viewpoint from many perspectives. Let's examine a few of those possibilities.

First, as mentioned above, you can transform your viewpoint from negative to positive. Or the reverse. If you were trying to determine the best marketing plan, you might determine all the reasons you want to market. Then again, you could determine all the reasons you do NOT want to market. How might this help you? Well, it might determine the things you would not want to do. For example, a radio or newspaper ad campaign might overwhelm your switchboard with calls, but result in clients who have too little money or are too small to use your services.

Second, you can transform your viewpoint to someone else. How would your clients look at your marketing strategy? How would your competitors view it? How would your mother view your strategy? How would your diversity coordinator view it? How about a CEO? A preschooler? A teacher? A musician? A soccer coach? Charlie Brown or Lucy?

Third, you can transform your viewpoint to another time. What would your marketing plan look like if you were developing it in 1899? 1944? 1959? 1976? What would your marketing plan look like if you were developing it in 2030? If you have been in business for a long time, how would you be developing it if this was your first year in business? If this is your first year in business, how do you expect to develop it once you are in business for ten years?

Fourth, you can transform your viewpoint by transforming the circumstances. How would you market your consulting practice if money were no object? How would you market if the U.S. Postal Service went out of business? How would you market if you were a cosmetics company? How would you market if you wanted to work just nine months each year? How would you market if you had too many customers?

Your Challenge Think of one of the marketing ideas you have. Then transform your viewpoint in two ways. Use some of the ideas above or create your own transformed viewpoint.

6. In Another Sequence

This technique suggests that you can generate a new way to accomplish something that may deliver different results. Everything we do has a process, and once we find the most efficient way to complete the process we rarely change our ways.

We tend to stay with the same order and, whether due to logic, habit, or stubbornness, we find suggestions to do things in a different order uncomfortable. But what would happen if we did the steps in the process backward? Or put the solution up-front instead of at the end of a problem? What if we mixed all the steps around? Might it save time or money?

A friend of mine who had never served stuffed turkey put the unstuffed bird in the oven to bake. While the turkey baked, he made the stuffing and baked it in a separate dish. He then stuffed the baked stuffing into the bird and continued baking until his guests arrived. His guests claimed that it was the best turkey and dressing they had ever had. It wasn't until cleaning up that guests discovered the extra dish he had used to bake the stuffing. And that's when he learned that his turkey baking process had been accomplished in an unconventional sequence of steps.

Prudential Insurance asked whether there was a better sequence for paying life insurance benefits. Typically people must die before receiving their benefits. What about those suffering a terminal illness? What if they received their death benefits before they died? Prudential asked this question and devised the living benefit life insurance. It pays death benefits when people who have a terminal illness need them, before they die. While this insurance has been with us for a while, it was a revolutionary idea in its time because the sequence was different.

How can this translate to marketing? What if you got information from potential clients before you made your first cold call? What if you marketed first and developed a marketing plan last? What if you sold something to your clients first and marketed to them last?

Your Challenge Think about the sequence that you are using for developing your marketing plan. Is there something that you might want to move up earlier or back later? What would change? What might be better? What might be the drawback?

7. Visit Other Places

Sometimes our physical surroundings may inhibit our creative ideas from flowing freely. Is your office conducive to creative thinking? Do you work in a busy office with the phone ringing constantly, interrupting your train of thought? Or perhaps the stimulation induces creative ideas?

You may want to determine what enhances your creativity. Does the noise level inhibit your creative thought process? Or does the activity stimulate it? Does a window in your office open you to new ideas? Or is it distracting? Does music disrupt your flow of ideas? Or does it enrich the ideas?

Get in touch with what makes you feel creative. What sights (picture of a lake, a tree waving in the breeze, vacation souvenirs); what sounds (jazz music, silence, ocean waves); what scents (spices, flowers, candles); what tastes (jasmine tea, chocolate, pretzels); or what feelings (autumn breeze, comfortable sweats, warm beverage) enhance your ability to think creatively? Then surround yourself with as many of these as possible before you settle into a creative idea–generating session.

Are you in touch with the times when you are the most creative? When did your last creative ideas occur? While you were running? Driving? In the shower? Mowing the lawn? All of these are times that we move into our right brain and the intuitive thought process takes over. At times like these be sure to capture your idea on paper so you don't forget it!

Knowing when you are the most creative helps. The office setting to which you aspire, the senses you require, and the opportunities you desire all help. However, you can still go someplace else. That may mean to physically move yourself to another location or to go someplace else in your mind.

What creative physical locations do people select? Walks on the beach or in the woods or even their neighborhoods; shopping in bookstores, toy stores, card shops, antique malls, or hardware stores; visiting museums, art galleries, libraries, a farm, or the zoo; enjoying nature such as a starry night, a rainy day, a park, or the sunrise; or something more personal such as lunch with a friend or taking a mini vacation.

Does this pay off in the business world? Hallmark Cards, Inc., must think so. They send their people on what may appear to be vacations, for example, two weeks in Mexico to "soak up inspiration." Hallmark must believe it is worth the investment.

How can you go to a creative place without leaving home? Try some of these ideas. Watch your favorite movie. Sit down with a stack of catalogs. Take a long soaking bubble bath and let the ideas flow. Page through a magazine like *Fast Company, Town & Country, Rolling Stone, Condé Nast Traveler,* or *Mechanix Illustrated*. Read a creative book. Start a journal. Join a creativity chat room. Listen to a day's worth of music you love.

Your Challenge Identify six places you could go (physical or not) this weekend for creative thinking time. Then select your top three and go to at least one of those. Save the other two for the next two weeks and use the rest as backups. When you get there, browse, walk, write, or do whatever is appropriate to generate at least two dozen marketing ideas. Think that's pushing too hard? It's not. Try it. The key is to write them all down without judgment.

8. Incubate

Remember all those times that your English composition teachers encouraged you to complete your assignments early so that you could "put them on the back burner"? Well, improving the product by allowing creativity to enter the process is one of the reasons. When creating something new, the results will improve in most instances if you start the project and then set it aside to allow the creative juices in your brain to gurgle and bubble, to splash and splutter about. What happens? Your subconscious gets involved; your teachers were allowing time for that to occur.

How do you implement this technique? Do your marketing planning early. Whether it is the entire plan or just one idea of the plan. Gather your data, define your idea, and design it as best you can. Now let it sit. Let it simmer on that "back burner." Go do something else. Think about a different problem. Take a couple days away from your plan. Uh uhh! No peeking!

You should sleep on it, though. And if you awaken in the middle of the night with new ideas, capture them. If you do not, you will most likely forget them by morning. So sleep with a pencil and paper (and maybe a flashlight) next to your bed. What's going on? Your conscious mind can focus on only one idea at a time. Your subconscious, however, can tap into everything that has ever happened to you at the same time. This is mega-combine technique! Sleep allows your mind to wander about and connect ideas in your brain to each other.

The 3M Company encourages employees to create new ideas. No, they don't allow employees to sleep at work. They do, however, encourage them to spend time on the job thinking of and creating new products for the company.

Your Challenge Remember the weekend when you were supposed to "visit another place" to generate two dozen marketing ideas? Examine those ideas now. Take one or two that you think have the most potential. Gather your data, define your idea, and design it as best you can. Then put it away for a couple of days. Let it incubate so that your subconscious can hatch another great idea.

9. Trigger Concepts

This technique is really powerful! Or maybe I think it is because I have used it for so long and have fantastic results. It is easy to personalize, and that also makes it a powerful creativity technique.

Using this technique, you will tap into a list of concepts that "trigger" new ideas for you. It is similar to the combine technique in that you have something (problem, product, thought, or challenge) that you want to think differently about. However, one big difference is that you will always have your lists available to you rather than thinking of something new each time. Here are some ways that you can create your personal "trigger lists."

You may want to create a list of your favorite words. These are words that may suggest actions or favorite nouns. It may, like mine, be a combination of both with some adjectives tossed in. My list includes words such as serendipity, ocean, hot fudge sundae, books, dancing, writing, design, Costa Rica, birds of paradise, destiny, exotic, snow, suspenders, avocado, sapphires, pink, profits, eat, magnify, dissolve, and gems. Update your list of words regularly, adding a word when you stumble on one you like, removing words as you tire of them.

Some people like to use a list of prepositions to trigger new ideas. A preposition list might include about, above, among, around, as, at, before, behind, between, beyond, by, despite, except, from, in, of, on, outside, to, under, with, and any others you choose. This list becomes action-oriented and may help you see the idea from a different perspective.

When it comes time to think of a new idea for anything, just pull out one of your lists and go through it, combining each word with your situation. As you use these trigger lists, allow your brain to rest for a time on each combination to allow inspiration to link the situation and the trigger word.

You may wish to refresh your entire list at least once per year. Some people use the items on their desks as a trigger list. You may choose some other place that has a variety of "things," such as your child's toy box or the supply cabinet in your office.

You may also use readymade lists. Roger von Oech has developed a *Creative Whack Pack,* a card deck that will stimulate ideas. I have developed a deck of Idea Sparkers that you can have in exchange for a marketing idea or story. E-mail your idea to us (remember to include your physical mailing address), and we will send you a set of Idea Sparkers. You might also pull up a chair to your computer and work with software programs that unleash creativity, such as the granddaddy of them all, IdeaFisher™. The *Chicago Tribune* called it a thesaurus on steroids. One model even has an advertising/promotion module. More information is available at www.IdeaFisher.com.

Personally I like to sit down with catalogs—a picture list that generates ideas for me. Your company probably receives corporate promotional catalogs and corporate paper catalogs. These are great for identifying a theme and a concept to get you started.

ebb associates also keeps boxes, files, and drawers full of ideas. It may be a cartoon someone read, an ad we clipped, a picture we found, a geegaw or gadget we purchased, or just the bud of an idea described in words. When we need an idea, we may turn to our idea files for inspiration.

Your Challenge Create at least one "trigger list" of your own. Personalize it for your use. If you have strong auditory senses, you may choose word lists. If you have strong visual senses, you may choose pictures or catalogs. If you have strong tactile senses, you may choose to collect a box of miniature things or toys. Then identify one marketing tool, for example, publicity, direct mail, or trade shows, and pair it with the items on your list. The challenge is to add at least four possibilities—no matter how wild and crazy—to your marketing ideas.

10. Youth's Advantage

Remember as a kid how creative and free you felt to put on a red cape (your mother's dishtowel) and imagine that you could fly through the air like Superman? Well, the "youth's advantage" creativity technique asks that you tap into that same Superman feeling. As a child you had the advantage that you had not yet been influenced by adult thinking that might have suggested that "You look ridiculous with that red dishtowel flying from your neck" or that "It isn't logical to think you can fly" or that "You should stop fooling around and get to work!" (All of which you may notice inhibit creativity.)

"Youth's advantage" suggests that creativity will flow (just like that red cape) if you think like a child. Look at your marketing plan and think "fun." Your brain is more likely to create new ideas when you are having fun. A child's thought process is innocent and curious. It asks lots of "why" questions. It is playful and spontaneous. There is an easy free-association of ideas. To emulate a child you will most likely need to loosen up a bit.

How can you loosen up? How can you get in touch with that child inside? Try doing what a kid does. Play. Get down on the floor and play with your own child or a niece or nephew or grandchild. You can always "rent" a kid from someone in the neighborhood. The idea is to find a playmate. You might remember that a NASA space telescope problem was solved while the scientist was playing with his child's Tinkertoys®.

Now you've got the kid, what can you do? Try crayons, Pla-Doh® clay, or bubbles. Build something (fort, truck, house, dog, castle) with anything (blocks, snow, sheets, straws, Legos®, or dirt). Play with a yo-yo, jacks, Nerf® ball, Frisbee®, or a jump rope. Learn to juggle or teach the child to whistle. Go fishing or camping. Pretend you're a bird or a dinosaur or a dump truck. Take a trip to the library or a toy store. Go for a walk around the block, checking all the sidewalk cracks, tree bark, and clouds along the way.

While you have a captive audience, why not involve the child in your idea? Present it in a simple way and then ask for advice or ideas. Maybe you will get a series of "Why's?" That's good. Follow the child's thought process and you may hear questions that you should have asked yourself.

Your Challenge Buy a box of crayons. Not just any box of crayons. Buy the big box with sixty-four crayons or buy some of the new glitter, metallic swirl, scented, fluorescent, color-change, or any of the others that are on the market today. Heck, why not buy one of every kind? After all, they are deductible as a marketing expense. Now sit down and start to doodle for at least twenty minutes. During that time let your mind wander on any pleasant thought you desire. What's the goal? Uh uhh! No goals. Just see what happens. And whatever it is, it will be the correct answer.

Ⓠuick tip . . .

> Go to your local bookstore and browse through the creative book section. Then go to the children's section and page through a few of the picture books. This should spark a few creative ideas.

Ten Successful Marketing Campaigns

You may be asking, "But do these techniques work?" The answer is a resounding "Yes!" Listed here are ten successful uses of the techniques by many consulting firms and training suppliers that you will most likely know by name. Although most were probably unaware that they were using a specific technique, their results were creative and the implementation successful.

Compare and Combine

Barbara Pate Glacel, co-author *of Light Bulbs for Leaders* and former CEO of VIMA International, Oak Hill, Virginia, needed a marketing piece that would address several needs and also be reasonable to produce. She needed a mailing piece to market her book, something that she could send to potential buyers as well as a thank you to those who purchased the book. She also needed something that could be used for corporate correspondence, something that could be used to jot a note off to a client. And in addition she needed something that could be mailed to clients as a follow-up to the workshops that VIMA conducted. Addressing all these needs with one useful product was the challenge.

Barbara combined the book with a need for correspondence. The result was one reasonably priced, customized, oversized postcard. One side of the card is an exact replica of the attractive cover of *Light Bulbs for Leaders*. The other side was printed in three different ways. First with advertising copy about the book, second with information about the company, and third left blank for a personal message written by the sender. In addition, the card has become a calling card at workshops and presentations and is useful as a bookmark. The company mails the card regularly, and it serves as a constant marketing tool and reminder of a good book to everyone—including the postman!

What problems could you combine toward one solution? What could you compare your company to for marketing purposes?

Risk Taking

Performance Systems Corporation (PSC) of Dallas, Texas, needed a trade show giveaway. PSC was a company that taught the importance of living their values to corporations, walking the talk. An employee of the company came across a set of plastic teeth with feet. When wound up, the teeth would open and close, hopping on miniature feet across any flat surface. What a way to visually display their favorite quote, "Walk the Talk!" Chomping teeth with feet seemed just too corny for a conservative consulting firm. Should they take the risk or not?

As time drew near and no other ideas surfaced, the employees started to accept the idea. The trade show attendees bit too. The teeth were a smashing success. They were printed with the company's 800 number so that clients and potential clients could reach PSC easily. In addition, PSC paid attention to the packaging to ensure that the message they were conveying was professionally presented.

The miniature walking teeth were nestled in red shredded paper and packaged in a glossy white box. Walk the Talk was emblazoned on the cover in metallic blue and gold on the lid. Accompanying the teeth was a printed fable about the importance of living your values, "The Legend of the Walking Teeth." On the back of the fable is this quote, "Words to live by are just words . . . unless you live by them. You have to Walk the Talk."

The teeth have impacted business significantly and changed the image of the company. In fact, the campaign was so successful that the company changed its name to The Walk the Talk Company! What a payoff for taking a risk.

What could you do that might be just a little risky but would attract client attention?

Expand and Shrink

MasteryWorks, Inc., was looking for something that could be mailed or used as an ad to hook people into the services they provided. They wanted something that would teach readers something about themselves and entice them to want to purchase more of their products. They had many books, articles, and workshops, but these were too large and valuable to give away on a large scale.

One day, Caela Farren, president of MasteryWorks, was sitting on an airplane and realized how much she enjoyed learning something about herself from the ten-question quiz she had just completed in a magazine. That was it! When she returned from her trip, she took some of the materials the organization presented and shrunk them down to a ten-question quiz that provided insight about the person who completed it.

Like MasteryWorks, you may have something that hooks potential new clients personally to your materials. For example, if you are a financial consultant it may be a quick assessment about your chances of retiring rich. If you are a nursing home administration consultant, it may be ten tips for selecting a nursing home for your parents. Look through your files. What do you have that could be expanded or shrunk to use as a marketing tool?

Ask What's Good? and What If?

The Times Mirror Group was a firm, like many today, that was created of several smaller firms. Each of the smaller companies had its own booth at trade shows. The group wanted to display teamwork and make the point that they were all a part of one company. How could they do that? One year at the American Society for Training and Development's (ASTD) Expo, they decided to ask the question: "What if we tried to get attendees to all of our booths?" They decided to play on attendees' love of gadgets and need for completing a project.

They decided that each of the companies would hand out one tool of a total toolkit. Attendees needed to visit all of the companies to complete a full tool set. Once attendees had all the tools, they would also receive a zippered case to hold all the tools. Because the companies shared the expense, the cost was reasonable. And the message was easy: "We have all the tools you need!"

Was it successful? Learning International, one of the companies involved, more than tripled inquiries from the year before. What "what if" question could you ask to boost sales? What barrier have you recently encountered to which you could ask, "What's good about it?"

Transform Your Viewpoint

There are many ways that this technique can be used. Eagle's Flight of Ontario, Canada, used it to help their clients transform their viewpoint of what was important to a consulting company.

Eagle's Flight's corporate values are not what you would expect of a successful consulting firm with employees numbering close to one hundred. Eagle's Flight wants its employees to love what they do and to express that in significant ways to its customers. In addition, they want their customers to know that life is for more than work. They remind their customers of this through their marketing campaigns. For example, on the inside back cover of their catalog they had printed, "P.S. Don't forget to call your mother!" to remind clients to remember people who are important to them.

In previous marketing schemes they sent greetings for Valentine's Day and Groundhog Day. When it was time for another message to their clients, they decided to play off their catalog and send a Mother's Day greeting complete with a ten-minute calling card so that clients could call their mothers on "Eagle's Flight's dime."

Eagle's Flight chose to use this creativity technique to help their clients view a training company as more than an entrepreneurial company that made money. You could use the technique in many different ways.

How could you transform your view of marketing to education? How could you change your view of cold calls to hot calls? How could you transform your view of selling? How would you view marketing if this was 1921? Or if you were the buyer instead of the seller?

In Another Sequence

Several years ago, Learning Solutions Alliance, Santa Clara, California, had initiated a service that was new to the industry. It began brokering other consultants' services. This required a new name, a new brochure, and a new way to explain its services to potential clients. While we as consultants always gather input about what the client needs (you do, don't you?) before beginning a project, few of us have ever asked our clients what they would like to see in our marketing materials. Well, Sally Ewald of Learning Solutions Alliance did just that.

Sally asked her potential clients not only what they wanted to have available in services, but also what they wanted to have in the company's marketing materials. And clients told them. They said, "We want something that is fast to read." They also wanted something that outlined the benefits in bullet format that they could use in their in-house proposals. Now that's a backward approach! The clients would use material from the marketing brochure to sell their own bosses on the services Sally and her gang provided. Quite a turnabout!

What could you rearrange or do in a different sequence that might lead you to a better marketing position?

Visit Other Places

Blanchard Training and Development is a name that you will recognize. Ken Blanchard, author of *The One Minute Manager* and more than a dozen other books, is a household name with most consultants. Even consultants who are well-known need to continue to market to keep their names in front of their clients. You can be assured that Ken and company do many things to keep the Blanchard name in front of clients and potential clients.

The company remembers the first time it hosted a client conference. They attribute the idea to attending an Instructional Systems Association (ISA) conference and hearing ideas from other participants. While attending the conference they conceived the concept of hosting a client conference. The result was an event that lasted over several days that was a cross between a client appreciation and a learning conference. The event has become the training supplier event of the year. Blanchard has purposefully kept it small with a limited number of invitations each year. This maintains the intimacy and the exclusivity of the event. And even though customers pay to attend this event, many more clamor for a chance to attend than can be accommodated.

Going to the ISA conference led them to a marketing solution that has paid off well for the company. Where could you go to be energized about new marketing ideas?

Incubate

This is the creativity technique that we, ebb associates inc, are best at doing. We constantly collect drawers and boxes, files and folders full of gadgets and geegaws, pictures and cartoons, advertisements and brochures. The entire staff has always been involved. When an occasion arises—a holiday, someone new joins the staff, or a special thank you is required—we turn to the collection. We pull items out of the collection, toss ideas about, sleep on them, and allow them to incubate until an idea is hatched.

So what might you expect to find in our collection? You've already read about some of the ideas we have implemented, but how might the thought process go with the items that are in the collection now? One item in the box right now is a miniature Swiss army knife. First of all, this is a good item because it passes the MUMU measure test. It is memorable (can be printed with the ebb logo), it will be useful to the recipient, it is easy to mail, and it is unique—meaning that it is unlikely the recipient would have received one in the past.

What message could a Swiss army knife deliver? How about a good-luck wish such as, "Good luck! You have all the tools for success!" How about a congratulations note that said, "Congratulations! Is there anything you can't do?" Or perhaps a customer appreciation gift that says, "Let's cut to the chase! You're a great customer!" And of course you can always use the "We have all the tools you need to . . . ," just as Times Mirror did in an earlier example.

What do you do to ensure your ideas have time to incubate?

Trigger Concepts

Sometimes an idea is so good it just must be used again. And that's the rest of the story from Debra Dinnocenzo, creator of the Times Mirror tool-kit example mentioned under the "ask what if" technique.

The idea had its beginnings when DDI (Development Dimensions International) first used the tool kit as an internal incentive to close a big sale, which also included hosting a team breakfast complete with "Team Flakes" and engraved spoons. The tools were representative of the "tool" each person would contribute to closing the sale. The twist in this case, however, was that the handles of the tools were not included in the kit. And they were not provided until the deal was signed—suggesting that all the "tools" had to do their part for the entire "kit" to be useful.

In this case the marketing idea itself was the trigger for another idea. That may not happen very often, but you can create your own trigger concepts. What triggers new ideas for you? What catalogs or idea lists do you have available to plant an idea seed for your next marketing campaign? What trigger system have you installed to keep marketing ideas flowing for your business?

Youth's Advantage

Hughes and Associates wanted to create a newsletter that was fun, youthful, easy, and colorful. They did not want the readers to be bored; they wanted a "ho-hum extinguisher"—one that clients would actually read. And they did just that with the creation of *News from the Jungle*, a newsletter that was exciting, bright, and colorful.

News from the Jungle had a different look and it was designed for a fast, easy read. The metaphors used were built around an "it's a jungle out there" theme. It had a collage and bulletin-board look. Many of the articles were less narrative and more brainstormed lists. How about results? The clients loved the lighter, less serious, yet helpful information. The company believes that the newsletter probably generates business, but more importantly, it met their criteria for being fun, both for the organization and for their clients. In addition, it was relatively inexpensive to produce. It was sent quarterly to about five hundred present and potential clients for the cost of copying and postage. Layout, design, and clip-art graphics were all done in-house.

Remember when you were young and life wasn't so serious? How have you used that childhood life-should-be-fun attitude in your marketing ideas lately?

MARKETING AND CREATIVITY: A PERFECT FIT

Marketing and creativity are a perfect fit. You need to grab your client's attention. Creativity is the tool that can help you do that. You need to stand out from the crowd. Creativity can do that. You need fresh, new ideas. Creativity is your answer again.

You've just reviewed ten creativity techniques. You can use them in almost every aspect of your professional and personal life. Let's examine how they might be used in the other aspects of marketing.

Practicing Creativity on Other Marketing Needs

As you implement your marketing plan, you will bump up against other aspects that will require your creative input; for example, how to make your package stand out in the mail or identifying a unique occasion to celebrate. I have identified some of these situations and have provided a half-dozen ideas for each. Some may be useful to you right now. Go ahead and use them. In addition, take a few minutes to identify another half-dozen. You may be surprised at how creative you can be using the techniques above.

Public Relations Ideas   This book suggests a number of occasions for which you may want to consider writing and sending a press release about you and your business. Chapter Five provides you with the categories that seem to appear interesting to the media. What can you submit that would be interesting enough to publish? Examine every item about you and try to connect it to your business. For example, if you are a computer consultant and your hobby is genealogy, you could write about how to design and file your family tree on a computer or how to use a computer to research a family genealogy. If you do volunteer work, write an article about something special you did, provide pictures, and mention your business. If a holiday is coming up, write an article connected to it. For example, to celebrate Martin Luther King Jr. Day you could write an article about the importance of vision to the success of a business. Submit a human-interest story about one of your clients (perhaps you could share the byline with one of their employees). Announce the publishing of a book or article. Submit an interview of a well-known individual in your field.

Creative Packaging   Getting your items to your clients safely is your first priority. But you can add an element of intrigue by sending items in a package that looks different. You could use a tube, brightly colored envelopes, stickers that signal the surprise inside, a brown paper bag, CD jewel cases, a paint can, or a coconut. (Yes, coconuts can be mailed.)

Trade Show Gotchas You will want to have something that will bring people to your booth. You could put intriguing messages under the participants' hotel doors. Candy is always a draw once they are in the area. You could send a piece of a puzzle before the show. You could send a series of postcards prior to the show that begin to build a story. You could offer a drawing. Have a celebrity appear in your booth to sign autographs.

Web Page Grabbers People will return to your website if you update it frequently and include something of value for each visit. These items could be a quiz, self-evaluation, quote of the day, crossword puzzle, tip about anything, time-saving idea of the month, or new business book review.

Reasons to Call You After Seeing Your Ad If you placed an expensive ad in the industry journal, you will want some way to know whether the ad garnered any interest. Give the reader a reason to call or e-mail you. Make it easy for the readers to reach you and have a way to obtain contact data from them. To do that you could offer something related to what you do, such as "Ten Tips to Solve . . ." or a free half-hour consultation. You could offer something indirectly related, such as an article about "How to Select a Consultant" or an ethics quiz. You could offer something from which they learn more about themselves or their companies, such as a self-assessment about their communication skills or how their companies rate against the top three in the industry.

Holidays Worthy of Celebration Early in this chapter I told you about how one organization celebrated Mother's Day with their clients. Here are some other days to celebrate, and this one is a bonus, because I have identified a full baker's dozen. Also, if you conduct business internationally, be sure to determine what holidays your clients in other countries celebrate and join in their fun as well. Try these here in the United States for starters: New Year's Day, Martin Luther King Day, Groundhog Day, Washington's Birthday, St. Patrick's Day, first day of spring, Secretary's Day, May Day, longest day of the year, Labor Day, Halloween, Thanksgiving, and Pearl Harbor Day.

Where to Look for New Ideas Sometimes the really creative ideas listed earlier in this chapter are more creative than you need. What other places can you look for ideas besides visiting toy stores? Check out the industry journals that are read by your clients, reading both the articles and the ads. Read the *Wall Street Journal*. Walk the floors of your industry trade show, collect brochures, talk to the sales reps, and ask questions. Attend presentations at local, regional, and national conferences. Listen to talk shows on radio. Take a tour of one of your client's plants, offices, or wherever the work is completed.

Marketing, Creativity, and Fun

So can marketing be fun? You bet! Remember to send me your most creative marketing idea and I will send you a deck of Idea Sparkers!

MARKETING: TAKE ACTION

1. Select one of the ten creativity techniques. Use it to attack your most difficult marketing challenge.

2. Select one of the ten successful marketing campaigns and adapt it to your situation. How could you use it?

3. Select one of the holidays worth celebrating and add it to your marketing plan. Highlight it on your office calendar and in your PDA or Day-Timer.

Lists, Plans, and Last-Minute Advice

Where's Your Opportunity?

O ne of the best things about writing a book is that I have the opportunity to include what I think is most important. In this case, a few things did not fit in the other chapters, so I have created a chapter just for these loose pieces.

LISTS

Several lists did not make it into other chapters. So they appear here. The Getting Unstuck list in Exhibit 12.1 can be used at any time, but is presented here for you to use, especially when you are stuck about any aspect of marketing. Use the suggestions to push you into a creative mode when you do not feel very creative. I originally wrote the list when I consulted for Land O'Lakes. The list later made it into a creativity book that I wrote called *The ASTD Trainer's Sourcebook: Creativity and Innovation*.

Exhibit 12.1. Getting Unstuck

Do Things Differently

- Visit a museum
- Take a different route to work
- Read a book you know you'll hate
- Visit a building you've never been in
- Make a phone call to a friend you've not talked to in over a year
- Visit a kindergarten
- Go for a swim
- Listen to a different radio station
- Walk around your block backward
- Cross your eyes
- Visit an art gallery
- Take a shower
- Watch a silent movie
- Go dancing

Visioning

- Think about your favorite sport
- See the task complete
- See the same situation in 1850 or in 2030
- Imagine yourself dancing with Fred Astaire or Ginger Rogers
- See yourself in a blizzard
- Envision yourself on a tropical island
- Imagine you are a millionaire

Word Ideas

- Play Scrabble®
- Read the dictionary
- Read the sports page—or not
- Do a cryptogram
- Read a comic book
- Visit a magazine stand; buy three magazines you've never read
- Look through the Yellow Pages

Exhibit 12.1. Getting Unstuck, Cont'd

Get Ideas From Others

- Hold a crazy idea meeting at lunch
- Offer to pay $10 for every idea you use
- Ask your child or someone under ten years young
- Ask your father-in-law
- Ask the librarian
- Ask a cab driver
- Start talking with someone, anyone, and ask the individual to challenge you and push you to continue

Time-Related

- Establish a completion time
- Break the task into small parts; assign a reward to the completion of each
- Establish a portion that must be done by a certain time. If successful, you quit; if not, work another hour.

Get Crazy

- Wear a costume to work
- Read only the ads in a magazine
- Watch TV with the sound off
- Blindly choose a word from the dictionary and list twenty-five ways it's related to your need
- Play a computer game
- Visit an arcade
- Read children's books

Stimulate Your Senses

- Eat an unusual fruit
- Eat chocolate
- Use an air scenting machine
- Burn a scented candle
- Go to sleep

(Continued)

Exhibit 12.1. Getting Unstuck, Cont'd

- Dream about it
- Listen to music you don't usually listen to
- Listen to your favorite music
- Listen to an environmental tape of the ocean or jungle

Writing-Related

- Create a mind map on a large piece of paper
- Start writing with crayons
- Write with scented markers
- Start writing and don't stop for twenty minutes no matter what is flowing from the pen
- Write about all the things you can't do
- Write the plan from your secretary's view
- Write with colored chalk on your sidewalk
- Write as fast as you can

Shock Your Dominance

- Cross your arms the opposite way for five minutes
- Cross your legs the opposite way for five minutes
- Use your more dominate eye to read a magazine article
- List ideas with your nondominant hand
- Doodle with your nondominant hand
- Call someone and keep the receiver on the opposite ear you usually use
- Breathe through only one nostril at a time for ten minutes

Your Favorites

-
-
-
-
-

3. *Share the load.* Find someone to partner with. We already mentioned partnering to sponsor an item for a conference. But you can partner in other ways as well. You could co-sponsor an ad or put a brochure together. I partnered with someone else when we wanted to send a direct mail piece to announce our books. We shared mailing lists and split the cost of the printing and mailing in half.

4. *Hire cheap labor.* Use college students to assist you with everything from doing your market research and developing your marketing plan to designing your website and packing and mailing a direct mail piece.

5. *Get your name in print.* Write your own public relations articles. Compose a letter to the editor. You can figure out how to obtain that free publicity.

6. *Send a freebie.* Create a handout of tips. No matter what your specialty, you can identify ten things that would help most of us. If you are an accountant, "Ten Tips to Organize for the Tax Season." If you are a time management consultant, "Ten Tips to Organize Your Office." If you are a computer consultant, "Ten Tips to Buying Your Next Computer." Send your tips to your clients. These tips will help to establish your credibility, and clients are likely to keep them around. They are practically free!

7. *Attend a free marketing seminar in your area sponsored by SCORE or SBA or* other nonprofit and government organizations.

8. *Give a cheap thrill.* Write thank-you notes to everyone for everything. The personal note is quickly becoming a lost art. You will be a phenomenon.

9. *Write.* Take stamps and a stack of client labels on your next vacation. Send your clients quick notes on postcards from your vacation spot.

10. *Speak up.* Find a way to be interviewed on television or radio.

You will find many more ideas in *The Business of Consulting* and *Marketing Your Services: For People Who Hate to Sell.*

MAKE MONEY MARKETING

Marketing is the vehicle to place you and your business in front of potential clients to ensure that work (and money) come through the door. But did you ever consider that you might be able to make money with your marketing tools? As a consultant

The Tightwad Marketing list in the next section is one I've been carrying around in my head for a long time. It was fun to put it on paper in this chapter.

Make Money Marketing is another list that just didn't quite make it to any other chapter, but you may wish to think about some of the items.

"ebb's 13 truths" (Exhibit 12.2) has been around for a long time. I put them together as a presentation for our company's first off-site retreat. They were meant as an overview for employees who had never been consultants. We initially used them as discussion starters. And I frequently use them in conference presentations. Until I wrote this book, I was unaware of the strong marketing focus each item has.

This chapter also includes several actual marketing plans. They do not present the assessment, but the plans help you see the direction the consultant wants to take. They also demonstrate that a few well-chosen ideas can provide a direction and focus for a consultant.

And of course, I end with "one last thing."

TIGHTWAD MARKETING

I suspect that this list has been formulating itself in my mind for nearly a quarter of a century. I have always had to do more with less, so being a tightwad comes naturally. Tightwad marketing requires more imagination than finances.

1. *Don't hire a marketing firm.* You can create great ideas. Just let your imagination flow. Or use some of the creativity techniques in Chapter Eleven. In the case of a holiday gift, forget developing the theme first. That's the way everyone else does it, but it's harder that way. Select the gift you like (and can afford), and then come up with the theme by brainstorming words or phrases. For example, a lighted magnifying glass could support a theme such as "finding something," "help with your big problems," "magnifying the best of . . . ," "light up your . . . ," or others.

2. *Make what you can't afford.* We wanted to send fortune cookies with customized messages. We learned that they would cost almost $1 each. We decided we could do it at a better cost. We bought the fortune cookies, used tweezers to pull the old fortune out, and inserted our own, all for less than 30 cents each.

the only time you usually make money is when you are working directly for a client, and usually that also means when you are physically on-site. You spend money and time creating marketing tools, but is there a possibility that they could also be sold to make money? Consider the following:

Your newsletter could be sold as a subscription. You may already write a newsletter as a marketing tool. People will subscribe to it if they believe it provides valuable information. Your newsletter will succeed if you offer information that is difficult to locate or if you compile it in a way that is useful to your subscribers. This means that you may need to ratchet up the level of sophistication, reliability, and content. It means more work, but it could also mean income.

You could become a paid speaker. You may already speak at conferences as one of your marketing tactics. You have many experiences from your consulting work, and perhaps your name can begin to appear on the speaker circuit and you can be paid for these presentations in a different venue. Depending on your expertise, experience, and skills, you could be paid anywhere from $500 to thousands of dollars for one speech. Many companies, clubs, and associations hire speakers for their conferences and special events. If you are interested, contact the National Speakers Association at 480/968-2552 or check their website at www.nsaspeaker.org.

You could charge for seminars. If you presently use showcases or demonstrations as a marketing tool, you might ask yourself if these could be expanded to be a full day or two-day workshop or seminar. Advertising to a cold list can be time-consuming and costly. But if you have a built-in audience with some of your clients, it could be worthwhile to check into this as another marketing tool turned into additional income.

You could write a book. You have been writing articles for magazines and journals to ensure that your name is in front of potential clients. Take a look at these articles—even the ones that have not been published. Could they be the beginning of a book? It is rare that you will make a large amount of money on the book unless it is a best-seller. But it will most likely at least cover costs, and it then becomes another marketing tool for you.

You could sell a special report. Perhaps you have conducted research and you are using it as leverage to obtain new clients. It could also be a spin-off from an article you wrote, for example, "A Dozen Ways to Increase Your Retail Sales." If it is valuable enough, clients may pay for it. The price can be as low as $5 or as high as $1,000 or more.

ebb's THIRTEEN TRUTHS

I introduced "ebb's 13 truths" to the ebb associates fledgling staff in 1990 at our newly opened Norfolk office. They have served me, ebb associates, and the consultants I coach well over the years. I had never analyzed them until I started writing this marketing book. I was fascinated to discover that nearly all of them are related to advice about marking! Let's take a look at them. They are listed in Exhibit 12.2 and explained in detail below.

Exhibit 12.2. ebb's Thirteen Truths About Consulting

ebb's 13 truths

1. You need clients more than they need you.
2. Listening is imperative.
3. Do your homework.
4. You must believe in what you do.
5. The more specialized you are, the more difficult it is to obtain business; the more generalized you are, the less credible you'll be in potential clients' eyes.
6. The time to market is all the time.
7. The most important time to market is when you're too busy to do so.
8. A billable day is a billable day.
9. If you're in it only for the money, you may not succeed.
10. Satisfying your client is your most important responsibility.
11. Your personality, not your expertise, will land most contracts.
12. Dress for success.
13. Quality: first, last, and everything in-between.

---

1. You Need Clients More Than They Need You

This is the entire purpose of marketing and selling your consulting services. You need clients or you will not be in business very long. Sometimes I talk to consultants who are certain that they have the magic elixir to solve every client's needs. That kind of attitude will get you in trouble and in debt. Your marketing should be focused on how you can serve your clients. Help your clients and they will help you with your marketing.

2. Listening Is Imperative

In Chapter Six I provided a list of natural marketing techniques, and "listening" was repeated again and again. Listening is the least expensive and most important marketing tool you have at your disposal. The payoff is immeasurable. A couple of years ago I was involved in a confidential survey of clients that confirmed how important listening is. One of the questions was: "What is the most important factor in a relationship with a consultant?" The second most common response (of twenty different responses) was: "Take time to understand our needs." The fourth most common was: "Listen to us." I consider both of these listening responses, and the fact that they were listed as two in the top four does not surprise me. I have often thought that every organization should have an official listener on staff. And when they do not, I serve that purpose.

3. Do Your Homework

Spend time finding out about your clients before you meet with them, and then don't ever stop learning. Everything that you learn will help you in two ways. Clients begin to trust you when they realize you have put effort into researching them. First, it is your responsibility to do the best job possible for your clients. You can't if you do not do your homework. Second, everything you learn about your clients personally and their organization is potential input into your next marketing idea. Keep your ears and eyes wide open and do your homework. Marketing is all about doing your homework.

4. You Must Believe in What You Do

Marketing and selling can come across as quite crass and pushy. But it doesn't have to be that way. If you believe in what you do and truly believe that you add value for your clients, you will see selling as providing assistance and help to your clients. Everyone has a great opening line, but the real test is behind the scenes and during the difficult times. Believing in what you do will come across sincerely in your work and in your marketing message.

5. The More Specialized You Are, the More Difficult It Is to Obtain Business; the More Generalized You Are, the Less Credible You'll Be in Potential Clients' Eyes

This has always been a dilemma for consultants. If you narrow your services too much, it may be difficult to find clients who require your services. On the other hand, if you claim to be able to do everything, your clients will wonder about your credibility. Finding the right mix—what you offer is what your clients need—is the key. In purest marketing jargon, this is called the product mix.

6. The Time to Market Is All the Time

More is written about this in Chapter Six. You simply cannot stop marketing. You are selling you and the image you project. That means you are "on" all the time—when you attend church or a service organization meeting, when you meet your children's teachers and friends, and when you are shopping or having your oil changed. You are marketing all the time. The secretary you were short with last week may be this week's gatekeeper who will not let you in to see his boss. Remember, you are your own marketing billboard.

7. The Most Important Time to Market Is When You're Too Busy to Do So

You are working on the biggest contract you've ever landed. You have lists of marketing activities to do, but the current client is counting on you and that marketing stuff seems so nebulous. Besides, you don't know if anything will come of it anyway. Well, without completing the marketing activities, nothing will come of it for sure. If you do not market yourself today when you are too busy to market, you will soon have plenty of time to market—all of it!

8. A Billable Day Is a Billable Day

Once a day is gone you can never have it back. If you are selling products and you stop selling for the day, you may be able to sell twice as many products the next day. But you are selling a service and that service is embodied in you. You can't sell two days' worth of yourself on the same day. This does not suggest that you should be billable full-time. It simply admonishes you to use your time wisely. And a very important part of that wise time use is marketing. Your billable time is critical to keep the cash flowing. And your marketing efforts ensure that your billable time is maximized.

9. If You're in It Only for the Money, You May Not Succeed

I believe in this one so strongly that I want to replace "may" with "will." You must be in consulting because you believe in what you are doing. Your marketing plan will have less of a chance of success if you are only trying to promote your business rather than provide a service.

10. Satisfying Your Client Is Your Most Important Responsibility

This cannot be emphasized too much. It is your job. But beyond that, it leads to more work. A satisfied client is your best marketing weapon. Your goal should be to have your clients marketing for you. A satisfied client leads to repeat work and referrals to other organizations. Satisfying your client is not only your most important responsibility, it is your only responsibility. Sage marketers know that to be a fact.

11. Your Personality, Not Your Expertise, Will Land Most Contracts

Unbelievable, but true. You will be promoting your services and your skills, but time and time again a client will hire consultants on "how they come across" rather than their expertise. You might be the best aeronautical systems engineering consultant in the world, but if you come across as arrogant, ignorant, or uninterested, you won't acquire much work. If you have a personality flaw, correct it. If you do not, no amount of marketing in the world is going to bring business your way.

12. Dress for Success

Although this one may sound a bit 1970s outdated, remember what was discussed in Chapter Four. You are selling you, so your image is critical to marketing your consulting services. While "dress for success" conjures up being concerned about whether you wear a navy blue or a gray suit, whether you should add a touch of red to connote power, or making certain your shoes are polished, it goes beyond that. Examine your marketing tools—your business cards, letterhead, brochures, fliers, and any other paper materials. Are they dressed for success? Designed and printed by professionals? Printed on high-quality paper stock? Do they have a consistent look? Make sure you are dressed from head to toe and from card to logo.

13. Quality: First, Last, and Everything In-Between

If I have not stressed how important quality is in everything you do as a consultant, I have not done my job. You should exude quality in all that you do from the first contact to the follow-up. With regard to marketing, if you can't do it well, don't bother doing it at all. A brochure with typos, a business card on cheap, flimsy cardstock, a poorly written yellow pages ad, or a poorly delivered conference speech will all detract from the message you are trying to send to your clients and potential clients. Go beyond that. Everyone connected to your office must have a professional demeanor and a client-centered attitude. If they do not, you are wasting marketing dollars.

The fact that all of these are related to marketing and selling in one way or another simply underscores the significance these activities have in your consulting practice.

MARKETING PLAN EXAMPLES

Example 1

This marketing plan is aimed at acquiring work for early next year. Other marketing efforts have been in place for months for the remainder of this year. Since estimates suggest that the cost to develop new clients is four to twenty times the cost to maintain present clients, a portion of this plan focuses on maintenance of present clients.

Goals

- To generate $150,000 in repeat business from 7/1 to 1/31
- To generate $120,000 in new business from 7/1 to 1/31

- To acquire five new clients by 1/31
- To present at one new conference next year
- To be published at least two times next calendar year

Focus

- *Geographic area:* the United States and Western Europe
- *Industry:* any new, different, exciting, profitable company that has high standards and expectations

New Clients

- Choose ten potential clients that we have never worked with, for example, Ciba-Geigy, or Pioneer. Work with Robin and Sonya to develop a personalized blitz over the next six months to include:

Identify the clients	July 5
Research the clients	July 15
Create six mailings for each	August 1
First mailing out	August 5
Continue mailings through	January
Make at least six phone calls to each	over the next six months

- Call five friends to ask for leads
    - Brainstorm with the WI office
    - Make phone calls by July 20
    - Research by July 30
    - Call by August 5
    - Continue to follow up
- Call four clients to ask for leads
    - Brainstorm with the WI office
    - Make phone call by August 30

- Research by September 10
- Call by September 15
- Continue to follow up
- Other contacts
  - Call two competitors for leads
  - Make four international contacts by January 1
  - Accept book offer by Wiley
  - Call Cat about writing another *Info-Line*
  - Submit proposals to at least four conferences
  - Make a list of people who owe me a favor (for potential clients)

Former Clients

- Contact nine former clients/contacts each month for four months, starting in August
  - Write initial contact note for each—something around "haven't heard from you in a while." Include something that encourages them to write back, e.g., a pen, SASE
  - Follow up all with a phone call
- Mail fifty Creativity brochures to selected past and present clients
  - Brainstorm list with WI office
  - Mail out by August 1

Ongoing

- Continue to send approximately one hundred articles and/or notes per month to present, past, and future clients focusing on their specific needs
  - Make monthly "how's it going?" phone calls to present clients
  - Maintain list of contacts

Other Collaboration

- Work with Dan on developing products
- Work with Dan to open Richmond
- Work with anyone who requests my assistance
- Begin a monthly circulated contact list to keep all consultants informed of everyone's activities

Example 2
New Clients

July–first three weeks

- Develop list of top thirty organizations in Tidewater, Williamsburg, and Richmond area that I want to target for new clients
  - Get names, addresses, positions, and phone numbers
  - Resources—Hampton Roads Quality Management Council roster, Richmond's Quality Council Roster, *Virginia* magazine, and Monday's Business Section
  - With Carol's help, devise a "phone call—then mail—then phone—then (hopefully) initial meeting" approach for each one with regular follow-up after that
  - Identify present friends and business acquaintances for personal introductions where possible—Jack Perry and others

July 26–August 27

- Work on ten potential clients from the list of thirty to develop a relationship utilizing the phone-mail-phone-meeting follow-up system

August 30–September 30

- Work on the next ten potential clients from the list of thirty

September 30–November 5

- Work on last ten potential clients

Objectives

- To have at least fifteen solid relationships by December 1
- Two to three contracts from the fifteen during first half of next calendar year
- Two more contracts during the rest of the year

Present and Past Clients

July–August

- Meet with present and past clients (lunch, breakfast, refreshments after work); discuss their plans for training and consulting. My approach to them will be: "In our efforts to continue to support you, what planning can we do so we can be better prepared to meet your needs in the coming calendar year?"

Local Networking

July–December

- Continue to network with local contacts via mail, phone, and meetings; maximum of sixty days between hearing from me

Associations/Councils

- Volunteer to present at local ASTD, ASQC meetings
- Investigate AQP, Quality Council in Richmond

Product Development

July

- Start patent development with lawyer
- Decide on a name

August

- Develop materials and packaging concept
- Research manufacturers, packaging companies
- Work with our advertising firm
- Develop positioning of product in marketplace, target customers, etc.

September–October

- Complete writing of the manuals, training materials, and so on . . .
- Finalize packaging, manufacturing, and marketing systems

November–December

- Start promotion of product; work the bugs out

January–June

- Heavily market product
- Display at trade show

Example 3

Industries to Target

- Financial services: banking, insurance
- ISO–9000

Lucrative Industries to Explore

- Proprietary chemical companies (soap, perfume, cosmetics, and drugs)
- Health care industries (pharmaceuticals, clinics, suppliers, and medical technology)
- Brokerage houses
- Insurance

Goal: Bring in Six New Clients per Year

- Financial services industry: Develop expertise in the area through work with present clients. Focus attention on opportunities for new work in the financial services area, target LocalLoans Bank as a new client
- ISO–9000: Send out letters for potential partnering, follow up on ISO leads, serve on the ASQC ISO–9000 Committee
- Community marketing opportunities: Take advantage of various marketing opportunities, through associations such as school activities, church, Masons, etc., . . . to let people know what we do and how we can help.

Other Activities

- Exhibit at Consultant's Showcase
- Partner with Better Business Bureau, Quality Awards Program
- Create a one-page quarterly newsletter to send to prospects, past clients, and current clients
- Send five prospecting letters each week
- Make ten follow-up phone calls every week
- Seasonal: Send appropriate greeting cards to every person on my database
- Hire marketing firm to develop a brochure last quarter

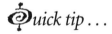 *uick tip . . .*

> Check out the Reading List at the end of this book. You still have much more to learn about marketing.

AND THE VERY LAST THING ...

Ever go off to a great conference or workshop? When you left you were all set to move forward, but in less than a week you had all kinds of excuses for why "it won't work here" or you "did not have enough time" or "I can't do it"?

What changed from the time you left the session? Probably nothing more than the fact that you stopped believing that it was a high priority in your life.

Marketing is a high priority for the success of your business. And you have a choice. You can either believe that the time is right, and you can make a difference in your business by developing and deploying a marketing plan and implementing some of the ideas in this book—or you can choose not to believe it. Whatever you decide, it will make a difference one way or another. The circumstances are the same. You will make a choice.

You can choose to see it as an opportunity whose time has come . . . or not.

Before You Turn the Page

Before you turn the page, please read this paragraph *completely*. When you turn the page you will see some letters in Figure 12.1 that spell a phrase. When you see the letters, *quickly* read the words out loud. Then look at them a second time.

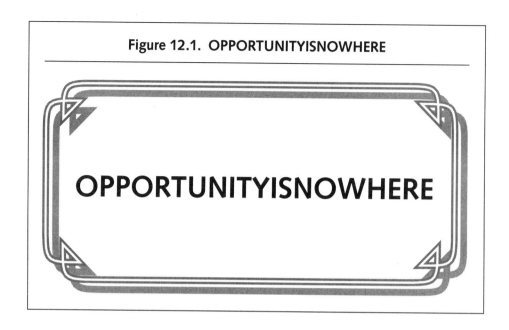

Figure 12.1. OPPORTUNITYISNOWHERE

OPPORTUNITYISNOWHERE

Now read the letters a second time. What do you read this time? Did the letters change? No. Did the message change? Yes.

It is all in how you interpret everything around you. You may view marketing as fun or not. You may view marketing as an opportunity or not. Either way you will prove your decision to be true. You have a choice to interpret things from a positive view or a negative view. You may either see that the opportunity for you to begin to market your business is "now here" or that the opportunity to market your business is "no where." Whatever you decide, you will prove the statement to be true. I hope you decide to prove that the opportunity is now here. Because I believe it is always here. Market like your business depends on it—because it does! Your opportunity is now here!

MARKETING: TAKE ACTION

1. Develop your own set of consulting truths. What do you "know" about consulting that guides you? Will all of these "truths" help you? Should you begin to incorporate other truths in your daily work?

READING LIST

Beckwith, H. (1997). *Selling the invisible: A field guide to modern marketing*. New York: Warner Books.

Bellman, G.M. (2002). *The consultant's calling* (2nd ed.). San Francisco, CA: Jossey-Bass, Inc.

Biech, E. (1996). *The ASTD trainer's sourcebook: Creativity & innovation*. New York: McGraw-Hill.

Biech, E. (1999). *The business of consulting*. San Francisco, CA: Jossey-Bass/Pfeiffer.

Biech, E. (2001). *The consultant's quick start guide*. San Francisco, CA: Jossey-Bass/Pfeiffer.

Biech, E., & Byers-Swindling, L. (2000*). The consultant's legal guide*. San Francisco, CA: Jossey-Bass/Pfeiffer.

Block, P. (2000). *Flawless consulting* (2nd ed.). San Francisco, CA: Jossey-Bass/Pfeiffer.

Carucci, R.A., & Tetenbaum, T.J. (2000*). The value-creating consultant*. New York: AMACOM.

Connor, D., & Davidson, J. (1997). *Marketing your consulting and professional services*. New York: John Wiley & Sons.

Crandall, R. (1996). *Marketing your services: For people who hate to sell*. Chicago: Contemporary Books.

Debelak, D. (2000). *Streetwise marketing plan: Winning strategies for every small business*. Holbrook, MA: Adams Media Corporation.

Decker, S. (Ed.). (1997). *301 do-it-yourself marketing ideas*. Boston, MA: Goldhirsh Group, Inc.

Fisher, D., & Vilas, S. (1995). *Power networking: 55 secrets for personal & professional success*. Austin, TX: Mountain Harbour Publications.

Fox, J.J. (2000). *How to become a rainmaker*. New York: Hyperion.

Franklin, R. (1996). *The consultant's guide to publicity: How to make a name for yourself by promoting your expertise*. New York: John Wiley & Sons.

Godin, S., & Peppers, D. (1999). *Permission marketing*. New York: Simon & Schuster.

Hiam, A. (2000). *Marketing kit for dummies*. Foster City, CA: IDG Books Worldwide.

Levinson, J., & Godin, S. (1994). *The guerrilla marketing handbook*. Boston, MA: Houghton Mifflin.

Levinson, J., & Godin, S. (1997). *Guerrilla marketing with technology: Unleashing the full potential of your small business*. Reading, MA: Addison-Wesley.

Lewin, M.D. (1997). *The consultant's survival guide*. New York: John Wiley & Sons.

Mackay, H. (1989). *Swim with the sharks without being eaten alive*. New York: Currency/Doubleday.

Mackay, H. (1997). *Dig your well before you're thirsty*. New York: Currency/Doubleday.

Michaels, N., & Karpowicz, D. (2000). *Off-the-wall marketing ideas*. Avon, MA: Adams Media Corporation.

Misner, I., & Davis, R. (1998). *Business by referral: A sure-fire way to generate new business*. Austin, TX: Bard Press.

Parinello, A. (1994). *Selling to vito: The very important top officer*. Holbrook, MA: Bob Adams, Inc.

Rackham, N. (1996). *Getting partnering right: How market leaders are creating long-term competitive advantage*. New York: McGraw-Hill.

Spoelstra, J. (2001). *Marketing outrageously: How to increase your revenue by staggering amounts!* Austin, TX: Bard Press.

Weiss, A. (2002). *How to establish a unique brand in the consulting profession*. San Francisco, CA: Jossey-Bass/Pfeiffer.

INDEX

C

Chamber of Commerce, 147

Charles, L., 215

Chicago Tribune, 234

Client base: building potential, 13–14; defining your company's, 25–26; positioning your, 44–46*e,* 47*e*–49

Client base building: excuses to stay in touch with clients, 97–99; marketing plan for, 118–120; marketing tools for, 74–76*e,* 77–97; MUMU Measure and, 100–102*e,* 101*f,* 241; taking action toward, 103; tips for sending "keeper" novelty item, 99–100; word of mouth, 73–74

Client Contact Log, 154*e,* 179

Client contact tracking, 30, 118, 179

Client gifts: MUMU Measure for, 100–102*e,* 101*f,* 241; selecting "keeper," 99–100; sending/giving, 81; sources for novelty, 82*e*–83

Client relationship building: communication styles model/communication and, 192–204*f;* as one of the four Rs, 207, 208*f;* suggestions for, 191–192

Client relationships: built with individuals, 191–204*f;* built with organizations, 186–189*e,* 190*e;* continuously improving the, 209*e*–210*e;* customer loyalty/retention through, 184–186; personal marketing tool through maintaining, 78–79; sales call and building, 178; techniques for maintaining, 80–84

Client retention. *See* Retaining clients

Client strategies: asking another consultant to review, 27; available choices for, 119*f;* for building relationship with organization, 186–189*e,* 190*e;* clarifying present preferences, 30–32*e,* 33; tracking successful, 30, 118, 179

Clients: accepting pro bono, 81–82; adapting to communication style of, 203–204*f;* assessing your, 42–43, 117–118; customer appreciation programs for, 84; customer satisfaction and, 205*e*–208; excuses to stay in touch with,

97–99; finding solutions for your, 176; fitting marketing tools to, 123–124; giving money-back guarantee to, 4; going for the big fish, 120; going to lunch/telephone contacts with, 83–84; keeping yourself in front of, 133–134; loyalty and retention of, 184–186; out-of-town, 179–180; referrals from, 85–86, 155–156, 206–207, 212; repeat work from, 206–207, 208*f;* sending congratulations, greetings, information to, 80–81; sending gifts to, 81, 82*e*–83, 99–102*e,* 101*f,* 241; testimonials from, 16, 63, 86. *See also* Potential clients; Prospecting for clients

Close-Up Position, 46*e*

Closing the sale, 175–176

Cold calls, 138–139

Collaborator communication style, 198*f,* 199

.com address, 214, 215

Communication style: adapting to client, 203–204*f;* benefits of taking course in, 200; described, 192–193; easygoing, 194, 198*f,* 199; grid showing four types of, 197–200, 198*f;* importance of flexibility in, 200–202; marketing actions on, 211; people oriented, 195*f,* 196–197, 198*f,* 199; Power Scale of, 193*f*–195; take-charge, 194, 198*f;* task oriented, 195*f*–196, 198*f*–199

Communication style grid: analyzer, 198*f,* 199; collaborator, 198*f,* 199; controller, 198*f;* illustration of, 198*f;* overview of, 197–200; socializer, 198*f,* 199–200

Communication style model: described, 192; Formality Scale of, 195*f*–197; observable behavior measured by, 193

Company name, 58–60

Company profiles, 143–144*e,*145

Compare and combine technique: generating marketing idea using, 225*f*–226; successful campaign based on, 237

Competition: assessing beyond immediate, 41; assessing your, 38–40*e,* 41; learning about

Q

R

S

Elaine Biech is president and managing principal of ebb associates inc, an organizational development firm that helps organizations work through large-scale change. Elaine has been in the training and consulting field for twenty-three years, working with business, government, and non-profit organizations.

Elaine specializes in helping people work as teams to maximize their effectiveness. Customizing all of her work for individual clients, she conducts strategic planning sessions and implements corporate-wide systems such as quality improvement, reengineering of business processes, and mentoring programs. She facilitates topics such as coaching today's employees, fostering creativity, customer service, time management, stress management, speaking skills, training competence, conducting productive meetings, managing change, handling the difficult employee, organizational communication, conflict resolution, and effective listening.

She has developed media presentations and training materials and has presented at dozens of national and international conferences. Known as the trainer's trainer, she custom-designs training programs for managers, leaders, trainers, and consultants. Elaine has been featured in dozens of publications, including the *Wall Street Journal, Harvard Management Update,* and *Fortune* magazine.

As a management and executive consultant, trainer, and designer she has provided consulting services to Land O' Lakes, McDonald's, Lands' End, General Casualty Insurance, PricewaterhouseCoopers, American Family Insurance, Marathon Oil, Hershey Chocolate, Johnson Wax, Federal Reserve Bank, the U.S. Navy, NASA,

Newport News Shipbuilding, Kohler Company, ASTD, American Red Cross, Association of Independent Certified Public Accountants, the University of Wisconsin, The College of William and Mary, Old Dominion University, and numerous other public and private-sector organizations to help them prepare for the challenges of the new millennium.

She is the author or editor of dozens of books and articles, including *The Consultant's Quick Start Guide*, 2001; *Successful Team-Building Tools*, 2001; the Pfeiffer *Annual* (1999, 2000, 2001, 2002, 2003); *The Business of Consulting*, 1999; *The Consultant's Legal Guide*, 2000; *Interpersonal Skills: Understanding Your Impact on Others*, 1996; *The ASTD Sourcebook: Creativity and Innovation—Widen Your Spectrum*, 1996; *The HR Handbook*, 1996; "Ten Mistakes CEOs Make About Training," 1995; *TQM for Training*, 1994; *Diagnostic Tools for Total Quality, INFO-LINE*, 1991; Managing Teamwork, 1994; *Process Improvement: Achieving Quality Together*, 1994; *Business Communications*, 1992; *Delegating for Results*, 1992; "So You Want to Be a Consultant," 1994; "Increased Productivity Through Effective Meetings," 1987; and *Stress Management, Building Healthy Families*, 1984. Her books have been translated into Norwegian, Chinese, and Dutch.

Elaine earned her B.S. degree from the University of Wisconsin-Superior in business and education consulting and her M.S. in human resource development. She is active at the national level of ASTD, serving on the 1990 National Conference Design Committee, a member of the National ASTD Board of Directors and the society's secretary from 1991–1994, initiating and chairing Consultant's Day for the past seven years, and as the International Conference Design Chair in 2000. In addition to her work with ASTD, she is also an active member of Instructional Systems Association (ISA), Organization Development Network (ODN), and the National Professional Speakers Association (NSA).

Elaine is the recipient of the 1992 national ASTD Torch Award. She was selected for the 1995 Wisconsin Women Entrepreneur's Mentor Award. In 2001 she received the Instructional Systems Association's highest award, the ISA Spirit Award. She is the consulting editor for the prestigious *Annual* series published by Pfeiffer. She can be reached at P.O. Box 8249, Norfolk, VA 23503; www.ebbweb.com; ebbiech@aol.com; or 757-588-3939.

Pfeiffer Publications Guide

This guide is designed to familiarize you with the various types of Pfeiffer publications. The formats section describes the various types of products that we publish; the methodologies section describes the many different ways that content might be provided within a product. We also provide a list of the topic areas in which we publish.

FORMATS

In addition to its extensive book-publishing program, Pfeiffer offers content in an array of formats, from fieldbooks for the practitioner to complete, ready-to-use training packages that support group learning.

FIELDBOOK Designed to provide information and guidance to practitioners in the midst of action. Most fieldbooks are companions to another, sometimes earlier, work, from which its ideas are derived; the fieldbook makes practical what was theoretical in the original text. Fieldbooks can certainly be read from cover to cover. More likely, though, you'll find yourself bouncing around following a particular theme, or dipping in as the mood, and the situation, dictates.

HANDBOOK A contributed volume of work on a single topic, comprising an eclectic mix of ideas, case studies, and best practices sourced by practitioners and experts in the field.

An editor or team of editors usually is appointed to seek out contributors and to evaluate content for relevance to the topic. Think of a handbook not as a ready-to-eat meal, but as a cookbook of ingredients that enables you to create the most fitting experience for the occasion.

RESOURCE Materials designed to support group learning. They come in many forms: a complete, ready-to-use exercise (such as a game); a comprehensive resource on one topic (such as conflict management) containing a variety of methods and approaches; or a collection of like-minded activities (such as icebreakers) on multiple subjects and situations.

TRAINING PACKAGE An entire, ready-to-use learning program that focuses on a particular topic or skill. All packages comprise a guide for the facilitator/trainer and a workbook for the participants. Some packages are supported with additional media—such as video—or learning aids, instruments, or other devices to help participants understand concepts or practice and develop skills.

- *Facilitator/trainer's guide* Contains an introduction to the program, advice on how to organize and facilitate the learning event, and step-by-step instructor notes. The guide also contains copies of presentation materials—handouts, presentations, and overhead designs, for example—used in the program.

- *Participant's workbook* Contains exercises and reading materials that support the learning goal and serves as a valuable reference and support guide for participants in the weeks and months that follow the learning event. Typically, each participant will require his or her own workbook.

ELECTRONIC CD-ROMs and web-based products transform static Pfeiffer content into dynamic, interactive experiences. Designed to take advantage of the searchability, automation, and ease-of-use that technology provides, our e-products bring convenience and immediate accessibility to your workspace.

METHODOLOGIES

CASE STUDY A presentation, in narrative form, of an actual event that has occurred inside an organization. Case studies are not prescriptive, nor are they used to prove a point; they are designed to develop critical analysis and decision-making skills. A case study has a specific time frame, specifies a sequence of events, is narrative in structure, and contains a plot structure— an issue (what should be/have been done?). Use case studies when the goal is to enable participants to apply previously learned theories to the circumstances in the case, decide what is pertinent, identify the real issues, decide what should have been done, and develop a plan of action.

ENERGIZER A short activity that develops readiness for the next session or learning event. Energizers are most commonly used after a break or lunch to stimulate or refocus the group. Many involve some form of physical activity, so they are a useful way to counter post-lunch lethargy. Other uses include transitioning from one topic to another, where "mental" distancing is important.

EXPERIENTIAL LEARNING ACTIVITY (ELA) A facilitator-led intervention that moves participants through the learning cycle from experience to application (also known as a Structured Experience). ELAs are carefully thought-out designs in which there is a definite learning purpose and intended outcome. Each step—everything that participants do during the activity—facilitates the accomplishment of the stated goal. Each ELA includes complete instructions for facilitating the intervention and a clear statement of goals, suggested group size and timing, materials required, an explanation of the process, and, where appropriate, possible variations to the activity. (For more detail on Experiential Learning Activities, see the Introduction to the *Reference Guide to Handbooks and Annuals*, 1999 edition, Pfeiffer, San Francisco.)

GAME A group activity that has the purpose of fostering team sprit and togetherness in addition to the achievement of a pre-stated goal. Usually contrived—undertaking a desert expedition, for example—this type of learning method offers an engaging means for participants to demonstrate and practice business and interpersonal skills. Games are effective for team-building and personal development mainly because the goal is subordinate to the process—the means through which participants reach decisions, collaborate, communicate, and generate trust and understanding. Games often engage teams in "friendly" competition.

ICEBREAKER A (usually) short activity designed to help participants overcome initial anxiety in a training session and/or to acquaint the participants with one another. An icebreaker can be a fun activity or can be tied to specific topics or training goals. While a useful tool in itself, the icebreaker comes into its own in situations where tension or resistance exists within a group.

INSTRUMENT A device used to assess, appraise, evaluate, describe, classify, and summarize various aspects of human behavior. The term used to describe an instrument depends primarily on its format and purpose. These terms include survey, questionnaire, inventory, diagnostic, survey, and poll. Some uses of instruments include providing instrumental feedback to group members, studying here-and-now processes or functioning within a group, manipulating group composition, and evaluating outcomes of training and other interventions.

Instruments are popular in the training and HR field because, in general, more growth can occur if an individual is provided with a method for focusing specifically on his or her own behavior. Instruments also are used to obtain information that will serve as a basis for change and to assist in workforce planning efforts.

Paper-and-pencil tests still dominate the instrument landscape with a typical package comprising a facilitator's guide, which offers advice on administering the instrument and interpreting the collected data, and an initial set of instruments. Additional instruments are available separately. Pfeiffer, though, is investing heavily in e-instruments. Electronic instrumentation provides effortless distribution and, for larger groups particularly, offers advantages over paper-and-pencil tests in the time it takes to analyze data and provide feedback.

LECTURETTE A short talk that provides an explanation of a principle, model, or process that is pertinent to the participants' current learning needs. A lecturette is intended to establish a common language bond between the trainer and the participants by providing a mutual frame of reference. Use a lecturette as an introduction to a group activity or event, as an interjection during an event, or as a handout.

MODEL A graphic depiction of a system or process and the relationship among its elements. Models provide a frame of reference and something more tangible, and more easily remembered, than a verbal explanation. They also give participants something to "go on," enabling them to track their own progress as they experience the dynamics, processes, and relationships being depicted in the model.

ROLE PLAY A technique in which people assume a role in a situation/scenario: a customer service rep in an angry-customer exchange, for example. The way in which the role is approached is then discussed and feedback is offered. The role play is often repeated using a different approach and/or incorporating changes made based on feedback received. In other words, role playing is a spontaneous interaction involving realistic behavior under artificial (and safe) conditions.

SIMULATION A methodology for understanding the interrelationships among components of a system or process. Simulations differ from games in that they test or use a model that depicts or mirrors some aspect of reality in form, if not necessarily in content. Learning occurs by studying the effects of change on one or more factors of the model. Simulations are commonly used to test hypotheses about what happens in a system—often referred to as "what if?" analysis—or to examine best-case/worst-case scenarios.

THEORY A presentation of an idea from a conjectural perspective. Theories are useful because they encourage us to examine behavior and phenomena through a different lens.

TOPICS

The twin goals of providing effective and practical solutions for workforce training and organization development and meeting the educational needs of training and human resource professionals shape Pfeiffer's publishing program. Core topics include the following:

Leadership & Management

Communication & Presentation

Coaching & Mentoring

Training & Development

E-Learning

Teams & Collaboration

OD & Strategic Planning

Human Resources

Consulting